How the Internet Changed America

Alexei Anisin

How the Internet Changed America

palgrave
macmillan

Alexei Anisin
Centre for Ethics as Study in Human Value Department of Philosophy and Religious Studies
University of Pardubice
Pardubice, Czech Republic

ISBN 978-3-032-02394-0 ISBN 978-3-032-02395-7 (eBook)
https://doi.org/10.1007/978-3-032-02395-7

This Palgrave Macmillan imprint is published by the registered company Springer Nature Switzerland AG.
The registered company address is: Gewerbestrasse 11, 6330 Cham, Switzerland

To Zoya

Foreword

An hour ago, while sitting in my living room compiling the bibliography of a political theory article I noticed that the entry *The Authority of the State* by Leslie Green had a missing year of publication. Even though I could have walked down the corridor to pick up the book with green glossy covers from the shelf, I googled the title to ascertain that it was published in 1988. Using the Google search engine was not prompted by my not having the book: I used the search engine despite having a physical copy of the book. Let us take another example—Winston is about to leave for work wondering whether it might be raining outside. Instead of walking to the front door just three feet away in order to check for signs of precipitation, he swipes the screen of his mobile phone to access the online weather channel. Doing so is not necessarily more efficient in terms of effort or time spent, it would have been faster to open the front door and look at the sky. Consider yet another case. Lucinda, an undergraduate, has to write a report on the 2015 European migration crisis this weekend. No physical books are available in her home and she has never been to the university library to read any. To get started on the topic, she switches on her tablet and logs onto the YouTube channel hoping to find some "shorts" (a short documentary). While such experiences are familiar to most of us as casual digital media users, it has been surprisingly hard for social scientists to pinpoint the exact reasons behind behavioral patterns of this kind. In *How the Internet Changed America*, political sociologist Alexei Anisin invites us on a journey that would provide some unusual and perhaps unsettling answers to this puzzle.

Social scientists usually seek to explain our ever-growing addiction to the digital world in either one of two ways. They either point to individual-level characteristics such as neurons firing in the brain or conversely, to structural-level characteristics represented by macro structures such as the market or even by micro structures such as habits that condition individual conduct. Against this bifurcation of structures and agents, Anisin makes a case for the duality of structure and agency drawing inspiration from Anthony Giddens' structuration theory (Giddens, 1984). The thrust of Giddens' argument is that structures are reproduced by recursively organized social practices over time. From the standpoint of structuration, internet usage is a social practice. This practice is constrained and enabled by background structures, and it comprises continuous but shifting patterns of usage by an enormous number of persons (agents) whose presence online is motivated by subjective preferences and values.

Within sociological theory, the idiom of structuration recognizes the import of structure while taking seriously the role of agents engaged in structural reproduction. The agent posited by this idiom is not the "dupe" of classical Marxism who remains unaware of the hidden workings of structural constraints. In this regard, Anisin departs from Pierre Bourdieu's concept of the habitus, as articulated in *Outline of a Theory of Practice* (1977). This key concept operates as a mediating link between individual wishes, desires, and thoughts, on the one side, and social structures, on the other. The habitus is the *microstructure* of an individual's character which mirrors background macrostructures exemplified by the state, the market, the academia, and the prison system. The habitus is unconscious and embodied; it captures how the person speaks and acts, a manner which is recognizable by the social scientist (as a marker of the person's class for example) but which remains opaque to the individual herself. In sharp contrast, structuration theory emphasizes the conscious aspect of agents partaking in structural change. In this sense, the digital world cannot be merely reduced to a constraint that operates without conscious input by agents. The question of why we are drifting away inside this world is intriguing because we knowingly take part in it in the first place.

A core notion within structuration is *recursivity*. A social practice designates not only an initial mode of interaction that constitutes an input for a given structure but also an *outcome* that serves as a recursive input to the structure at a later time. Patterns of interaction, or practices, feed pre-existing structures via a loop or recursively. Hence, at least in theory, structures can shift over time depending on whether or not significant changes in the patterns of usages, or practices, materialize—that is to say, depending on what the agents tend to be doing. Structuration signals that structures persist over time because of practices that possess the feature of recursivity. In sociological theory time as a factor in the explanation of social structure has been linked to modernity (Dupre, 1993, p. 158). Giddens himself adopts this line of reasoning when claiming that the two basic elements of structure—rules and resources, where rules are understood as norms governing action and resources as materials that allow us to navigate the physical world—are located in space and time. The idea that, as theorists, we are *reflexively aware that* our theorizing is relative to a locus in time (and space) is an awareness that symbolizes modernity. Similarly, Niklas Luhmann (1995) has theorized social systems as recursive and reflexive, categorizing these properties as an aspect of modernity. Giddens and Luhmann both accept the twin notions of modernity and reflexivity as benchmarks of their preferred mode of theorizing. But whereas for Giddens the reproduction of social structures relies on the category of action, for Luhmann it relies on the category of observation. Social systems are seen as observational systems. Social theory in Luhmann's account becomes a metatheory of society, where society encompasses different systems that observe one another. The main unit of analysis is communication where communication is reduced to information in a binary sense (a system encountering another social system poses a question about the latter's identity and has only two answers, "Yes" or "No," or "Similar" or "Different"). This highly abstract notion of communication is symptomatic of Luhmann's antihumanism. An antihumanist standpoint can be used to analyze the digital realm, but the book under discussion adopts the contrary, humanist standpoint, and thus accords significance to agency.

The concept of digital realm is central to the book. The primary technological manifestation of this realm is the internet. Under one description, the internet is a technology for information processing and transmission grounded in logic, mathematics, and cybernetic theory. Under an alternative description, favored by the book's author, it is a technology for information *production and consumption*. This production depends on human input and indeed on the inputs of billions of users (and content creators, viz. programmers). Anisin has chosen structuration theory as a framework to show that the actions of some odd billion users have a recursive effect on extant structures in a pragmatic sense over and above the formalized sense attributed to the internet as a digital space. In other words, it is necessary to distinguish the internet in terms of concrete social practices related to how human beings are using digital technologies online and the internet as a formalized space full of zeroes and ones. The two domains are interrelated in terms of a common function, as is the interface of the computer on which I am typing the current sentence in English (which sentence is "seen" by the computer as a binary string of zeros and ones), but analytically and normatively they reflect different perspectives. Only the (non-formalized) pragmatic perspective is relevant in what follows.

Pragmatically, then, the internet can be construed as a digital realm inside which human users create, seek, disseminate, and consume information. Human actions and interactions, once they become patterned and turn into distinct, relatively stable practices, begin to exert recursive effects over a set of structures. What structures can these be? To begin with, there is the already mentioned formalized, logico-mathematical structure of code. Next, the internet requires a physical infrastructure or hardware in the form of microchips, modems, computers, wires and cables, power lines, cooling towers, and buildings. Further, there are interface structures or software that enable programmers to translate a deep mathematical model into "surface" models, readily interpretable by an average human intelligence and translatable into natural languages such as Hindu, French, English, or Afrikaans. Hovering above all those are macro structures, including rules and resources that enable and constrain specific modes of human interaction within a historically situated society, including its domains of ethics, law, and politics. *How the Internet Changed America* focuses on such rules and resources related to practices of internet use in advanced modern societies of which the United States is an obvious (but not sole) example.

The leitmotiv of the book is that the increasing immersion of users in the digital realm has generated social practices that are complex and ambiguous. On the positive side, it is much easier to search for and obtain information online without leaving the premises of one's home or workplace. Because the digital realm is global in scope, the physical networks that undergird it are always "on" in real-time and users in technologically advanced countries have instant access to the data they need. However, such developments generate alternative social and political costs. Current surveys show that an American spends an average of seven hours per day online, mostly looking at digital screens, a staggering increase from just a decade ago. The problem can be analyzed in terms of a "budget" of feasible interactions and actions that are pragmatically available to us as finite human beings. Being hooked to the net for half of the day means spending less time with one's children, spouses, colleagues, and neighbors. This trend is perhaps not entirely novel. In his well-known study *Bowling Alone* (2000), Robert Putman observed that at the turn of the twenty-first century, Americans have become isolated from their local communities, preferring a mode of self-sufficiency over communal association and civic engagement. But once associational life takes a back seat, there is a real danger of social atomism. The puzzling aspect of the internet is that social atomism in real life seems to be accompanied by enhanced presence in online communities. Should we worry about abandoning one platform of participation (real-life associations) and joining another (virtual associations)?

Three negative trends represent a particular source of concern, Anisin claims. The first is the emergence of echo chambers which has implications for political polarization, the second is digital capitalism, and the third is the decline in the practice of reading and individual reflection.

Echo Chambers and Polarization

Echo chambers are subject-specific domains inside the digital space that allow users to associate exclusively with like-minded individuals, leading to the recursive reinforcement of prejudice. If your only audience comprises replicas of yourself, then the possibility of critical discourse is precluded from the very inception. Diversity of opinion and viewpoints however remains indispensable for personal self-development and the growth of liberal societies, as JS Mill observed in Chap. 2 of *On Liberty* (1978). To accept the prevailing custom or sentiment that asserts what counts as true, Mill maintained, is to embrace a dogma. The genuine pursuit of truth involves a process of finding out what *may* count as true, and this should be treated as an open question. To settle it, autonomous agents should engage in an uncoerced process of deliberation that involves alternative viewpoints. Inside the digital realm, Anisin argues, this seldom happens largely because our identities are concealed. As a result, individuals will tend to unreflectively accept the viewpoint of unknown others (heteronomy) or engage in exchanges motivated by incivility and ill will. All too often, the anonymized structure of online platforms brings out the worst in human nature.

What is more, as Chap. 4 illustrates, digital technology in advanced societies has amplified the uncritical reproduction of prejudice and has contributed to political polarization and the erosion of trust in public institutions. This conclusion needs to be qualified by noting that the talk of causality (as a counterfactually validated relationship) may seem exaggerated—at most, we can talk about influence and concretely about multifactorial influence. While the current wave of polarization sweeping the US and certain European countries has been affected by developments in the digital realm, it has been no less affected by factors such as populism, a sense of uncertainty in the wake of volatile global financial markets as well as nuclear and environmental risks (Beck, 1992), transborder migration crises, and identity politics.

Digital Capitalism

Because technology nowadays is embedded in a global capitalist system, algorithms seek to promote rather than challenge our settled views as internet users. Targeted reinforcement via recursive loops is not limited to echo chambers. Even with respect to users who search the internet by themselves (without taking part in online communities), algorithms typically create individualized user profiles which are then recursively employed to reinforce previous search patterns. The positive reinforcement of settled views prompts the user to consume more data—data of the same kind mind you. Targeted data consumption that is uniform is good for business. It is less certain whether it is good for the pursuit of knowledge and truth considering that users end up obtaining repetitive information.

The repercussions of the above-mentioned trends transcend the domain of economics and spill over into politics. Tech giants such as Google, Meta, Twitter (or *X*), and Amazon are profit-seeking enterprises. Their enormous market power has a clear political dimension and has enabled them to keep issues off the agenda by supplying specific types of information to end users while bracketing other types in a non-transparent, largely unaccountable manner. This capacity to restrict discussion to a set of issues that count as "safe" for the power wielder represents the so-called second face of power (Bachrach & Baratz, 1962, p. 948). Tech giants have not only been able to exert influence over political outcomes including national elections but continue to maintain an ambivalent connection to the military-industrial complex. It should be remembered that back in the late 1960s the internet began its life—under the rubric of *ARPAnet*—as a technology designed by the US Defense Department.

The Practice of Reading

One of the core insights of the book is that the relationship between the digital realm and our practices that recursively reproduce it, exhibits complexity. Certain aspects of this relationship, as we have seen, are political, others are economic, some concern the conduct of individuals in online groups, others concern their conduct when considered as solitary consumers of digital content. What bears emphasis in this context is the practice of reading non-digital media and its exponential decline in recent years. It is a disconcerting fact that young people in the US spend multiple hours daily on platforms such as Meta and TikTok, but only seven minutes reading a physical text (2024 data). Why is this an issue—why should the medium, virtual and digital, as opposed to physical and analog, matter?

Chapter 5 of the book argues that the observed decline in reading physical texts in print media is an issue for two main reasons. One is the deep human need to interact with the physical world. Humans, as Marx noted, are not just thinkers but actors who, in acting, transform their physical and material environment, thereby constituting themselves as makers. Second, the digital world contains deliberately shortened messages that are easily digestible. In contradistinction, a physical text is not subject to the instantaneous logic of digital media, nor does it have to be a snippet—it allows for reflection and temporal deferral of interpretation. Physical texts enable us not merely to think, but to rethink an idea or argument and to reach a more refined stage of reflection. To this, we might add two further reasons why the physical world matters. One such reason is that a human being cannot be reduced to an abstract Cogito or a thinking process, *pace* Descartes: humans are physically embodied. The philosopher of mind John Searle has argued that even if the thoughts, feelings, and desires of a human person were stripped down to their bare propositional content ("I want a new Mercedes" or "This sunset is beautiful"), such consciously articulated propositions must still be considered mental states multiply realizable inside the human brain as a biological structure (Searle, 1997, p. 17). This means that purely syntactic operations which typify AI cannot be a match for the semantic constitution of human consciousness nor for its biological basis. At most, Searle claims, AI can *simulate* the operation of human consciousness, but a simulation of a nuclear disaster is not itself a nuclear disaster. Last but not least, because we are physically embodied actors with a capacity for consciousness and self-consciousness, it makes a difference whether the input content that feeds into our conscious processes is physically manifest or not. Reading a physical text, touching the pages of a book, for example, makes us think, feel, and perceive in a different way than the way of perceiving a digital text. A digital text is "flat": it has no determinate beginning or end, the pages have no visible imperfections and appear more or less the same. My physical copy of the *Authority of the State* appears different: it has a glossy green paper that is cold to the touch. Some pages bear pencil markings, each page has a determinate beginning and end, and this reminds me that the text in front of me constitutes an object set apart from me as a reader and thinker. In lieu of being a physical artifact, the text has the capacity to resist the flow of consciousness that is attending to it.

Anisin's account is multifaceted—the sociological trends concerning the ubiquitous digital realm it illuminates do not spring from a single foundation; they remain diverse in their sources, nature, and implications. And yet there is an overarching message articulated in Chap. 1—namely, "Get outside!" Getting outside means getting in contact with the physical world populated by analog artifacts and embodied human beings who are not replicas of our digital selves and with whom we may not always see eye to eye. Such a complex human world will at times be dangerous and it will certainly contain a myriad of disappointments: but it is the only place that allows us to disclose our creative capacities and our autonomy as agents: no digital realm can be a surrogate for it.

King's College London
UK & Anglo-American University—Prague
Germany

Silviya Lechner

Bibliography

Bachrach, P., & Baratz, M. S. (1962). Two faces of power. *American Political Science Review, 56*(4), 947–952.

Beck, U. (1992). *Risk society: Towards a new modernity* (M. Ritter, Trans.). Sage Publications.

Bourdieu, P. (1977). *Outline of a theory of practice* (R. Nice, Trans.). Cambridge University Press.

Dupre, L. (1993). *Passage to modernity: An essay in the hermeneutics of nature and culture*. Yale University Press.

Giddens, A. (1984). *The Constitution of society: Outline of the theory of structuration.* University of California Press.

Green, L. (1988). *The authority of the state.* Clarendon Press.

Luhmann, N. (1995). *Social systems* (J. Bednarz Jr., & D. Baecker, Trans.). Stanford University Press.

Mill, J. S. (1978). *On liberty* (Elizabeth Rapaport, Ed.). Hackett.

Putnam, R. D. (2000). *Bowling alone: The collapse and revival of American community.* Simon & Schuster.

Searle, J. S. (1997). *The mystery of consciousness.* The New York Review of Books.

Preface

The internet was once a communication technology that was reserved for academic or military purposes. By the 1980s, it began to be commercialized and the private sector in the United States ended up putting forward one of the key technological marvels to the world which would later go on to dominate societies through platforms such as Google, YouTube, Facebook, Instagram, etc. The internet underlies every digital interaction and many cultural experiences that take place across most societies in the world. For all its ubiquity, the internet's transformational impact on American society has been relatively under-theorized. This book conceptualizes various outcomes that the internet has induced on American society. It utilizes a sociological approach based on Anthony Giddens' structuration theory. The goal of this book is to both theoretically account for and discover how the internet has reconfigured conditions of social life through altering civic and cognitive behaviors and through reshaping cultural and institutional landscapes. The internet has forced masses of people to spend more time inside than ever before, and most importantly, to spend time immersed in an evolving digital realm. The internet thus serves as a structural force. Within this structure, agency is exercised by people, companies, corporations, and government—all of which interact with the overarching structure and a disaggregated but active digital realm. The internet has thus fostered a dialectical relationship that has, over a few short decades, completely reorganized social life.

The questions that this book addresses are not whether the internet has induced good or bad outcomes in American society, but rather, it seeks to explain how it has changed society and to theoretically account for these changes. To accomplish this, I rely on Giddens' theory of structuration which is a classical framework that offers a middle ground between deterministic accounts of technological change and agency-focused accounts. The latter tend to overlook the role of institutional and structural constraints and their impact on social behavior. The chosen theoretical framework emphasizes the duality of structure and agency providing a template to explain and assess how the digital realm is mutually a product of human action as well as a conditioning force that influences behavior. For example, much of society currently spends swaths of time on social media and online communication platforms. It is now common for people to engage in behavior when offline that is connected to their behavior online. The classical example of this (which is, unfortunately, becoming more prominent as time goes on) can be observed in the extent to which individuals use their smartphones to film, photograph, and record their day-to-day lives. Whether attending concerts, festivals, or even sometimes in sports events, it is common to see that nearly every single person in a crowd will have their smartphone out filming the event. Such developments are historically new, but importantly, they are in no way simple phenomena. They represent incredibly significant changes that have been induced by the evolution of the digital realm. From weddings to child births to graduation ceremonies, content about a given event gets instantaneously streamed or uploaded into one of the systems and structures of a given digital platform, and concurrently, large amounts of people end up experiencing and spending some of the most important portions of their physical lives either directly immersed in the digital realm or with background knowledge and expectations of how the event will be interpreted online.

To explain these complex and highly transformative dynamics, I have framed the analyses and order of chapters in this book thematically rather than chronologically. Each chapter captures a specified set of aspects or outcomes of social life which range from changes to patterns in civic engagement in the United States to increasing levels of political polarization, declining rates of traditional reading, the rise of influencer culture, as well as the phenomenon of digital surveillance. These topics enable me to provide, what to the best of my knowledge, is among the more multifaceted accounts of how internet technologies have impacted and reshaped social practices. This book relies on different methodological approaches which include combinations of qualitative and quantitative data. In some cases, comparisons are made between contemporary patterns in relation to patterns that were salient in earlier periods of American history. These comparisons help to clarify what has changed and how it has changed through new dynamics and mechanisms that have transformed society in what truly has been rapid fashion. Finally, although the focus of this book is on the United States, I strongly believe that its findings have much broader implications and can be applied to most post-industrialized economic societies, especially those that are liberal-democratic. The numerous recursive processes identified in this book capture large-scale shifts that have arisen from physical to digital association; they likewise capture how algorithmic reinforcements of beliefs and self-righteous behavior have become prominent online, along with how social attention is becoming increasingly commoditized. Such outcomes are likely observable in other countries with similar digital infrastructures.

I hope that this book will help scholars, students, and interested members of the public develop their understanding of how the internet has changed society and enhance their future pursuits of understanding technological change. I also hope that we will not be passive recipients of rapidly changing digital technologies, as we must keep in mind that we can contribute to the reproduction and transformation of the digital systems we populate.

Pardubice, Czech Republic — Alexei Anisin

Funding Statement

This book was financially supported by the Ministry of Education, Youth and Sports of the Czech Republic within the specific funding program ERC CZ, Grant No. LL2308, Combatting self-righteousness—a vice of the digital age.

Acknowledgments

The finishing point of this book would not have been possible to reach without the support and inspiration of my close family members and friends as well as colleagues, some of which I spent extensive time debating the complex nature of technological change with. I appreciate all who have contributed to the realization of this project.

Competing Interests The author has no competing interests to declare that are relevant to the content of this manuscript.

Contents

1	Going Outside	1
2	Structure and Agency: The Digital Realm and Society	17
3	Civic Engagement and Social Interactions	49
4	Political Polarization and Trust in Institutions	75
5	Reading	105
6	Idols as Influencers	123
7	Digital Surveillance Structures	145
8	Conclusion: Going Inside	167
	Index	177

List of Figures

Fig. 3.1	People can be trusted in the United States 1972–2022 (n = 12,857)	64
Fig. 3.2	Spending evenings with friends (1972–2022) (N = 29,484)	65
Fig. 3.3	Spend evenings with relatives (1972–2022) (N = 63,015)	66
Fig. 3.4	Time spent with neighbors (1974–2022) (N = 33,457)	67
Fig. 3.5	Trust in neighborhood (WVS—2005–2022) (N = 5998)	68
Fig. 4.1	“Hardly Any” confidence in the press (1973–2022)	94
Fig. 4.2	Confident in television (hardly any) by political affiliation (1973–2022) (N = 24,194)	95
Fig. 4.3	“Hardly any” Confidence in the Executive Branch of the Federal Government (1975–2002) (N = 23,064)	97
Fig. 4.4	“Hardly Any” Confidence in Congress (1975–2002)	97
Fig. 4.5	Box plot	98
Fig. 5.1	Average time spent reading (2003–2023)	115
Fig. 5.2	Average time spent reading all age groups (2003–2023)	116
Fig. 5.3	Average time spent reading by age group bar chart (2023)	117

List of Tables

Table 3.1	People can be trusted in the United States 1972–2022 (n = 12,857)	63
Table 3.2	How secure do you feel in your own neighborhood (WVS) (N = 4828)	69
Table 4.1	ANOVA results for confidence in television by political affiliation	96
Table 4.2	How often respondent discusses political matters with friends 1981–2022 (N = 9502)	98
Table 5.1	Average minutes spent reading female and male (2003–2023)	115
Table 5.2	Average time spent reading all age groups (2003–2023)	117
Table 6.1	Top 25 influencers (2024)	133
Table 6.2	Top influencers health and fitness (2024)	134

CHAPTER 1

Going Outside

A drizzle falls on the screen of a dusty NOKIA 6110 cellular phone perched on a rock in a wooded area in Northern California. A group of kids is playing on the banks of the creek bed nearby. One kid is hauling stones while the other is digging mud from the creek. Emma is sitting on the creek bed alongside her friend Becca, who is chewing on some freshly picked blackberries. An attempt at building a dam is being carried out by their friends, several boys, and another girl, so that the kids' plan of hanging a makeshift rope swing on a tree above can be realized. It's the beginning of a three-day weekend in autumn and curfew is sundown. These were days in Emma's early life that were marked by an organic type of human interaction with nature—one that millions of children and young people across historical time have engaged in. Actions of building, constructing, tearing down, ripping, hanging, digging, and tying objects in nature constitute a fundamentally important set of characteristics that forge our relationship to the physical world early on in our lives. Of course, not all kids around the world have had the privilege to play in clean and safe outdoor settings, but most readers of this book will probably recall that things used to be quite different in our childhood. Why has this happened? What caused this to occur? How has digital media consumption affected cognitive and social behaviors? These are all questions that warrant a deep reflection into our way of life and the role that technology plays in it.

A. Anisin, *How the Internet Changed America*,
https://doi.org/10.1007/978-3-032-02395-7_1

It seems that something strange appears to have happened sometime in the late 1990s and early 2000s, something which surpasses generational differences and is greater than any single person, group, society, or state. This book argues that the internet, as realized, engineered, and utilized through digital technologies, has fundamentally transformed the ways that hundreds of millions of people in the United States (and billions more across the globe) live their lives. From spending significant periods of our lives outside, we have incrementally been encouraged to go inside—to immerse ourselves in digital reality in which time moves faster, entertainment is more accessible, and individualism is more expressible. The internet has fundamentally transformed some of the most salient aspects about our lives, our communities, and the larger society in which we live.[1] Most of us now have what was once a "super" computer in the palm of our hands, and many urban areas across the Northern Hemisphere have 5G networks, which means that high-speed internet is now literally mobile—we (including teenagers and in some instances, even young children) carry around a world of information in our back pockets on a daily basis. There are some truly astounding patterns and changes to social behavior that have arisen alongside Americans' entrenchment into digital reality—as the amount of screen time increases, the more profound many of these processes are turning out to be.

This book uncovers some of these patterns through analysis of data drawn from large-scale surveys and other data sources. For example, while digital media and internet communication have expanded access to information, broadened people's social networks, and created new opportunities for civic engagement, they have also contributed to isolation and weakened community ties in the process. The percentage of Americans who believe that most people in their society can be trusted dropped sharply from 46.1% in 1972 to just 10.2% in 2022. Likewise, the frequency with which individuals engage in physically real social interactions has weakened, with fewer people spending evenings with friends several times a month compared to past decades. Along similar lines, recursive interactions between digital media structures and user agency have driven

[1] This is emulated through the story of Emma—a fictional character and girl whose common experiences in life will be brought up and referred to throughout introductory sections of chapters in this book—beginning with her bright and vibrant childhood, then shifting into her turbulent teenage years, a struggle with an eating disorder, young adulthood, mental illness, prescription meds, a spiral into addiction, recovery, and enduring struggles in her middle ages.

individuals in the U.S. are engaging in remote work and several scholars have conceptualized the rise of the gig economy to changing dynamics of work in the digital age. Healthcare has also seen the advent of telemedicine which has enabled sick patients to consult with doctors on a remote basis and access medical information and services online. Personal finance has also been transformed with the rise of online banking, digital wallets, and even alternative forms of currency (crypto). Most recently, the advent of publicly accessible and useable artificially intelligent chatbots and systems (i.e., ChatGPT, OpenAI) has further altered the ways how individuals create content, analyze information, and operate throughout digital reality. The ways in which individuals manage and transfer money have changed, and recent conflicts (such as the Russia-Ukraine war as exemplified by the latter's usage of Starlink) provide many glimpses into how satellite-based internet connectivity and drones have (and will continue) to transform the nature of modern warfare.

Decades ago, Putnam observed that Americans were "Bowling Alone" and were increasingly isolated from what used to be common activities found throughout America's communities, town halls, malls, and associations. The internet has further exacerbated the tendency to go *Bowling Alone* by shifting individual consciousness on a mass scale into digital forms of community, into a non-stop virtual reality that comprises both real and fictitious entities and experiences. In this sense, it is not the case that Americans are *Bowling Alone*, but rather, they are *Bowling Inside*.

Much of humanity is currently on track to journey deeper into the digital age—an age that is marked by increasing amounts of technology that most commonly manifests itself through high-definition screens that range from smartphones to tablets, to computers, to smart televisions. With more and more people spending portions of their day looking at screens, the distinctions between our physical and virtual lives are beginning to blur. Throughout modern history, few technological developments have brought about as much change in social behavior as the internet. What began as a loose network of computers that were stationed at a handful of universities in the 1960s has grown into a pervasive force in daily life. From altering the way we communicate and interact with one another to restructuring economic, political, social, and cultural structures, the internet has become an integral part of billions of peoples' daily reality. This book analyzes internet-induced social change in the United States. Anthony Giddens' structuration theory is drawn on to theorize a heterogeneous collection of societal and interpersonal changes. Over time, many different recursive relationships have arisen and continue to evolve as societal behaviors and structures get continuously shaped and reshaped by interactions with digital internet technologies.

This book takes readers through common experiences that people tend to come across on a daily basis throughout modern and highly technologically dominated societies. By the latter, I refer to contexts that are not necessarily "Western" in nature but societies that are marked by high levels of urbanization and possess electrical grids that power and sustain megacities of tens of millions of people and above all, societies in which a majority of the population spends multiple hours looking at screens throughout their day. On this basis, the American-centric theme of this book will not necessarily be tied to only the United States—as many areas of the world have experienced similar technological processes. With this being said, this book is focused on America, the USA, the U.S., the United States, or "the States"—all terms will be used to reference the same country. Why explain how the internet changed America, and not another country? The U.S. significantly influenced the historical development of the internet through funding early projects across military and defense industries. Specifically, through projects carried out by the Advanced Research Projects Agency (ARPA) and the Department of Defense (DOD), state agencies held the initial impetus for contributing to the development of internet technologies with the overarching purpose of ensuring robust and reliable communication systems that could withstand potential threats amidst potential nuclear conflict during the Cold War (Ruttan, 2006), particularly during the Cold War era. ARPA's work led to the creation of ARPANET, which was the precursor to the modern internet—it enabled some of the first internet-based communications to take place between different computer networks around the country. At the time, many of those who worked and knew about these projects had envisioned internet communication to function as a critical strategic defense mechanism, yet as these technologies advanced, the internet transitioned away from being a strictly military tool and into a commercialized and privatized entity that could be used by the public.

Retrospectively, such a shift was pivotal as it allowed for widespread public access and the eventual commercialization of the internet into the private sector. An unprecedented boom in technological development followed and Silicon Valley led the way. From America Online to Yahoo and then Google, Facebook, Twitter, Instagram to eBay, Amazon, and Netflix, the global dominance of American internet corporate technologies helped propel the nation to hegemony and power status that is difficult to find historical parallels with. Indeed, at the time of writing this book, this power status is hastily dwindling in light of China (whose economy is at least as large and by some estimates, even larger than the US) along with fundamental changes in global political power positioning—changes that many plausibly argue are leading to the formation of multi-polar world order.

Internet technologies constitute diverse structural forces that influence our consumption of modalities of content and information. This monograph demarcates these structures within a conceptual framework. By focusing on the relationship between the constraints imposed by extant structures and responses exhibited by human agents, this book demonstrates that internet-induced social changes are both dynamic and evolving. It carries out quantitative and qualitative inquiries and draws on a range of interdisciplinary research spanning sociology, political science, psychology, media studies, and cultural studies to explain social transformations and the changing nature of human interactions in the digital age. For example, in recent decades, the United States has experienced a plethora of changes that range from the decline of community engagement, the erosion of interpersonal trust, the rise of social isolation, polarization, declining reading rates, among a number of other factors ranging from decreased digital privacy to heightened state surveillance. There are profound statistical trends that are inherent to some of these changes, and many are identified and illustrated throughout this book.

The study of internet technology is vast and rich—it is probably the most thought-provoking field currently being researched by social scientists. Carr's (2020) and Alter's (2017) works elucidate a frequent approach that places emphasis on neurological dynamics and how the internet can propel different types of addiction to technology. I don't disagree or take issue with these insightful works—they touch on a key component of internet technology, and there of course are sub-sets of society that are highly addicted to screens, video games, social media, etc. Yet neurologically based accounts only scratch the surface as they are reductionist in their assumptions. Graham and Dutton's edited volume (2019) does resemble the present monograph and comprises more than a dozen different contributions that shift focus away from the purely neurological approach to gauging the internet's transformative cultural potential. However, the volume does not present a unified theoretical framework as is done in the present book. Turkle's (2017) monograph likely offers the closest approaches to the one taken in this book, but does not present any data on trends associated with technologically induced social change. My aim in this book is to analyze the interplay between structure and agency and to offer statistical evidence of trends that have been salient since the rise of the commercialized internet. In this regard, this book puts forward a different perspective that, to the best of my knowledge, has not been utilized in other noteworthy works on internet technology and its relation to social change (Shirky, 2008; Castells, 2010; Lanier, 2010; Turkle, 2017; Morozov, 2011; Rainie & Wellman, 2012; McChesney, 2013; Zuboff, 2019).

Most of these contributions elucidate a collective set of trends in books on technology that are prevalent in popular culture right now. On the one hand, emphasis is commonly placed on scientific interpretations of neurological dynamics and how the internet can propel different types of addiction to technology. On the other hand, many are pointing toward the potentially exploitative nature of internet technologies such as algorithmic manipulation based around data commodification. I don't disagree or take issue with these insightful works—they do indeed touch on important and salient components of internet technology. There are many highly engaging but addicting properties associated with digital media and digital reality more broadly. But with this being said, it is important to consider the fact that the addictive, coercive, and transformative processes that have arisen due to the internet's impact on our world are not simply limited to the neurological functions of our brain. There have been several fascinating developments that can be traced through analyzing the structures and systems found in digital reality and how they have interacted with human agency, with individuals and groups—from young to old.

Wide-reaching changes have arisen in the U.S. either as a direct result or as an ongoing set of processes associated with the internet. Back in 2001, flip phones were becoming standard and people were spending more time using electronic devices, but the total amount of an average person's day spent looking at a screen was minuscule in comparison to what we are currently seeing in 2024. It is estimated that the average internet user spends an estimated 6 hours and 40 minutes a day online and in the United States, the average American spends an estimated 7 hours and 3 minutes per day on screens (Moody, 2024). In contrast, back in 2000, the average person experienced significantly less of their day looking at screens—it is estimated that the average American spent 2.7 hours watching television and only 30 minutes per day online (Backlinko, 2024).

Most importantly, at the time of writing this book, Gen "Z"—the generation of individuals born from 1997 to 2012 (who will soon be tomorrow's leaders, parents, and adults)—spend 7.2 hours per day watching video-specific content across platforms such as TikTok, YouTube, and Instagram (SlickText, 2024). On both quantitative and qualitative levels, these are profound shifts that create different constraints and opportunities for individuals.

Theoretical Framework

In contrast to approaches that assume technology functions as either a deterministic force that one-sidedly shapes social outcomes or as a tool that gets used solely by individuals, the theoretical framework adopted in this book should be of broad interest to readers because it captures dynamic interactions between digital structures and human agency. This book demonstrates how internet-based digital technologies both shape and are shaped by societal behaviors according to specific contexts. In this sense, the chapters and their accompanying analyses presented in this book are not intended to span the entirety of social science, but rather, each chapter is relevant to particular academic literature and knowledge. Although this book is centered on the U.S. context, the findings and implications of my inquiries are clearly applicable to other technologically advanced societies. As digital connectivity continues to grow and network speeds and computing power increase, the trends and patterns that are identified in this book likely will become more pronounced, albeit the trajectories through which this will occur will probably turn out to be much more contingent than can be predicted with statistical analyses.

This book is not meant to prescribe any concrete set of recommendations for how we should live our lives or interact with internet-based technology. I am to map out what I believe are among the most prominent changes that have arisen in the last several decades across American society. These changes reflect patterns that have arisen in other parts of the world, especially countries with a similar human development index (HDI) and similar political systems (i.e., advanced liberal democracies). Moreover, one of the keys to explaining the internet's transformative impact on society lies somewhere in the middle of the theoretical prism between structure and agency. This book accounts for both of these factors and in doing so, it offers a perspective that can be considered to represent a middle ground between works that have emphasized biology, neurology, and individualism and those that have emphasized societal structures and culture.

The time we are currently living through will be looked back on as a massively transformative era of human history. Many things we once thought were science fiction are now becoming a reality. At the beginning of July 2024, I was flipping through channels in a seaside resort hotel room, one particular story was being re-run over the course of an hour about how scientists were able to extrapolate chromosomes from dried-up ancient mammoth skin through artificially intelligent algorithmic systems—with the overarching purpose of potentially being able to recreate the mammoth itself. Earlier that month I had also, out of randomness, re-watched a movie that I enjoyed as a kid, *Jurassic Park* (1993), which was premised on what at the time was considered to be complete science fiction, wherein dinosaurs were cloned by a company in a remote tropical island for touristic purposes and revenue via DNA strands that were preserved for millions of years in amber. Scientists collected fossilized mosquitoes that were trapped in amber (having fed on dinosaur blood before becoming fossilized). DNA was then extracted from these amber-trapped mosquitoes and supplemented with frog DNA to complete the missing chromosomes. This DNA is then injected into eggs that are incubated until dinosaurs hatched. In comparison, contemporary attempts to "de-extinct" the mammoth feature scientists utilizing a new technique "Hi-C" to analyze the 3D structures of the mammoth genome. Through a private company's venture with a university, Professor Pask (head of the Thylacine Integrated Genetic Restoration Research lab) noted that "I hope we act responsibly with all the powerful technologies at our disposal — de-extinction being one of them" (Bowler, 2024). What we consider to be science fiction now, may become reality down the line. The societal changes identified in this book are not interpreted in a deterministic manner, but rather, are best viewed in open-ended form.

Discoveries of this sort do not rise out of thin air but are made possible by internet-reliant structures and systems and their recursive relationships and interactions with human agency. Theoretically, this book delves into historical and contemporary experiences and situates itself within a classical sociological approach to explaining social change known as structuration theory—an approach that seeks to highlight the duality between structure and agency (Giddens, 1984). Structuration theory is adopted to assess the ways which digital structures and individual agency interact and transform social practices. For analytical purposes, this book will categorize subjective experiences within the broader concept of agency—which itself will be contrasted to structure. As noted by Giddens (1984), "agency concerns events of which an individual is the perpetrator, in the sense that the individual could, at any phase in a given sequence of conduct, have acted differently" (Giddens, 1984, p. 9). Social structures tend to be shaped by organized frameworks, institutions, rules, and other forces that exist within the societies in which we live. Giddens' theory emphasizes the duality of structure and a central assumption is that social practices are produced and reproduced through the continuous interaction with individual actions (agency). Giddens noted that "the constitution of agents and structures are not two independently given sets of phenomena, a dualism, but represent a duality" (Giddens, 1984, p. 25). In drawing from structuration theory, I do not intend this book to only be for scholarly audiences. The usage of this theoretical framework will be articulated in the most basic of forms to account for societal change induced by the internet.

Some may wonder, why adopt such a complex theoretical framework at all? Others may ask whether this framework is outdated in light of computational social science, and especially social network analyses. There is no straightforward answer to either of these questions, but readers must consider that complex social processes warrant complex theorization. Along similar lines, sometimes frameworks that were articulated decades ago and remain relevant have stood the test of scholarly time—there is still great utility in explaining the world by considering social change via duality between structure and agency. According to structuration theory, structures constitute both the medium and the outcome of the practices they organize. Giddens argued that individuals are not passive recipients of structural influences, but rather, individuals possess agency which reflects a capacity to act independently and make choices across a complex set of social situations and contexts. Agency allows individuals to navigate and even transform the structures in which they operate. Importantly, structures are not static but are dynamic and constantly evolving. Through such processes, subjective experiences get intertwined with and influenced by structural contexts, while at the same time, individuals, through their actions and behaviors, contribute to the ongoing construction and transformation of these structures.

Internet technology has led to the formation of many different structures. Empirically, these structures both constrain and get shaped by our behavior(s). Our heterogeneous usage of these technologies constitutes agency. The interaction of structure and agency has been multifaceted since the 1990s and the onset of internet-based communications and the formation of a way of living that is completely digital—a reality that billions of people spend swaths of their daily time engaged with. Chiefly, the internet is not a superstructure that funnels specific behavioral patterns downward at us, nor is it a coercive structure that incentivizes us to behave in certain ways. Rather, it is representative of a structural set of changes that have already started to form. Digital reality gradually came into existence as more and more information made its way onto the internet. High-speed internet access has made its way into nearly all households in the country and nearly 100% of the population is covered by 4G internet, and upward of 93% already have 5G access (Dine & Kane, 2022). Meanwhile, a diverse set of advancements in artificial intelligence have increasingly started to operate largely beyond the conscious awareness of the average person and social media user. Processes and interactions are driven by complex algorithms and machine learning systems that are reliant on continuous human interaction from users of different platforms and applications.

Our daily lives are increasingly influenced by systems and structures we do not fully understand or control. No single person or entity oversees the digital realm which is infinite in capacity. Yet our behavior is of massive importance to these systems, and over time, it has shaped their makeup and output.

Despite the digital realm's reliance on electricity, historical evidence shows that energy grids and the internet remain operational continuously if viewed from a global scale. This near-constant availability has become a defining characteristic of modern society—it has enabled an incessant flow of digital information and services to subsist. We have likewise seen the rise of what Lippitt (2023) neatly conceptualizes as self-righteous behavior and different vices of virtue signaling. These have arisen on a mass scale, as online interactions increasingly seem to be marked by moral grandstanding and a lack of moral accountability. Consistent access to information is a key feature of many of the structural characteristics of digital reality. The non-stop iterative functionality of countless applications influences and gets influenced by agency across social, economic, and political contexts. The digital realm is accessible through screens, the most common of which include smartphones, tablets, smartwatches, automobile screen interfaces, computers, and smart televisions. The digital realm is simply an alternative world that intersects with our real or physical world but also exists externally from it—on its own as an entity that is propelled by billions of people's interactions with different applications and networks. If the digital realm is structural and is underpinned by the existence of the internet, then agency is the opposite—agency is subjective and through subjective practices, we influence the structure of the digital realm. This is particularly what has and continues to underpin societal change induced by internet connectivity in America.

Order of Chapters

My aim is to offer theoretical and empirical analyses throughout this book that touch on what I believe to be among the more important outcomes that the internet has brought about across society. This book concerns regular people and should not be treated as being innately an academic work. It necessarily should be read by those who seek to understand why things don't seem quite the same in today's world as they once were, by those who are struggling with finding themselves in a world that is full of an abundance of information that seems to be never-ending, and for those that simply hold an interest in the nature of technology and its relation to society. Along similar lines, this book is not just about the internet, it is about common people who use it, about societies that have been (and will continue to be) transformed by it, as well as about theoretical knowledge on digital technology. Regardless of whether you are a scholar, a student, or simply a curious reader who has an interest in technology, this book will deepen your understanding of the internet's broad impact and hopefully, this book may inspire you to think critically about the role that technology plays in your own life.

I begin my inquiry with theory and the duality of structure and agency. The second chapter lays out the theoretical groundwork of this book via the duality of structure and agency and explains how the digital realm empirically functions via societal behaviors and structures that are shaped by digital technology in a reinforcive nature. Chapter 3 then presents the first empirical analyses of this book by placing focus on civic engagement. It traces the decline of traditional forms of civic association which include changes in patterns of neighborhood gatherings and community organization and links them to increases in digital interactions. It draws on a large number of observations of survey data to illustrate how a heterogeneous set of factors has led to decreases in face-to-face interactions and interpersonal trust. More people are turning to online communities which, although broadening an individual's digital social network, often bring about feelings of isolation and reduced community ties.

The fourth chapter analyzes political polarization and trust in government. Here I argue that digital media and structures and systems of internet platforms have exacerbated polarization and have contributed to the formation of alternative discursive narratives, which in turn have dampened trust in the state and its institutions. The chapter demonstrates how algorithms on social media platforms can foster the commonly discussed echo chamber which reinforces a person's existing beliefs and amplifies antagonistic rhetoric. The chapter presents data that reveal a decline in trust across various institutions and an increase in politically charged discussions. The latter are increasingly marked by polarization. Next, Chap. 5 examines societal-wide declines in traditional reading habits and attributes these outcomes to the rise of digital media, which has shifted individual behavior toward consuming fast-paced and easily digestible content. I explain how the widespread adoption of digital technologies has led to a significant decrease in the time people spend reading, especially among younger generations. Empirical analyses of data reveal that Americans spend less time reading today than ever before in modern American history (data go back to the early 1970s).

Chapter 6 analyzes the increasingly prevalent phenomenon of internet influencers and argues that these entities represent digital idolization. The cyclical relationship between influencers and the digital structures they operate within is premised on the commodification of social relationships—many of which have profound impacts on individuals' lifestyle choices. Several case studies of influencers who have manipulated their audiences are put forward to illustrate the real-world consequences of the influencer phenomenon. Chapter 7 addresses the topics of privacy and surveillance capitalism. It engages with Zuboff's noteworthy framework and argues that while technological advancements have enabled pervasive surveillance, individuals still retain agency within structures and systems that are dominated by tech corporations. I raw on high-profile cases including Wikileaks, the Cambridge Analytica scandal, and the Twitter files to analyze complex power dynamics that have driven among the more important political outcomes about digital privacy.

The concluding Chap. 8 summarizes the findings of this book and explains how these chapters contribute to our understanding of internet-induced social change. If the conceptual starting point of this book begins with going *outside*, the logical conceptual endpoint of this book is going *inside*. This is what has happened since the rise of digital-based internet connectivity to populations across the United States. The concluding chapter of this book summarizes the many different associations that internet technologies investigated in this book have had with on societal change.

References

Alter, A. (2017). *Irresistible: The rise of addictive technology and the business of keeping us hooked*. Penguin.

Backlinko. (2024). *Revealing average screen time statistics for 2024*. https://backlinko.com/screen-time-st

Bowler, J. (2024, July 11). 52,000-year-old woolly mammoth chromosomes reconstructed from 'jerky-like' skin. *ABC News Australia*. https://www.abc.net.au/news/science/2024-07-12/woolly-mammoth-chromosomes-resconstructed-from-skin/104059130

Carr, N. (2020). *The shallows: What the internet is doing to our brains*. WW Norton & Company.

Castells, M. (2010). *The rise of the network society* (2nd ed.). Wiley-Blackwell.

Dine, J., & Kane, J. (2022, December 5). *The state of US broadband in 2022: Reassessing the whole picture*. Information Technology & Innovation Foundation. https://itif.org/publications/2022/12/05/state-of-us-broadband-in-2022-reassessing-the-whole-picture/

Giddens, A. (1984). *The constitution of society: Outline of the theory of structuration*. University of California Press.

Graham, M., & Dutton, W. H. (Eds.). (2019). *Society and the internet: How networks of information and communication are changing our lives*. Oxford University Press.

Lanier, J. (2010). *You are not a gadget: A manifesto*. Knopf.

Lippitt, J. (2023). Kierkegaard, "the public", and the vices of virtue-signaling: The dangers of social comparison. *Religions, 14*(11), 1370.

McChesney, R. W. (2013). *Digital disconnect: How capitalism is turning the internet against democracy*. The New Press.

Moody, R. (2024, March 20). Screen time statistics: Average screen time by country. *Comparitech*. https://www.comparitech.com/tv-streaming/screen-time-statistics/

Morozov, E. (2011). *The net delusion: The dark side of internet freedom*. PublicAffairs.

Rainie, L., & Wellman, B. (2012). *Networked: The new social operating system*. MIT Press.

Ruttan, V. (2006). *Is war necessary for economic growth?: Military procurement and technology development*. Oxford University Press.

Shirky, C. (2008). *Here comes everybody: The power of organizing without organizations.* Penguin Books.
SlickText. (2024). *30+ Average screen time statistics for 2024.* https://www.slicktext.com/blog/2024/01/average-screen-time-statistics/
Turkle, S. (2017). *Alone together: Why we expect more from technology and less from each other.* Basic Books.
Zuboff, S. (2019). *The age of surveillance capitalism: The fight for a human future at the new frontier of power.* PublicAffairs.

CHAPTER 2

Structure and Agency: The Digital Realm and Society

Structural changes have been induced by the creation and subsequent commercialization of the internet. Many of these developments are not deterministically connected nor can we assume that they are causally interlinked in any antecedent way(s). Nevertheless, the age of digitalized information has enabled information to become widely commoditized. Additionally, there are palpable parallels between the development of the World Wide Web (internet) and artificial intelligence (Halpin, 2004). Americans now spend much of their day scrolling through sites that rely on artificial intelligence to curtail informational content to their users. These sites, through algorithmic systems, monitor their users' actions; pick up, track, and record their location and previous search histories; and then from a vast amount of data, dictate what piece of information a user will be exposed to next. Through reliance on publicly accessible data and ongoing non-stop interactions with hundreds of millions of users, AI is on track to outpace and surpass human intelligence in a short number of years (Anisin, 2025). Moreover, internet users contribute to a globally connected web and interconnected network of machines and humans. This is the digital realm—a realm that comprises material, physical, and symbolic properties. The digital realm was created (and is currently sustained) by individual and group actions—through structures and physical properties including hardware, microchips, processors, cables, and satellites.

A. Anisin, *How the Internet Changed America*,
https://doi.org/10.1007/978-3-032-02395-7_2

This book draws from Anthony Giddens' structuration framework—a sociological framework that was initially articulated in the 1980s to address the key dichotomy between macro-level structures and micro-level actions of individuals. Among the more historically salient cleavages in social science has been whether or not causality and social processes are brought about by structural or individual (agency) factors. Often, theories were (and still are) developed based on assumptions that are akin to structural characteristics, functionalist frameworks, or even age-old Marxist reasoning which contrast when compared to frameworks that emphasize individual-level characteristics such as those based on utility maximization, methodological individualism, and emotional, neurological, or psychological dynamics. Social reality is more complex than can be captured by any single structural or agency-based framework. For this reason, the theoretical approach adopted in this book does not privilege either structure or agency over one or the other. Giddens posited that structure and agency are not separate entities but are interlinked in a duality where they continually influence and shape each other in society. This chapter will conceptualize how this duality is applicable and observable in the digital realm, which in turn will then be linked to subsequent chapters' analyses of internet-induced societal change in the United States. Among the more widely used examples of a system of interaction is speech in which a speaker's monologue is understood by the audience if they comprehend the language—this is what Giddens referred to as a basic example of structure. Languages typically feature strict guidelines or rules that ensure what is being expressed are understood by the interpreter. Through the use of the speaker's voice and their knowledge of the language (structure), speech (system of interaction) is thus understood. As such, structuration is the process through which structures reproduce systems and systems of interaction exist as a result of the structure of the language spoken (Lamsal, 2012). Rules and resources established by structures facilitate and reproduce social interaction. Giddens argued that structures are created and maintained through repeated empirical actions of individuals and groups. This duality implies that while individuals navigate their social world with some degree of autonomy, their actions are deeply influenced by structures that may encompass social norms or institutional resources that have been established in a given context over previous periods of time (Giddens, 1984). Structure is also assumed to be the basis of what provides conditions for action. Specifically, Giddens noted that "agency concerns events of which an individual is the perpetrator, in the sense that the individual could, at any phase in a given sequence of conduct, have acted differently" (Giddens, 1984, p. 9). This entails that structures are not external to individuals or groups but are internalized and expressed through their actions. A key characteristic of this theoretical framework is in how agents themselves perceive structure—it is not the case that agents are blind to the structure(s) within which they operate or exist in. They are well aware of the rules and norms and because of this, Giddens' conception of a social system entails that individual action is always patterned by structure and the overarching institutional reality (King, 2010).

A key conceptual differentiation can be observed in how Giddens treats systems in comparison to structures. Systems are marked by patterns and networks that are spread across space and time—here, cycles of actions are reproduced over time through individual actions, behaviors, and practices. In contrast, structures constitute the rules and resources that underpin social practices. As noted by Giddens, structures "exist only in and through the activities of human agents" (Giddens, 1984, p. 25), which entails that structures are continuously recreated. Structures comprise resources (material resources and resources of authority) as well as rules (procedural rules and moral rules) which are combined according to context. Human agency reproduces and, at the same time, maintains these different components.

Giddens neatly argued that time and space both need to be considered for understanding the continuity and discontinuity of activities in society. Social practices are always situated within temporal and spatial contexts. Thus, the duality of structure is reliant on space and time, as it is here where social structures serve as both the medium and the outcome of the practices they recursively organize. Moreover, for Giddens, time is of conceptual relevance because continuity and change are dependent on the temporal ordering of events and processes. In this sense, this theoretical framework is not antagonistic to statistical analyses or general understandings of causal inference that will be applied in later chapters of this book.

Nearly four decades ago, Giddens (1984, 1990, 1991) already had a hunch that technological change and advancements in technology would fundamentally alter what at that point in history were traditional constraints of time and space (Giddens, 1984, p. 45). Giddens (1984) initially noted that technology would stretch out the fabric of social systems (Giddens, 1984, p. 154). The basis of his argumentation was in a cross-historical comparison between modern and pre-modern societies. In the latter, social practices and individuals interactions were very much linked to local areas and highly interpersonal forms of exchanges that took place in limited temporal sequence (Giddens, 1991, p. 18). However, with the onset and creation of modern technology, this all changed as interactions began to transcend local contexts. Modern technology enabled communication to take place over vast distances and diverse time zones. Technological developments such as mass telecommunication infrastructure, networks, global transportation, and above all, the internet—all contributed to an explosion of human interaction across the world. Giddens already foresaw that such a set of processes would constrict time and, in the same vein, expand spatial reach (Giddens, 1990, p. 20). Social systems would be stretched as actions and events that would occur in one location could have rapid and immediate impacts on locales far away. Likewise, social practices would get transfigured away from their localized contexts and would undergo a process of restructuring across swaths of space and time. Some practices would be lifted out of their local contexts and restructured across indefinite periods and space.

Indeed, although Giddens foresaw how the world would grow to be more interconnected and interdependent than ever before, what he did not (and out of all fairness, simply could not) foresee was that the future would be marked by an incredibly complex and dynamic duality between structure (the digital realm) and agency (individual and group-based actions) that would subsist 24 hours a day and 7 days a week in a seemingly infinite manner.

Scholarly Applications of Structuration Theory

Structuration theory has been applied across a diverse array of scholarly fields in interdisciplinary inquiries by scholars. The most common sphere of application has been in the study of organizations wherein the theory has been used to analyze how organizational structures are transformed. It has also been applied to educational studies, media and communication studies, political sociology, healthcare, among others. For example, in education studies, structuration theory has been deployed to assess to the ways that educational policies and practices get shaped by broader social structures and interactions with individual behavior. Datnow et al.'s inquiry (2002) investigated thousands of American schools' educational reform policies and asked what happens when reforms get devised by external organizations? The authors argue that a rise in pre-packaged curricular and instructional models is closely tied to the increasing political pressure placed on educators to boost test scores. Schools that were labeled as struggling or failing often ended up facing an ultimatum from district or state administrators to either revamp their approach or adopt a proven educational improvement model. Many principals ended up opting for the latter. Interestingly enough, it was found that the ultimate success rate of any school redesign effort was dependent on teachers—if teachers perceive that changes are being imposed on them, then they are likely to resist and interpret reform as a temporally constricted trend that can be overcome. The authors' application of the theoretical framework enabled them to identify the reflexive nature underlying educators' perception of own roles in relation to students and larger structural and cultural factors.

Structuration theory has also been applied to the study of healthcare. Waring and Bishop's (2013) inquiry assessed the implementation of patient safety initiatives in hospital settings. This framework enabled them to account for how safety protocols were designed to create safer healthcare environments and, at the same time, to observe empirical practices used by healthcare professionals. Here it was found that such practices were critical in their role for how protocols were enacted and subsequently sustained. The analysis was rooted in the interaction of corporate structures and medical practices within Independent Sector Treatment Centres (ISTCs). The authors argued that social practices are influenced by prevailing social structures which include institutionalized rules, resources, as well as shared interpretative schemas. In turn, these impact and shape how individuals act and interpret their world (Waring & Bishop, 2013, p. 149). The inquiry highlights the duality of structure and agency by demonstrating the different ways in which doctors' responses to corporate changes in healthcare are shaped by their structured positions within organizational settings. For example, the authors observed how doctors' reactions to new corporate norms varied based on their professional autonomy and the unique value they brought to the ISTCs. This allowed some to resist and reshape their working conditions while others had different experiences (Waring & Bishop, 2013, p. 154). The utilization of structuration theory enabled the authors to move beyond a simple dichotomy of managerial hegemony versus medical resistance by emphasizing the dynamic interplay between structure and agency (Waring & Bishop, 2013, p. 155).

Giddens' framework has also been applied in the study of media practices. Couldry (2004) utilized structuration theory to investigate how media impact everyday life and shape consumption practices. Here, the interactive nature of the media industry was related to individual behavior and agency. The author discovered that media consumption is structured by both industry norms and individual behaviors. In turn, the analysis implied that media practices are not just determined by technological affordances or industry standards but also shaped by the everyday actions and choices of media users. For example, Couldry observes a recursive set of dynamics through media actions, representations, rituals along categories—all of which feed into a mechanistic set of functions that enable media practices to increase authority and influence in society. Couldry described this as "the anchoring role of media practices at work" (Couldry, 2004, p. 128). Additionally, it was observed that "media practices are crucial in ordering other practices through authoritative representations" (Couldry, 2004, p. 127). The key theoretical dynamic here is that media practices are not only reflective of existing social structures, but they also contribute to the reproduction and transformation of those structures through non-linear and mutually constitutive relationships between structure and agency.

In shifting disciplines, structuration theory has also been utilized to study mass-scale processes of social changes by political sociologists. Specifically, Sewell Jr.'s (1992) widely cited inquiry explored how social movements are formed and sustained. Sewell's inquiry started with the French Revolution in which it was argued that although the structures of the regime set the stage for revolutionary actions, these actions ended up transforming the very structures that had initially constrained them. This was a historical recursive process. Sewell put forward a general template for understanding the ways in which social movements can emerge and subsequently alter political systems. Historical agents' thoughts and motives are often shaped by their cultural and social institutions which are also reproduced by the structurally shaped actions of these agents. Importantly, under certain circumstances, agents can innovate in ways that reconfigure the very structures that constitute them (Sewell Jr., 1992, p. 4). Sewell also argued that structures must be understood as both schemas and resources. The former are the virtual aspects of structure which include rules and norms that guide behavior, while the latter are the material means through which power is exercised. Conceptually, Sewell emphasized the importance of recognizing the multiplicity and intersectionality of structures. Different structures such as those influencing kinship, religion, or economic production operate at various levels and modalities and often intersect and interact (Sewell Jr., 1992, p. 16). In reformulating structuration theory to include a more robust conceptual basis around the multiplicity and intersectionality of structures, Sewell put forward an updated framework for understanding historical change.

When it comes to how researchers have applied Giddens' ideas to explore technology and its transformative impacts on social practices within organizations, Orlikowski's (1992) inquiries are well known. Orlikowski assessed how technological practices get deployed in organizations. Emphasis was placed on the reciprocal relationship between technology use and organizational structures. Here it was argued that technology is not just a tool used by organizations but actively shaped by the social practices and contexts within which it is used. As expected, Orlikowski's perspective went on to be influential in the study of information systems (IS). This perspective, at the time, challenged what were overly deterministic views of technology. The author emphasized the recursive relationship between technology and social practices. The initial model drew heavily from Giddens' theory to argue that technology is socially constructed by human actors through the meanings they attach to it and also through a heterogeneous collection of ways they use it. Through observation of Computer-Aided Software Engineering (CASE) tools in a software consulting firm, Orlikowski demonstrated that once structural properties get institutionalized within an organization, tools that get initially developed by technical consultants become institutionalized (this happened within Beta Corporation) and in turn influence and standardize development practices (Orlikowski, 1992, p. 23). Technology can thus enable and constrain human action, as CASE tools were observed to facilitate a rapid design of screens, but they also limited the consultants to predefined templates. In turn, this shaped consultants' work practices and interactions with clients (Orlikowski, 1992, p. 24). The latter process exemplifies a duality in how technology mediates human activities and is itself shaped by the social and organizational context in which it is used (Orlikowski, 1992, p. 12).

Another noteworthy study by Orlikowski (1996) explored why technology's effects were not uniform across an organization—some employees adopted groupware in ways that reinforced existing work practices, while others used it to experiment with new forms of collaboration and communication. This variation in use demonstrated the contingent nature of technology's impact and revealed how it was shaped by the specific contexts and practices of its users (Orlikowski, 1996). Technological artifacts cannot be understood independently of the social practices they are part of. This perspective challenged traditional distinctions between the social and the material by proposing that they are inextricably linked and co-constitutive. This socio-material view later became quite salient as it broadened the scope of organizational studies to include a more cohesive understanding of technologies and their relation to social practices (Orlikowski & Scott, 2008). Furthermore, Orlikowski and Scott (2008) utilized structuration theory to examine relationships between technology and work in organizations. Here it is argued that technology is not a static artifact but constantly shaped and reshaped through its use in practice (Orlikowski & Scott, 2008, p. 434). Through the concept of technological enactment, the authors demonstrate how technologies become integrated into organizational practices. This occurs through continuous human interaction via a Black-Scholes financial model that they demonstrate had influenced the options market. This occurred not only by shaping the market dynamics through its application in trading algorithms and financial practices but through a mutual constitution of technological utilization and individual agency (Orlikowski & Scott, 2008, p. 462). A key implication of this analysis is in their critique of previous research on technology and organizational studies wherein a dominant assumption of treating both factors as separate entities was common. Orlikowski and Scott (2008) call for greater integration between these two factors as they are empirically deeply intertwined (Orlikowski & Scott, 2008, p. 453).

Finally, Jones and Karsten (2008) also applied Giddens' framework to study the adoption of new technologies in organizations. Here the aim was to bridge a gap in knowledge about technology and social systems within the field of information systems (IS). Focus was placed on how IS researchers have employed structuration theory to understand the interaction between technology and organizational change (Jones & Karsten, 2008, p. 130). The authors demonstrate that technologies are not simply external forces that act upon organizations, but rather, technologies are engrained in ongoing practices and routines of social actors. This obviously echoes Orlikowski's (1992) aforementioned theorization on the duality of technology. Jones and Karsten also emphasize contextual dynamics of interactions because within the sphere of information technology, social systems and technology co-evolve over time (Jones & Karsten, 2008, p. 134). The latter is a key insight I will draw from later on in this chapter and more broadly, in empirical analysis of this book. Likewise, Boyd and Ellison (2007) utilized structuration theory to explore relationships between social structures and individual agency within social network sites (SNSs). Although quite early in the history of these sites and networks, the authors' inquiry identified how SNSs can simultaneously shape and are shaped by the interactions of their users. Profiles, friend lists, status updates, and other similar features provide users with structures that in turn guide user behavior and interactions (Boyd & Ellison, 2007, p. 213). These structures, importantly, are not static as they are continuously reproduced and modified through user practices. Boyd and Ellison's (2007) inquiry neatly revealed how users adapt to technological features in innovative ways and transform the intended use of SNSs. These processes, as subsequent chapters will reveal, are now much more embedded within the habitual nature of the digital realm and specific mechanisms are linked to outcomes that operate within the duality of the structures of the digital realm and individual behavior and agency.

Theoretical Drawbacks and Conceptual Comparisons

We now turn to an examination of the drawbacks of this chosen theoretical framework, and while doing so, I will explain why structuration theory was adopted in this book versus other possible approaches. First, the drawbacks to structuration theory are well known. While I will not delve into the extensive literature on these drawbacks, especially the many different points raised in debates on the philosophy of social science, it must be acknowledged that the chosen framework has been criticized for vagueness with regard to its method and the concept of duality. Archer notably argued that the concept of duality lacked clarity and analytical utility (Archer, 1995). In putting forward her own morphogenetic theoretical framework, Archer argued that Giddens' framework ran the risk of conflating structure and agency. It suffered from a lack of ability to be able to distinguish between the two, especially because of the latter's multi-nodal nature and applicability. Put differently, Archer believed that both structure and human agency have distinctive purposes (King, 2010), and because of this distinction, Archer aimed to maintain a clear distinction between the two and argued we should aim to explore and understand their interactive properties. Possibly a more significant critique Archer posed was aimed at rule-breaking—since conditions are assumed to be simply internalized rules, then an individual theoretically possesses the freedom to interpret and follow these rules differently at any given moment. Such a critique, in my view, is important but is ultimately not damaging to Giddens' overall framework because it does not consider the necessity of free will—without being able to account for individual free will (which can manifest as agency), any framework will eventually fall into determinism.

Furthermore, there have been scholars who have criticized Giddens' conceptualization of structure also primarily due to its multifaceted nature—with a lack of clarity being observed in how different aspects of structure (such as patterns in social practices or rules and resources) differ from one another in their analytical and causal propensities (Chatterjee et al., 2019, p. 68). The lack of analytical distinction and direction within the framework's concepts is probably most evident in the overall lack of methodological guidance provided by Giddens, which Chatterjee et al. (2019) believe boils down due to its absence of a detailed methodology. This has led critics to argue that it serves more as a meta-theory that is absent of important details.

As time has gone on, these drawbacks, in my view, have proven to be somewhat advantageous to the longevity of this theoretical framework. Leaving space open for the development and potential applicability of different methodological tools was a wise maneuver by Giddens, as methodologies have advanced in sophistication as time has gone on, especially in quantitative research, computational methods have become more prominent as has the combining of different datasets. Likewise, it is arguably better for a given theoretical framework in the social sciences to be conceptually stretched out because that makes it more reflective of social changes and ironically, makes it more suitable to capture the complexity of social reality. As subsequent chapters of this book will reveal, there are heterogeneous processes and forms of causality that have arisen in different spheres of life for individuals and groups as a result of internet-induced social change.

As to be expected, many different frameworks can be compared to structuration theory. Bourdieu's (1977, 1990) theory of practice is of course relevant to consider right off the bat. Here, the concept of habitus captures how individuals develop ingrained habits, skills, and dispositions through their interactions with social reality. This is similar to Giddens' conceptualization of agency. Bourdieu articulated the idea of fields which he described as being structured social spaces that have their own rules, norms, and power relations. One can easily see the parallels to structuration theory in this regard. Bourdieu even emphasized how social structures can shape individual practices and how these practices, in turn, either reproduce or transform structures. Specifically, through the concept of the field, Bourdieu claimed that structured social spaces have their own rules and various forms of capital ranging from economic to social, cultural, and symbolic—either of which can enable individuals to navigate their way through interactions in fields. The habitus was described by Bourdieu as consisting of "systems of durable, transposable dispositions, structured structures predisposed to function as structuring structures" (Bourdieu, 1977, p. 72). Via the habitus, a given individual's positionality in various fields is influenced by his or her capital. The latter echoes the logic underpinning Giddens' conceptualization of knowledgeable agents that internalize and reproduce social structures.

A critical point of difference between the two frameworks is in how Bourdieu emphasizes that social practices and interactions are epistemically driven by unconscious and embodied dynamics that guide individual behavior. These dynamics are engrained and operate beneath individuals' conscious awareness. In contrast, Giddens' framework emphasizes a reflexive set of dynamics in which individuals consciously reflect on and adjust their behavior. In other words, Bourdieu's framework is premised on the assumption that social practices are unconscious and embodied in nature which in turn suggests that individual behavior across a given society gets driven by ingrained dispositions that function beneath the level of our conscious awareness. Such temperaments get formed throughout a person's lifetime, past experiences, and during processes of socialization and then go on to shape how individuals perceive their world and act in it. The key dynamic here, again, is that this is assumed to transpire by and large without individuals' overt awareness. From these assumptions, Bourdieu then contends that an internalized habitus can lead to a naturalization of social structures that feature individual activities and behaviors getting repetitiously reproduced. Giddens' viewpoints differ as he places greater emphasis on the reflexive monitoring of actions in which individuals actively and consciously reflect on their behavior throughout different social contexts. This reflexive dynamic is key to understanding duality. For example, as Giddens argues that people continually evaluate and adjust their actions based on their understanding of the rules and resources available to them, this deliberative and reflexive underpinning of social behavior entails that individual behavior is malleable.

As already mentioned, Archer's (1995) morphogenetic framework was premised on criticism of structuration theory largely due to Archer's argument that Giddens conflated different facets of structure and agency. In putting forward the morphogenetic framework, Archer sought to separate structure and agency through different analytical categories that were observed over different temporal periods. This in turn enabled the framework to offer greater analytical precision about how different factors change and interact according to the transformative potential of individual agency. King (2010) makes a notable set of claims by arguing that the fundamental contours of structuration theory were always close to morphogenesis. While novel, I did not decide to adopt Archer's framework, considering it is overly complex for the broad set of topics that this book covers. Furthermore, Luhmann's (1995) social systems framework also categorized society and emphasized the communication of individuals and processes that are self-referential and self-organizing. Due to its emphasis on communicatory dynamics, this framework would not be applicable to the range of topics analyzed in this book, as many of the factors we will come across in subsequent chapters intersect between symbolic and material components of the digital realm. Similarly, Cohen's (1985) notion of the symbolic construction of community featured intriguing assessments that captured the different ways in which individuals draw upon symbols and meanings to create a sense of community. Here, the role that culture and shared meanings play in enabling people to construct social identities and establish social cohesion was a key topic of analysis.

Further, Beck's (1992) framework on risk society investigated how modern societies are increasingly preoccupied with managing risks and uncertainties in light of fast-paced changes, especially in the spheres of technology and environment. Beck emphasized how risk can shape social structures and individual behavior. In detail, Beck's (1992) framework captures how transitions in modern societies have arisen from industrial-based risk to new globally oriented forms of risk that are at their core, difficult to predict and feature complex mixtures of technological development, industrialization along with globalization. The reflexive character of contemporary risks are a result of human actions and feature (but are not limited to) climate change, nuclear disaster, as well as financial crisis. In comparison to previous risks in history, such dangers transcend national boundaries and disproportionately impact highly disadvantaged and vulnerable populations.

This brings us to Castell's network society framework, which is probably the most relevant competing framework to consider. Castells' widely cited theoretical framework (1996) sought to assess how information and communication technologies impact social structures. Similar to Giddens, this framework also examines the relationship between structures and individual agency. Castells put forward a plausible and innovative set of explanations about how technological changes transform society. Castells predicted that new forms of social organization would emerge, namely, through the "network society"—a society that would function through informational networks based on the concepts of space of flows and timeless time. Castells explained how digital technology can enable the instantaneous transmission of information and continuous global operations that never stop. Similar to Giddens, Castells emphasized how this would reconfigure spatial and temporal categories of social reality. However, the most palpable difference between the two frameworks can be observed in how Castells placed a greater weight on the role of technology and networks and how they can spur economic and social inequalities by leaving people out of key processes. In detail, Castells had an interesting take on the relationship between power and counter-power, which he examined through salient contradictions that arose between multinational corporate media networks and creative audiences. Focus was placed on the concepts of framing and counter-framing. Here, Castells introduced four types of power in the network society: networking power, network power, networked power, and network-making power. Network-making power is considered the most significant form of power in Castells' network society—this form of power is held by programmers who possess the authority to establish networks and to program or reprogram these networks according to different objectives that get assigned to them. Switchers are also important as they hold the power to connect different networks, and in turn, they manage competition from other networks by setting up strategic collaborations (Fuchs, 2009).

Fuchs describes Castell's notions of power as being inspired by Weber because they have a clear relational capacity that features asymmetric influences of one group of actors over another through coercion, domination, and violence. Giddens, in contrast, does not conceive power to be necessarily coercive and violent—social situations can have power that is more symmetrically distributed (Fuchs, 2009, p. 95). Giddens also spends significant time differentiating his framework away from Weberian-based approaches. These are important conceptual points that are necessary for us to consider about theory on understanding how the internet has (and continues to) induce major social change in the United States. If technological network-based power were only coercive and violent, it would have a much more limited set of impacts across society. Individuals' involvement in the digital realm is often voluntary and reciprocal—it is through such involvement that the duality between structure and agency functions. For example, Chap. 8 of this book will dive much deeper into these dynamics via the dialectic of control, which will be utilized to explain contemporary practices of surveillance and privacy.

Giddens' conception of power in structuration theory does not necessarily entail that social reality is marked by coercion and violence. Asymmetric distribution of power is key to the functionality of the structure of the digital realm and its relationship with billions of users that interact with the digital realm on a daily basis. Importantly, this does not mean there are not exploitative and dominative aspects of the digital realm—surveillance capitalistic processes are salient and there are clear and easy-to-observe mechanisms of domination that exist throughout the internet, especially about social network technological corporations and their propagation of algorithmic addictive properties. Yet there is much more that goes on in the digital realm, and by limiting a given analysis to examining the exploitative and coercive nature of different processes, we will fail to observe cooperative outcomes that are driven by individuals' interactions with one another and with social structures. The duality between the digital realm and individual agency encompasses much more than power, domination, and coercion.

The Rise of the Internet and the Digital Realm

The digital realm is an electronically dispersed set of structures and systems that has been active and evolving for decades. As more of the world's population gets access to high-speed internet connectivity and as smartphones and other devices become both cheaper and more materially accessible, the digital realm continues to grow in scope and capacity. The digital realm functions through internet connectivity, ranging from 3 g to 5 g, from dial-up internet to the Global System for Mobile Communications (GSM), long-term evolution (LTE), and Starlink satellite-based technologies. In 2018 alone, 3.7 billion people used the internet across the world; Google processed over 40,000 searches every second (over 3 billion a day), and every minute of each day saw 46,000 photos get uploaded to Instagram, 456,000 tweets sent on Twitter, and over 4 million videos watched on YouTube. What's more, each minute more than 156 million emails get sent. The weather channel receives an estimated 18 million requests per minute (Marr, 2018). While statistics of this sort are of course indicative of a great extent of digital activity by human societies, the most increases in political polarization, which in turn have deepened ideological divisions and antagonisms throughout society. This has occurred alongside significant declines in the population's trust in the press, television, the executive branch, and Congress. Concurrently, major high-profile cases, such as the release of Wikileaks, the Twitter Files, and the Cambridge Analytica scandal, have revealed how data commodification and political manipulation of democratic processes have been driven surveillance capitalism and the interrelations of external political actors collaborating with tech firm executives.

When it comes to how individuals consume and come across information, major changes to reading patterns have also arisen. There has been an intense shift in individual behavior across American society toward consumption of fast-paced and easily digestible video content. Specifically, a 22.2% decrease in average daily reading time across all age groups can be observed over the last 50 years. While older adults read more than younger generations (65–74 age group averaging 39.6 minutes per day), the 15–19 age group averages just 7.8 minutes. When compared to how much screen time teenagers and young adults experience per day, they spend 3500% less of their day reading (7.8 minutes vs 5 hours). Socio-cultural power dynamics have also changed—especially with the rise of social media influencers. Influencers navigate digital structures to build their online presence by creating sensational and engaging content that aligns with user demands. Although not all influencers manipulate their audiences for material gain and profit, it is evident that many significantly influence the social behaviors of their followers.

There are of course many other considerable changes that can be observed in Americans' tendencies to engage in. People now use digital technology for basic tasks like paying bills, grocery shopping, dating, planning funerals and vacations, schooling, and entertainment among a plethora of other activities. This shift from face-to-face interactions to digital communication has led us to share our data and personal information with companies and governments without much thought about the consequences this poses for our privacy. There are, indeterminately, many more different aspects of societal change related to the internet that could be identified (but were not given attention in this book) such as changes to medicine, transport, space exploration, sports, and many other topics. The internet has also fundamentally altered the how societies engage in commerce—the birth of e-commerce giants such as Amazon has led to changes in retail landscapes. At the time of writing this book, more and more robust proxy of assessing how much a given society is immersed in the digital realm is in the amount of time people spend looking at screens per day.

Two decades ago, the total amount of screen time in an average person's day was minimal compared to screen time in 2024. Currently, it is estimated that Americans average around 7 hours and 3 minutes per day on screens which marks a dramatic increase. Generation Z (individuals born between 1997 and 2012) spend an average of 7.2 hours per day consuming video content on platforms like TikTok, YouTube, and Instagram. What's more, recent data from the American Psychological Association reveals that American teenagers are spending an average of 4.8 hours per day on social media platforms and 37% of teens exceed 5 hours of daily usage (DeAngelis, 2024). This trend highlights a broader societal shift toward increased digital engagement; it also indicates that a larger set of processes have occurred in which more and more people are getting immersed in the digital realm. Through this immersion, human agency contributes to the reconstitution of structures and systems via the digitalization of social interactions. Virtual connections are replacing face-to-face interactions in a rapid pace.

The internet is a necessary condition that enables the digital realm to persist and evolve in complexity through time and space. Over time, the internet has grown into a global network of interconnected computers that communicate using standardized protocols, specifically the common internet protocol suite (TCP/IP). This consists of four layers which include (1) the Link Layer, (2) the Internet Layer, (3) the Transport Layer, (4) the Application Layer. The Link Layer includes local network technologies, notably Ethernet; the Internet Layer handles packet forwarding through IP (Internet Protocol); the Transport Layer manages end-to-end communication through TCP (Transmission Control Protocol) as well as the UDP (User Datagram Protocol); the Application Layer supports services such as HTTP for web browsing, SMTP for email, and FTP for file transfer (Comer, 2018). Further, the internet is built on a mainstay of high-speed data lines which enable connections between cities and countries. Such data lines are made up of fiber optic cables that transmit data as light signals. As such, data on the internet are divided into packets that comprise small units that travel independently across the network and are reassembled at their destination. The common household router is a device that directs data packets between networks and ensures that data reach the correct destination via the best path for each packet based on the current network conditions (Kurose & Ross, 2017). The internet also features the Domain Name System (DNS) which translates human-readable domain names (e.g., www.google.com) into IP addresses which computers (or smartphones or tablets) use to identify one another on the network. This allows users to access websites and services using easy-to-remember names instead of numerical IP addresses.

In its early stages, the digital realm was most commonly accessed by users (regular people) through desktop computers, then through laptops, and subsequently through smartphones and tablets which are now found in houses, cars, and businesses. Indeed, the smartphone is currently the hegemon when it comes to screens and access to the digital realm. Two particular transformative developments were responsible for the rise of smartphones, the first of which was the transition from telephones into button-based Dialpad mobile phones that arose on a mass scale in the late 1990s and into the early 2000s. The second transition occurred with the launching of the Apple iPhone and subsequent models. Accompanying these transitions were swift developments in telecommunication technology, specifically the rise of 2G, 3G, and 4G connections.

The widespread reach of technology and our current entrenchment into internet technologies cannot be disconnected from one another—this is a key facet of the digital realm, in that it is not limited to one set of behaviors or practices but is all-encompassing. Durante's (2022) conceptualization of the ontology of virtuality and reality is worth mentioning here. This framework begins by considering a distinction between what is real and what is virtual. Durante argues that the virtual has always been a part of human experience through language and imagination. He refers to the ability of humans to imagine non-existent entities as a fundamental evolutionary asset that has been utilized time and time again. It is also argued to have paved the way for technological and philosophical advancements (Durante, 2022, p. 319). Traditional boundaries between the real and the virtual are increasingly blurred by digitization. Durante correctly claims that the virtual has acquired its own form of reality, which is independent of human perception and interaction. This entails that it challenges conventional ontological categories (Durante, 2022, p. 322). Virtual reality is demonstrated to have the propensity to modify human experience into three main forms: (1) augmentation or enhancement of reality, (2) re-engineering of the world, (3) construction of counterfactual realities for improvement of actual reality (Durante, 2022, p. 323). A new ontology of the virtual, argues Durante, challenges us to rethink the nature of existence and how we construct and interact with our world (Durante, 2022, p. 322).

Ravi and Cherukuri (2021) note that the emergence of big data (which is necessarily shared and computed via internet connectivity) has revolutionized development sectors and public planning. Smart cities function alongside computing which enables enhanced data management and processing. AI and big data have played a critical role in creating inclusive digital ecosystems through advanced tools such as AI-based exoskeletons and IoT-enabled smart environments. The authors categorize what are described as essential attributes of big data—the "5Vs" include volume, variety, velocity, veracity, and value. Importantly, applications that rely on real-time data processing function largely through cloud computing, which is argued to provide sufficient infrastructure that can handle the massive volumes of data generated by IoT devices. We all use the cloud, knowingly or not. I am writing this book in the cloud and have written my other works in the cloud as well. For around a decade, I have utilized Google Drive to store all my files across different laptops and desktops. I have been using Google Sheets instead of Microsoft Word because it has saved me during computer crashes. I tell all of my students to do the same, to eliminate the stress of losing a file, having their computer crash, or having something else happen that would entail their hard-earned intellectual effort would be in vain. Cloud computing, in essence, might be the most straightforward and easy-to-grasp function found in the digital realm.

The digital realm is marked by different cloud networks wherein information always hovers around. It is fruitful to think of it as constituting what Vallor (2022) describes as a fusion of artifacts and social practices that both influence and are influenced by human behaviors and societal structures (Vallor, 2022). The internet extends the life of information, things never really vanish. Danaher (2022) conceptualizes the usage of big data in society as algocracy and argues that big data, predictive analytics, machine learning, and AI are increasingly being utilized to govern human behavior. Importantly, it is argued that algocracy can both promote and undermine freedom. On the one hand, computer-coded algorithms can structure, constrain, incentivize, nudge, manipulate, and encourage human behavior. For instance, algorithms used in predictive policing and credit scoring can perpetuate existing biases and inequalities and in turn spur unfair outcomes (Danaher, 2022, p. 251). On the other hand, algocracy can also promote freedom by filtering choices and reducing cognitive overload by helping individuals make better decisions via relevant information and recommendations, which can promote rational decision-making and reduce the paradox of choice (Danaher, 2022, p. 264).

There are of course countless other examples that can be observed throughout the vast stratosphere of contemporary society in the United States and other comparable countries with advanced economies and high levels of internet connectivity. The wide-reaching transformative potential of technology, especially internet-based technologies, are crucial to theorize if we are to form an understanding of the different structures inherent to the digital realm. Along these lines, Bruun et al. (2022) make an important set of claims by noting that technological progress is not linear as technologies spread and often develop in unpredictable fashion—technological development gets influenced by social relations and technological choices across different societies (Bruun et al., 2022). The authors critique previous deterministic narratives around emerging technologies by arguing that the integration of technologies into a given society is accompanied by the co-production of social practices and technological usage. For example, the rise of digital platforms such as Uber and Deliveroo brought about restructuring processes for labor relations via algorithmic management and datafication but did so through complex social interactions with organized interests, institutions, and legal rules. This is just one example out of many of the duality between structure and agency in the broad scope of internet-induced societal change. Kristensen (2022) investigates how individuals engage in self-optimization through what she accurately conceptualizes as enhancement technologies. In many developed societies and economies, there now is a hegemonic and pervasive desire for self-improvement that is deeply embedded in expectations. From plastic surgery and neural implants to psycho-pharmaceuticals and genetic interventions, individuals are seeking to "enhance" themselves through digital technological processes. This is most evident in the usage of tracking devices, apps, wearable devices, mindfulness practices, and app-based meditation techniques—all of which are argued by Kristensen (2022) to symbolize a moral imperative for continuous self-improvement.

These developments are a part of individuals' immersion in the digital realm. Importantly, many of the aforementioned processes feature individual behavior that is not necessarily coercive in the sense of being brought about or caused by profit-seeking motivations of tech corporations or health applications. This does not mean there is no coercion or power-based dynamics within the duality of structure of the digital realm and agency; rather, the digital realm encompasses all of social behavior that functions through internet connections, applications, smartphones, computers, tablets, smartwatches, satellites, and many other devices.

The Duality of Structure and Agency

The concept of structure is more specific and detailed than that of a system as Giddens conceptualized the former, "structure exists, as time-space presence, only in its instantiations in such practices and as memory traces orienting the conduct of knowledgeable human agents" (Giddens, 1984, p. 17). What this entails is that structures are both the medium and the outcome of the practices they recursively organize. Since rules (normative guidelines and conventions that inform social action) and resources (capabilities or means individuals draw upon in their social practices) are the two primary factors that makeup structure, we must keep in mind that structures thus "do not exist in a time-space vacuum" but are "deeply embedded in the social systems they shape" (Giddens, 1984, p. 25). The aspect of duality here is in how structures are both constituted by human agency and at the same time are the medium of this constitution. In contrast to structures, a system constitutes the patterned relations and regularities that emerge from ongoing interactions between individuals within a given social context. Giddens describes systems as "reproduced relations between actors or collectivities, organized as regular social practices" (Giddens, 1984, p. 26).

Systems are best viewed as empirically observable outcomes of the application of structures in social interactions. The digital realm comprises numerous heterogeneous structures, which themselves have systems attached to them. Systems feature concrete patterns and regularities that result from practices stemming to a given structure. Within social systems are different kinds of structures (signification, legitimation, domination). Giddens goes to great lengths to stress that these three types of structures are not empirically static but are continuously produced and reproduced through social practices. Individuals behave within these structures and through their actions they reinforce or transform the structures over time. *Signification* structures are related to the production and communication of meaning and include symbolic orders and interpretive schemes that individuals use to make sense of the world and communicate with others. Language, symbols, and discourse make up signification structures. These structures provide the frameworks through which people interpret social reality. For instance, the shared understanding of words and symbols in a language allows individuals to convey and interpret meaning effectively during interactions (Giddens, 1984, p. 29).

Throughout the digital realm, signification structures are widespread on different platforms and applications that are used by billions of people. For example, the classical Twitter (now known as "X") platform created character limitations on posts back in 2006 when it was launched. These character limitations subsequently had a profound impact on digital discourse as shortened statements became a norm on the platform which also carried over to other platforms and online discourse in general. At its peak, hundreds of millions were using Twitter and many more were reading public tweets. Initially, a 140-character limit was set for tweets based on similar constraints of SMS text messaging (which at the time were limited to 160 characters for each message). In 2017, Twitter expanded the character limit from 140 to 280 characters; then in 2020, Twitter began allowing users to include voice tweets (of up to 140 seconds of audio). Within this platform, signification structures that were created by engineers and software programmers ended up operating through countless empirical interactions with users of the platform who adapted to the structure(s) and eventually these structures through engagement and feedback. The key observational point here is in how users created their own shortened words to save space in their tweets—such as "gov" instead of government. Many other examples of adaptations to signification structures across social media and other forms of digital communication platforms can be observed ranging from memes to short video clips.

On the one hand, technological structures may feature algorithmic curation that plays a substantial role in determining the content presented to users. Such algorithms are designed to optimize engagement by prioritizing content that matches users' past behaviors and interests for the overarching purpose of keeping that user on their platform. On the other hand, users also actively make choices about the content they engage with which is driven by their desires and preferences. This selective exposure further reinforces the type of content they are shown in the future because algorithms learn from these interactions. Such interactions result in a recursive ordering of social practices within the digital realm. This is not to say that algorithms are neutral. Indeed, many of American society's inherent problems, especially those surrounding race and racism, also manifest and get exemplified through algorithmic biases. Noble (2018) observes how search algorithms are not purely objective technologies, but rather, they are rooted in societal structures, some of which exacerbate power dynamics and contribute to the reinforcement of inequality through stereotypes. Moreover, as users continue to engage with content that resonates with their views, algorithms continuously refine and personalize the content they deliver—creating a continuous cycle of adaptation and continuity. These outcomes are clearly observable in the continuity of digital activity, where both technological and human factors are in constant play with one another.

Next, *legitimation* structures involve norms, values, and moral positions that justify and sustain social practices. Here, Giddens included rules and standards that define acceptable or unacceptable behavior within a social context. Legitimation structures can thus be assumed to provide a basis for the establishment of norms and expectations that guide individual and group-based behavior. From legal systems to religious doctrines and cultural traditions, sources of legitimation in a given society help maintain social cohesion and regulate conduct (Giddens, 1984, p. 31). Throughout the digital realm, we can observe how legitimation structures are widely active—in many ways, they simply get carried over from the physical world and real-life in-person social interactions. Although arguments can indeed be made that there are different moral considerations in an online world where people can post anonymously and create content under fake identities, there are, at the same time, clear examples that illustrate major platforms ranging from Amazon to Facebook and YouTube all adhere to standards that generally reflective regulatory and legal parameters that are prevalent in American society. Content that is "illegal" is removed and is done so quite rapidly due to algorithmic detection mechanisms.

Finally, the third type of structure for Giddens is *domination*, which captures how dynamics of power and control function via the exercise of resource-based authority. Domination structures determine how power is distributed and influence who can make decisions, allocate resources, and enforce rules in a given social setting or context. Empirically, these types of structures tend to be linked to political institutions that govern the distribution of resources within a given state (Giddens, 1984, p. 33). Similar to legitimation structures, domination structures feature traditions and doctrines, but with the domination structure type, power dynamics get exercised. This is where, for example, one could possibly observe political influences from lobbyists, interest groups, and other actors that come into play in an attempt to sway online behavior. This is also where censorship and manipulatory practices can be observed along with what most likely are a large number of latent processes that go on behind the scenes between state agencies and private technological corporations. Along these lines, domination structures are clearly present and relatable to T. Kant's concept of algorithmic personalization which reveals how personalization is not simply representative of a technical feature but constitutes broader cultural and social processes that can shape user experiences and even identities. Algorithms shape user experiences by curating user preferences through reinforcement of specific behaviors and worldviews that often can directly impact how individuals situate their identity and place in the world. The various personalization systems that currently exist across major technological platforms and search engines reinforce societal biases and have major implications for upholding normative assumptions on identity and social behavior. Kant notes that "the verified self cannot be considered inner or holistic, as Facebook and Google try to reinforce, but rather inherently iterative and relentlessly reworkable—a recursively flexible identity that must constantly prove its worth as a verified subject within the global flows of capitalism" (Kant, 2020, p. 76).

Furthermore, developers and data scientists design algorithms to optimize user engagement based on platform usage patterns. Widely utilized recommendation systems in streaming services such as Hulu, YouTube, or Netflix operate through complex structure(s) that function as machine learning models, data storage solutions, as well as Application Programming Interface (API) designs that facilitate continuous improvement and integration. Companies heavily invest in the development and refining of such structures and associated systems. This promotes growth through collaborative projects and funding. Industry norms and standards also influence their design and application and are particularly focused on best practices in content recommendation and data analysis. Recommendation algorithms that get used by such companies are developed and implemented by data scientists, engineers, and computer scientists for the purposes of analyzing a vast array of data including user history, user ratings, and even the time of day users watch certain types of content and their location. Such data are then used to create a personalized viewing experience for each user with the ultimate aim of keeping them engaged on a given platform or service for longer periods. Personalized approaches are formed as a direct result of the interactions between users (agency) and the algorithmic structures in place. The more users interact with a given platform, the more data get generated, which in turn allows algorithms to become more refined and accurate over time—this is structuration in the digital realm.

Technical Components of Structure and System

To better understand how structuration occurs throughout digital space and empirical time, we have to consider the duality of structure and agency and technical aspects that are built into digital media platforms that provide informational content to users. The system(s) inherent to digital and social media platforms are built on a for-profit logic—none of the mentioned social media applications and websites are state-run or non-profit. As such, digital and social media platforms are based on the utilization of advanced algorithms that are implemented by computer scientists and engineers to maximize user engagement and retain users on their platforms. Here, both signification and legitimation structures are created. This is achieved through a heterogeneous collection of strategies including personalized content recommendations, social validation mechanisms, intermittent reinforcement, among others. Such methodologies are rooted in psychological and behavioral principles which are designed to appeal to human tendencies and keep users engaged. Algorithms analyze user behavior and interactions to curate a content feed that is tailored to individual tastes which is representative of a digitalized personalized approach and significantly increases the likelihood of prolonged engagement. This is particularly why nearly all of the aforementioned platforms have similar content presentation—a given user is very unlikely to come across a string of content or stories that substantially deviate away from their past interests. Socially dominant platforms such as Facebook or YouTube extensively implement machine learning techniques to present content that users are likely to enjoy based on their past interactions and viewing history. This method creates a feedback loop—in which the greater interaction from a user, the better a platform will become at delivering predictive content.

Machine learning algorithms play an important set of functions by processing large volumes of data to identify patterns and make predictions. These algorithms use technical methods such as clustering, classification, and collaborative filtering for the overarching purpose of analyzing user behavior. These actions are carried out within each respective system(s) that is associated with a given digital media platform. With collaborative filtering, users are identified with similar preferences and content that they have enjoyed in the past. For example, Spark's MLlib library can provide scalable implementations of such algorithms and in turn enable the development of personalized recommendation trajectories. This particular library is widely used at the time of writing this book and includes tools for regression analysis, predictive pathways, as well as classification, clustering, and collaborative filtering. In utilizing such techniques, digital and social media platforms, in real time, engage in the continuous refinement of algorithms to improve the accuracy of their content recommendations. For instance, Ali et al. (2021) provide evidence for how MLlib 2.0 can handle large-scale data analytics tasks through reference to six datasets drawn from the University of California Irvine's machine learning repository. The authors carry out experiments on a standalone Spark cluster with particular configurations to test the performance of MLlib compared to the Massive Online Analysis (MOA) library. The latter is a prominent Java-based machine learning library. Along similar lines, Singh and Verma (2022) draw on real-time sentiment analysis on Twitter and demonstrate multifaceted ways in which it is possible to process large volumes of tweets for gauging sentiment polarity. This is done by leveraging machine learning models and parallel processing frameworks. Through analysis of 100,000 tweets that were collected in Twitter's API (and were stored in a MongoDB database), Sing and Verma deploy machine learning algorithms such as support vector machines, LightGBM, as well as long short-term memory to carry out predictions of user sentiment based on different characteristics that they derived from tweets. The latter included post content, embedded images, URLs along with profile information from users that posted. Without getting into the advanced technicalities of their actual analysis, this particular study is among many that exemplify how parallel processing can improve the performance of sentiment analysis frameworks when applied to social media data. Importantly, the authors note that even organizations that have limited hardware and resources can extract large-scale insights from social media platforms.

Furthermore, on a more psychological level, Fernández-Rovira and Giraldo-Luque (2022) put forward a plausible argument that tells us that social media platforms gain traction through leveraging an innate human desire for social connection and self-expression. Subsequently, as the platforms evolved they began to integrate more sophisticated data collection techniques. The advent of predictive models in the late 2000s classified users into advertising clusters and anticipated their behaviors, which the authors believe mirrors some of the predictive strategies that are used by

Amazon. These platforms also rely on the construction and implementation of reward systems that comprise likes, comments, and shares. All serve as rewards that reinforce user behavior and create a feedback loop that encourages continued engagement (Fernández-Rovira & Giraldo-Luque, 2022, p. 29). This has causal implications as such a mechanism is demonstrated by the authors to resemble and even parallel Pavlovian conditioning wherein the anticipation of social rewards drives users to interact more frequently with the platform. Along similar lines, systems developed within social media platforms rely on the concept of "fear of missing out" to also maintain user engagement through constant updates and notifications which create a psychological sense of urgency (and even anxiety among some users). By and large, this compels users to check their feeds regularly to stay updated on trending topics (Fernández-Rovira & Giraldo-Luque, 2022, p. 30). These examples illustrate the complexity inherent to systems and structures in the digital realm.

Developers and data scientists make decisions on algorithms to include for optimization on user platform usage patterns. If we turn back to the MLlib example, we can observe that there are technical aspects that necessarily would have to go into the structure(s) of social media platforms that rely on this framework—it functions through architecture known as Apache Spark, which includes core components and integration capabilities. More specifically, there exist computational models, storage mechanisms, as well as API designs that influence how MLlib is used and continuously developed in relation to new input. On an organizational level, companies that use, support, and subsidize MLlib's development contribute to the creation of a technical environment that shapes the library's growth over time. Development of such projects typically includes funding as well as collaborative projects and even community-driven contributions that provide resources to a digital library. Previous norms and standards also shape how MLlib gets designed and empirically utilized—norms are generally centered on what at any given point in time are best practices in a given industry, which, in the context under attention, focus mainly on machine learning and other data processing norms.

The empirical continuity of these algorithmic processes and mechanisms functions through interactions between structure and agency as developers build and improve MLlib based on their understanding of current technical capabilities and user needs. As a framework such as MLlib evolves, its technical landscape (structures) also evolves through the enabling of new forms of data analysis, which in turn also end up influencing how users engage with content on a given platform.

Methodological Approach

Having laid out the characteristics that encompass the duality between structure and agency in the digital realm, several things need to be considered about causality and this book's assumptions on how theory is linked to method. I assume that different outcomes are driven by different causal processes and mechanisms according to the context being studied. In this sense, my usage of structuration theory serves as a theoretical backdrop to conceptualize duality between structure (digital realm) and agency (individual and group behavior). As such, structuration theory is not a predictive framework. Since the subsequent chapters that form this book's empirical analyses are largely based on observational data which encompass surveys and other forms of commonly used observational and investigative techniques in social science such as King et al.'s (1994) widely cited work. King et al. (1994) outlined a framework of statistically based casual inference, which then developed into a unified empiricist approach that still remains widely used throughout qualitative and quantitative methodological inquiries in social science. King et al. (1994) argued that both qualitative and quantitative approaches can benefit from the application of scientific principles to ensure validity and reliability in causal inference. Mixed-methods approaches can be used as part of clear and replicable research designs (Brady & Collier, 2010). King et al.'s (1994) framework has also been influential in spurring the usage of case studies and other methods in complex social settings (Morgan & Winship, 2014).

The connection between Giddens' framework and commonly used empiricist approaches that feature statistical analyses can be observed in their shared emphasis on understanding mechanisms that bring about outcomes in the social world. Structuration theory provides a conceptual framework for understanding how structures and agency interact to produce social phenomena. Statistically oriented methodological approaches are tools that can be used for empirical investigation of these phenomena, to identify causal relationships, and to ensure that research findings are robust and transparent. Giddens' structuration theory and statistical analyses are not at odds with one another as in each perspective, many have recognized the complexity of social life and reality. Along similar lines, it is important to consider that among traditional views on causation in the philosophy of social science, some may believe that structures are static and can only unilaterally influence individual actions. Giddens' framework offers a different take as it emphasizes that individual action continually produces and modify structures. In this sense, causation is continuous and interactive in the empirical world. As noted by Giddens, "social structures are both constituted by human agency and at the same time are the very medium of this constitution" (Giddens, 1984, p. 25). Understanding causation through the lens of this framework's concept of duality can help to untangle the complexity of social reality, while, at the same time, it can provide us with an ability to observe a variant set of trajectories on how agents act with relation to structural constraints and opportunities.

When it comes to agency, I assume that it constitutes behavior of what will be referred to as an actor(s) throughout the empirical analyses carried out in subsequent chapters. For my purposes, the concept of an actor is utilized in a game-theoretic sense as an actor can be an individual, group, corporation, organization, armed insurgent group, state, among other entities. Agency will be observed through actors and viewed among broad patterns of group-based social behavior. Where necessary, I will draw on empirical observations of different stratospheres of individual and group behavior—some may reference neurological characteristics and studies, while others may feature broader societal-level data. In this sense, I do not privilege one form of agency-based explanation over another.

The methodological heterogeneity that is prevalent throughout different chapters of this book is reflective of the complexity that underlies internet-induced social change in the U.S. Adopting different methodological approaches is also meant to not fall into reductive or deterministic forms of explanations on internet technologies' impact on American society. Many of the phenomena that are captured in the chapters ahead are dynamic and are driven by co-constitutive processes between structures and human behavior. Internet-based technologies and advancements, which range from the spread of 5G connectivity to widely implemented algorithms and AI, interact with human agency in recursive ways and spur fascinating outcomes and social transformations. Structuration is the theoretical base through which every empirical inquiry in the chapters of this book is carried out. Importantly, however, the analytical strategy of each chapter can differ and the datasets that are drawn upon are also different in what they encompass, their scope, and their sampling methodology. The aim of drawing on quantitative analysis and data, where necessary throughout this book, is to unpack the complexity that is inherent to structures and the relation that they have with agency. Agency is not only an abstract topic—as it is directly observable and applicable throughout the social world and empirical outcomes and processes. Social behavior is of course theorized in this book antecedently, in theoretical terms, but critically, this is done deliberately to contextualize social changes induced by the internet according to the theoretical framework via empirical analyses. In this sense, the empirical analyses that are present in some of the chapters in this book feature datasets and large-scale survey data that are meant to complement the theoretical framework and conceptual basis of the chapters, rather than make up their totality.

Along similar lines, the methodological approach adopted in this book is not meant to focus on or put forward predictive output. The aim of drawing on datasets is to complement theory on how structuration empirically operates and to identify recursive processes that have unfolded in recent decades as a result of an evolution of internet technologies in the highly diverse American societal context. Identifying large-scale social changes is fruitful through the usage of big data. With this being said, importantly, the analyses carried out in this book are not planned to put forward narrow statistical-based accounts of social reality—such accounts cannot capture the complexity that underlies internet-induced social change nor can they capture the contingent nature of structure and agency. Data are utilized to complement the theoretical underpinning of this book, not vice versa. In Chap. 3, data are drawn from two different large-scale surveys: the General Social Survey (GSS) (featuring U.S. specific data) ranging from 1972 to 2022 along with the World Values Survey (global survey data along with U.S. specific observations) ranging from 2005 to 2022. The usage of both datasets enables the chapter to investigate social changes on the topics of civic engagement and societal trust. Chapter 4 likewise draws from the same datasets, albeit with relation to political polarization and trust in government institutions. Preceding both chapters' inquiries, structuration theory is conceptualized in relation to the main variables that are drawn from the data. While most of the data analyses that are carried out in this book are mostly descriptive, there also are several instances where more sophisticated statistical techniques are drawn on including ANOVA and follow-up assessments such as the Kruskal-Wallis test. Furthermore, Chap. 5 also draws on a big dataset, but from the U.S. Bureau of Labor Statistics' American Time Use Survey. Here, reading rates are investigated across American society ranging from 2003 to 2023.

In Conclusion

This chapter has explained and developed the theoretical framework of this book and has related it to profound socio-cultural transformations that have thus far arisen due to the commercialization of the internet. I have argued that many developments are not causally linked in a deterministic manner but have concurrently emerged with the rise of digitalized information and the evolution of the digital realm. Giddens' framework has been explained and contrasted with other theoretical frameworks, such as Bourdieu's theory of practice and Castells' network society framework. This was done to differentiate variant noteworthy perspectives that have been used throughout social science to explain major processes of historical and social change. This chapter has also addressed the critiques and shortcomings of structuration theory, especially about its perceived vagueness and what some believe to be a conflation of structure and agency. In acknowledging these criticisms, I argued that the framework's adaptability and openness to methodological advancements has sustained its relevance for contemporary social inquiry. This chapter has also engaged in theorization in relation to the concept of duality—duality between the digital realm where structures, systems, and interactions with artificial intelligence and social networking sites experience a dynamic interplay between individual actions and societal configurations. The digital realm represents a complex interplay between technological structures and human agency that influences and reshapes social practices. The next chapters of this book will unpack how this has all occurred throughout daily life.

References

Ali, A. H., Abbod, M. N., Khaleel, M. K., Mohammed, M. A., & Sutikno, T. (2021). Large scale data analysis using MLlib. *Telkomnika, 19*(5), 1735–1746.

Anisin, A. (2025). The humility problem and imminent ascension of artificial intelligence. *Studies in Christian Ethics*, Onlinefirst. https://doi.org/10.1177/09539468251347499.

Archer, M. S. (1995). *Realist social theory: The morphogenetic approach*. Cambridge University Press.

Beck, U. (1992). *Risk society: Towards a new modernity* (M. Ritter, Trans.). Sage Publications.

Bourdieu, P. (1977). *Outline of a theory of practice* (R. Nice, Trans.). Cambridge University Press.

Bourdieu, P. (1990). *The logic of practice* (R. Nice, Trans.). Stanford University Press.

Boyd, D. M., & Ellison, N. B. (2007). Social network sites: Definition, history, and scholarship. *Journal of Computer-Mediated Communication, 13*(1), 210–230.

Brady, H. E., & Collier, D. (Eds.). (2010). *Rethinking social inquiry: Diverse tools, shared standards.* Rowman & Littlefield Publishers.

Bruun, M. H., Wahlberg, A., Douglas-Jones, R., Hasse, C., Hoeyer, K., Kristensen, D. B., & Winthereik, B. R. (2022). *The Palgrave handbook of the anthropology of technology.* Springer.

Castells, M. (1996). *The rise of the network society.* Blackwell Publishers.

Chatterjee, I., Kunwar, J., & den Hond, F. (2019). Anthony Giddens and structuration theory. In Management, Organizations and Contemporary Social Theory (pp. 60–79). Routledge.

Cohen, A. P. (1985). *The symbolic construction of community.* Routledge.

Comer, D. E. (2018). *Internetworking with TCP/IP: Principles, protocols, and architecture* (6th ed.). Pearson.

Couldry, N. (2004). Theorising media as practice. *Social Semiotics, 14*(2), 115–132.

Danaher, J. (2022). Freedom in an age of algocracy. In S. Vallor (Ed.), *The Oxford handbook of philosophy of technology* (pp. 250–270). Oxford University Press.

Datnow, A., Hubbard, L., & Mehan, H. (2002). *Extending educational reform: From one school to many.* Routledge.

DeAngelis, T. (2024, April 1). Teens are spending nearly 5 hours daily on social media. Here are the mental health outcomes. *American Psychological Association.* https://www.apa.org/monitor/2024/04/teen-social-use-mental-health

Durante, M. (2022). Technology and the ontology of the virtual. In S. Vallor (Ed.), *The Oxford handbook of philosophy of technology* (pp. 318–339). Oxford University Press.

Fernández-Rovira, C., & Giraldo-Luque, S. (2022). *Predictive Technology in Social Media.* CRC Press.

Fuchs, C. (2009). Some reflections on Manuel Castells' book "communication power". tripleC: Communication, *capitalism & critique. Open access journal for a global sustainable. Information Society, 7*(1), 94–108.

Giddens, A. (1984). *The constitution of society: Outline of the theory of structuration.* University of California Press.

Giddens, A. (1990). *The consequences of modernity.* Stanford University Press.

Giddens, A. (1991). *Modernity and self-identity: Self and Society in the Late Modern age.* Stanford University Press.

Halpin, H. (2004). The semantic web: The origins of artificial intelligence redux. In *Third international workshop on the history and philosophy of logic, mathematics, and computation (HPLMC-04 2005).*

Jones, M. R., & Karsten, H. (2008). Giddens's structuration theory and information systems research. *MIS Quarterly, 32*(1), 127–157.

Kant, T. (2020). *Making it personal: Algorithmic personalization, identity, and everyday life*. Oxford University Press.

King, A. (2010). The odd couple: Margaret Archer, Anthony Giddens and British social theory. *British Journal of Sociology, 61*(1), 253–260.

King, G., Keohane, R. O., & Verba, S. (1994). *Designing social inquiry: Scientific inference in qualitative research*. Princeton University Press.

Kristensen, D. B. (2022). The optimised and enhanced self: Experiences of the self and the making of societal values. In M. H. Bruun, A. Wahlberg, R. Douglas-Jones, C. Hasse, K. Hoeyer, D. B. Kristensen, & B. R. Winthereik (Eds.), *The Palgrave handbook of the anthropology of technology* (pp. 585–607). Springer.

Kurose, J. F., & Ross, K. W. (2017). *Computer networking: A top-down approach* (7th ed.). Pearson.

Lamsal, M. (2012). The structuration approach of Anthony Giddens. *Himalayan Journal of Sociology and Anthropology, 5*, 111–122.

Luhmann, N. (1995). *Social systems* (J. Bednarz Jr., & D. Baecker, Trans.). Stanford University Press.

Marr, B. (2018, May 21). How much data do we create every day? The mind-blowing stats everyone should read. *Forbes*. https://www.forbes.com/sites/bernardmarr/2018/05/21/how-much-data-do-we-create-every-day-the-mind-blowing-stats-everyone-should-read/?sh=359e856b60ba

Morgan, S. L., & Winship, C. (2014). *Counterfactuals and causal inference: Methods and principles for social research*. Cambridge University Press.

Noble, S. U. (2018). *Algorithms of oppression: How search engines reinforce racism*. New York University Press.

Orlikowski, W. J. (1992). The duality of technology: Rethinking the concept of technology in organizations. *Organization Science, 3*(3), 398–427.

Orlikowski, W. J. (1996). Improvising organizational transformation over time: A situated change perspective. *Information Systems Research, 7*(1), 63–92.

Orlikowski, W. J., & Scott, S. V. (2008). Sociomateriality: Challenging the separation of technology, work, and organization. *The Academy of Management Annals, 2*(1), 433–474.

Ravi, V., & Cherukuri, A. K. (Eds.). (2021). *Handbook of big data analytics: Methodologies*. The Institution of Engineering and Technology.

Sewell, W. H., Jr. (1992). A theory of structure: Duality, agency, and transformation. *American Journal of Sociology, 98*(1), 1–29.

Singh, R. K., & Verma, H. K. (2022). Effective parallel processing social media analytics framework. *Journal of King Saud University-Computer and Information Sciences, 34*(6), 2860–2870.

Vallor, S. (Ed.). (2022). *The Oxford handbook of philosophy of technology*. Oxford University Press.

Waring, J., & Bishop, S. (2013). McDonaldization or commercial re-stratification: Corporatisation and the multimodal organization of English doctors. *Social Science & Medicine, 82*, 147–155.

CHAPTER 3

Civic Engagement and Social Interactions

When Emma was in her pre-teen years, she often accompanied her mother to a local community association that set up summer camps for children and helped those in need by collecting canned goods, going door-to-door, and printing flyers to post around neighborhood electricity poles to spread word about poverty. This association served as a beacon of community spirit for more than half a century in her town. It was especially helpful in a particular neighborhood where kids often would roam the streets and not eat for days, as parents were either working, on drugs, or simply absent. Crime and poverty were not sky-high in this neighborhood but were nevertheless more frequent and palpable than in the nice part of town. The one-story plywood houses with peeling and faded paint built in the late 1950s had seen their best days. Unkept lawns filled with brush growing over scattered old bicycles and broken toys were common to see. By the time Emma became a teenager, the community association that used to help the poor was shut down due to a lack of participation. People stopped showing up, stopped volunteering, and no one wanted to undertake board positions. By the time the financial crisis of 2007–2008 arose, many people in Emma's town lost their homes. Crime increased in the city and more homeless appeared. Synthetic drug overdoses started becoming common, and many people simply stopped going out as often. In the years before shutting down, the community center saw fewer and fewer people attend—especially during what were once popular parts of the year such as

A. Anisin, *How the Internet Changed America*,
https://doi.org/10.1007/978-3-032-02395-7_3

4th of July and Labor Day holidays. One of the community meetings in the local recreation center ended up in a fistfight, as two parents started bickering over politics—"It was the first time something like this happened," said Henry, an elderly man who had been tasked with cleaning up the center for more than 20 years.

By the time the COVID-19 pandemic arose, the recreational building that the association was housed in ended up being encircled by tents and the homeless; it was broken into numerous times which forced local police to have to patrol the area constantly. Needles and syringes were not uncommon to come across around the building, and in the summer of 2020, the building was burned down to the ground by masked rioters during nationwide BLM protests. As readers will probably acknowledge, the events described above are not unique to the Northern Californian context where Emma lived. The year 2020 went down in history as the year of the pandemic, but it likewise was a year that saw great political turbulence and many cultural and political cleavages that had been boiling up to that point. The year 2020 and beyond—2021, 2022, and 2023—all were clearly more polarizing than the years prior. Changes to civic association relate to changes in trust and to changes in polarization. Downturns in voluntary civic association elucidate a growing trend in America. Yet at the same time, there has been an ongoing transformation in the nature of how people engage in civic association and voluntary behavior. More and more digital interactions unfold on a daily basis than ever before. This ongoing transformation is indeed vast, it pertains to how people interact, and specifically, some of its primary implications can be observed in the amount of time individuals spend with their friends, relatives, and neighbors.

Broadly speaking, the United States is and has been, since its founding era, among the more diverse countries in the world when it comes to ethnicity, religion, ideology, and a range of geographical parameters. Vast mountain ranges, warm sea ports, cold sea ports, deserts, tropics, beaches, geysers, and the Great Plains make up the large territory of the United States. Within these places, populations sharing a common language have lived for centuries, and through different tumultuous periods of political history, the country has remained intact, although many (at the time of writing this book) would agree with the statement that society is as polarized as ever now since the civil war of the 1860s. If we glance deeper into some key historical dynamics that were prevalent across early periods of American history, we can observe that within the bedrock of America's historic social fabric is gold, which itself symbolizes opportunities to acquire material wealth and liberal freedom—in the mid-nineteenth century, hordes of Americans ventured out West as a part of a long stemming process known as Manifest Destiny. Territories were rapidly being incorporated into the United States alongside a massive push westward that was heavily encouraged by the Federal government. People of all backgrounds from far-off places in the world came in search of a better life. Many had a dream of getting rich quickly, while others fled persecution in their home state whether for material, religious, or ideological motivations. Indeed, many of the state-sponsored processes of removal of native populations from their land during the creation of the U.S. were incredibly coercive (Anisin, 2017). The latter, however, is not the focus of this chapter. We must consider that during the early era of U.S. history, most of what was at that point in the United States (and territories that would soon be incorporated into statehood) were vastly rural outside of cities and towns—there were no highways and roads connecting one state to another were often demarcated based on geographic terrain. There were substantial challenges of travelling that would often involve crossing fast-flowing rivers or going through contested and unpoliced territory filled with outlaws and bandits. Nevertheless, across areas in which collections of people settled, social interactions were marked by high rates of civic association. Helping each other, coalescing with neighbors, and contributing to one's community were all factors that went into early American enterprise and freedom. Civic associations facilitated opportunities to form new communities, towns, and cities across a diverse and vast geographic landscape.

Social scientists describe the practice of civic association as one that involves volunteering, debating, and amalgamating with other members of society without government encouragement or coercion. Civic association has long been argued to be a central component of democracy and liberal democratic freedom. Yet with the emergence and subsequent evolution of the digital realm, the internet has fundamentally altered the landscape of how people interact with one another. This chapter presents readers with an explanation of a rich set of foundational academic texts on civic association—ranging from Tocqueville to Robert Putnam. It then presents a conceptual and statistical set of analyses of processes that are associated with structures, systems, and mechanistic interactions in the digital realm.

Historically Contextualizing Civic Association

Civic association constitutes a set of interactions and social practices that are carried out by individuals and groups. It is known for its voluntary characteristics which most commonly manifest in the formation of voluntary associations. Throughout social science, civic associations have been operationalized through several different methods and concepts. On one hand, in quantitative injury, surveys tend to be the gold standard as they enable time series and large-scale temporal variation to be considered. For the U.S. context, the General Social Survey (GSS) is widely utilized, especially questions on respondents' participation in civic associations, which in turn enables researchers to trace participatory rates and engagement over different periods (Smith et al., 2019). On the other hand, in qualitative inquiry, interviews and ethnographic methodologies typically have been utilized to investigate sub-national variation in particular communities' and groups' preferences in civic engagement. A critical component of these associations is that they are formed without any outside or exogenous forms of coercion. Individuals and groups voluntarily come together to pursue common interests. Civic associations have included professional organizations, charitable groups, neighborhood associations, clubs, religious organizations, advocacy groups, environmental groups, among a plethora of other issue-based associations. For example, Skocpol's (1997) study of the "Golden Age" of civic association identifies a plethora of different organizations that played significant roles in fostering civic engagement and specified whether each organization had a local-state-national (Federal) structure (indicated as either Yes or No). The latter entails that the organization ended up establishing links to the Federal government. Below all organizations are listed from the founding era of the U.S. to the post-New Deal era (1945+), which had an enrollment of at least 1% or more of the U.S. adult population from 1790 to 1997 (Skocpol, 1997, pp. 464–5).

Aid Association for Lutherans—No
American Anti-Slavery Society—No
American Association of Retired Persons—No
American Baptist Women Ministries—No
American Bowling Congress—Yes
American Farm Bureau Federation—Yes
American Legion—Yes

American Temperance Society—Yes
Ancient and Accepted Free Masons—No
Ancient Arabic Order of the Nobles of the Mystic Shrine—No
Ancient Order of Hibernians in America—Yes
Ancient Order of United Workmen—Yes
Benevolent and Protective Order of Elks—Yes
Boy Scouts of America—No
Catholic Golden Age—No
Christian Coalition—Yes
Christian Endeavor—Yes
Citizen Action—No
Colored Farmers' Alliance—Yes
Farmers Alliance—Yes
Fraternal Order of Eagles—Yes
General Federation of Women's Clubs—Yes
General Union for Promoting the Observance of the Christian Sabbath—No
Grand Army of the Republic—Yes
Improved Order of Redmen—Yes
Independent Order of Good Templars—Yes
Independent Order of Odd Fellows—Yes
International Brotherhood of Teamsters—No
Junior Order of United American Mechanics—Yes
Knights of Columbus—Yes
Knights of Labor—No
Knights of Pythias—Yes
Knights of the Maccabees—Yes
Loyal Order of Moose—Yes
Modern Woodmen of America—Yes
Mothers Against Drunk Driving—No
National American Woman Suffrage Association—Yes
National Congress of Mothers (PTA from 1924)—Yes
National Education Association (formerly National Teachers' Association)—Yes

Of course, this is not a comprehensive list but does provide us with a good glimpse into the fundamental nature of civic associations in the U.S.; other noteworthy associations include the Women's Christian Temperance Union (WCTU), among many others, such as the American Red Cross,

League of Women Voters, Rotary International, Kiwanis International, Lions Clubs International, Boys & Girls Clubs of America, Habitat for Humanity, 4-H Club, Sierra Club, United Way. Some of the aforementioned associations played crucial roles in promoting social change and defending disadvantaged groups in society. The NAACP (National Association for the Advancement of Colored People) was created in 1909 and ended up playing a vital role during the struggle for civil rights in the 1940s, 1950s, and 1960s. The Rotary Club is also an interesting association—originally established in 1905, it has long pursued global humanitarian aims and peace.

Skocpol demonstrates how these organizations reflect heterogeneous outlets that Americans have pursued to engage in civic association. The interesting (and overarchingly important) component for our consideration here is that this has been done in the absence of Federal (and often state-level) government involvement. Often, these associations arose specifically due to a lack of state public goods and service provisioning. Rather than the government forcing or creating programs and implementing them from the top-down, civic associational activity and practices throughout American history have been able to organically reflect regular peoples' demands and interests toward the state in cases where the latter was unable to address key public needs and issues. Numerous associations provided essential social services such as education and even welfare support. The Women's Christian Temperance Union (WCTU) advocated for social reforms and provided community services. As noted by Bordin (1981), "the Women's Christian Temperance Union (WCTU) not only campaigned against the evils of alcohol but also engaged in a wide range of social reforms, including labor rights, women's suffrage, and public health initiatives, thereby providing various community services and advocating for societal improvements" (Bordin, 1981, p. 45).

Civic associations played a major role in historical struggles for civil rights. It provided organizational support and encouraged community solidarity. Associations including the National Association for the Advancement of Colored People and the Southern Christian Leadership Conference were especially important in their mobilizing efforts across predominantly Black communities. The NAACP's function was critical as it effectively carried out legal strategies that were used to contest discrimination on state and Federal levels, which eventually led to the monumentally important case of Brown v. Board of Education to demonstrate that racial segregation in public schools was unconstitutional (Kluger, 1975).

Along similar lines, the Southern Christian Leadership Conference was headed by figures such as Martin Luther King Jr. and organized mass nonviolent protests across the South, including other noteworthy events such as the 1963 March on Washington. Fairclough (2001) makes a plausible argument by noting that civic associations brought about legal and social advancements while simultaneously, they laid groundwork for future advocacy in the United States (Fairclough, 2001).

Many of the associations fostered community solidarity, advocated for necessary reforms, and provided direct services, which in turn helped shape the civic landscape of the nation. Through their efforts, these associations not only filled gaps in public service provision but also empowered individuals and communities. Again, this is not to say that U.S. history was absent of institutional racism, antagonistic racial cleavages, ethnic violence, racism, or any other adverse phenomena. These were all prevalent, and many remain salient today. Nevertheless, American society has also experienced fruitful civic association for multiple centuries. Skocpol correctly points out that organizations of this sort were historically vital to the fabric of American democracy and reflect the concepts of civic participation that Alexis de Tocqueville observed in his *Democracy in America*.

From Tocqueville to Putnam and Beyond

To date, social scientists have studied civic associations alongside a broader discourse on civil society and social capital. Putnam (2000) defined social capital as a phenomenon comprises networks of people who trust and cooperate with one another organically than for a given mutual set of benefits (2000). It has long been known that societies with high levels of civic association tend to experience a greater rate of social capital. Putnam's *Bowling Alone: The Collapse and Revival of American Community* (Putnam, 2000) was (and still is) a monumentally important text for understanding social order in the American context. The text is foundational for knowledge of civil society and its importance to liberal democracy. Before delving into this text and many of its empirical observations of twentieth-century trends on civic activity in the U.S., Tocqueville's work must be given detailed consideration.

Tocqueville was an early French social theorist and philosopher who traveled through the U.S. in the early 1830s and subsequently produced two volumes that ended up serving as a foundational international text about the nature of American democracy, the country's social structures, as well as civic associations. Tocqueville's central claim was that America was blossoming because of civic associations and that civic activity was directly connected to democratic functionality. Unlike what was occurring in Western Europe at the time, Tocqueville had a very positive evaluation of the U.S. context wherein,

> Americans of all ages, all conditions, and all dispositions constantly form associations. They have not only commercial and manufacturing companies, in which all take part, but associations of a thousand other kinds, religious, moral, serious, futile, extensive or restricted, enormous or diminutive. (Tocqueville, 2000, p. 513)

At a time when revolutions against monarchical regimes and empires were prevalent in Europe, Tocqueville observed that civic associations in America served a counter-balancing function that fostered pervasive cooperation and mutual assistance. Tocqueville (1835/1840) stated,

> as soon as several of the inhabitants of the United States have taken up an opinion or a feeling which they wish to promote to the world, they look out for mutual assistance; and as soon as they have found one another out, they combine. (Tocqueville, 2000, p. 517)

The latter was geared toward establishing common perceptions of public goods. Additionally, Tocqueville notably stated that "in democratic countries, the science of association is the mother of science; the progress of all the rest depends upon the progress it has made" (Tocqueville, 2000, p. 514). There also was an egalitarian attitude that was observed throughout his travels which was equated with a liberal notion of equality, "If men are to remain civilized or to become so, the art of associating together must grow and improve in the same ratio in which the equality of conditions is increased" (Tocqueville, 2000, p. 516).

Along similar lines, among the more salient differences that were prevalent during Tocqueville's ethnographic expedition was the separation of church and state. On this topic, it was noted that "religion in America takes no direct part in the government of society, but it must be regarded as the first of their political institutions" (Tocqueville, 2000, p. 518). At the time, theistic worldviews were still heavily prominent, but the key dynamic here is that the state was not a sponsor of any particular form of Christianity, nor were there any restrictions on religious practice that could compare to what was going on in Europe at that time. Finally, perhaps Tocqueville's most quoted statement about civic association and democracy in America told his readers that "the health of a democratic society may be measured by the quality of functions performed by private citizens" (Tocqueville, 2000, p. 519). This timeless statement is of utmost importance for understanding social and political behavior in today's world. The nature of what constitutes quality of functions performed by private citizens has fundamentally transformed from being physical to digital—it may even be more fruitful to consider this transformation a metamorphosis, as few could have imagined back in the early 2000s (when the usage of flip phones was only starting to become a new norm), that just two decades later, individuals would spend most of their day looking at a screen, scrolling through endless content curtailed to their unique interests.

Now shifting onto Putnam's seminal studies on civic decline in the United States, here, the central claim that Putnam advanced back in the late 1990s was that the United States had, up until that point, experienced deterioration in social capital and civic engagement when compared to previous eras. The implications of this argument were massive—civic association and social capital are critically important for a range of societal functions, argued Putnam. Specifically, it was noted that "civic engagement and social connectedness are practical preconditions for better schools, safer streets, faster economic growth, more effective government, and even healthier and happier lives" (Putnam, 2000, p. 326). The approach that Putnam adopted was simple and empiricist in its character—extensive analyses of survey data and membership records of social participation were drawn upon. Putnam broadly observed that changes in social structure(s), advancements in technology, as well as shifts in cultural norms all negatively impacted community ties and in turn spurred a decline in civic engagement. Conceptually, many believe that Putnam's inquiry successfully linked Tocqueville's theoretical intuitions with empirical data.

Some noteworthy findings from Putnam's analyses included participation in partisan political activities significantly decreased from the 1950s to the 1990s—a decline that coincided with a shift from active participation in election campaigns to a more passive character of observation by the general population. Putnam also found a substantial reduction in grassroots democracy—between the mid-1970s and the mid-1990s more than a third of America's civic infrastructure vanished. Across 12 separate civic activities, Putnam observed an average decline in participation of 10%

between 1973–1974 and 1983–1984. This subsequently accelerated to a 24% decline between 1983–1984 and 1993–1994. Such a trend illustrated a diminution in social capital and community involvement in the U.S. Ultimately, Putnam's observations were markedly different when it comes to twentieth-century civic engagement and participation in community activities (from the mid-twentieth century to 1997) in comparison to Tocqueville's observations of a pulsating trend of civic engagement that was observed in the nineteenth century. If individuals were still "Bowling Alone" during the time which Putnam wrote his seminal work, today they are bowling inside, physically, and more specifically, they are entrenched in the digital realm.

Recent Social Inquiry on Civic Association

Subsequent to Putnam, a noteworthy perspective was put forward by Skocpol (2003) who argued that a shift in civic associations occurred from mass-membership-based organization to professionally managed advocacy groups. Such a shift, contended Skocpol, was brought about due to a decline in grassroots participation, which itself was driven by weakened civic and democratic engagement. Along these lines, Warren's (2001) extensive ethnographic inquiry involved attending meetings, rallies, and civic associational events along with text-based reviews of organizational records, meeting minutes, reports, and other relevant documents produced by community organizations. Organizations included the Industrial Areas Foundation, which is a network of faith-based community organizations that seek to address socio-economic topics as well as the Greater Boston Interfaith Organization, which similarly focuses on socio-economic issues that range from healthcare reform to affordable housing and education. Warren also extensively investigated the Pacific Institute for Community Organization, which works on issues of immigration reform and economic justice. Warren found that relational organizing through building personal relationships and community ties enabled individuals to achieve collective action and effectively address local issues. For example, Warren demonstrated how community groups such as the Greater Boston Interfaith Organization have successfully enacted policy changes and revitalized grassroots democratic participation. This showcases the powerful role that strong social connections have in fostering civic engagement (Warren, 2001).

Analogous to Putnam, Warren contends that community ties positively contribute to democratic processes. Warren's analysis reveals a central logic that underpins theoretical assumptions on civic association, social capital, and their linkage to democratic functionality. Here, individual activities that are aimed at achieving cooperative norms and social cohesion based on specific goals and issues tend to have a positive spill-over effect for society at large. Warren's inquiries were carried out at a time that was marked by the beginning advent of the digital realm. With the arrival of Facebook (back in 2006–2007) and the subsequent emergence of social media hegemons (including Twitter, YouTube, then Instagram, TikTok, etc.), it appears that more and more people are engaging in different activities that can potentially be classified as belonging to the umbrella of civic engagement, but their engagement is not necessarily physical and interactive in the classical sense of these terms.

Furthermore, Skoric et al. (2016) carried out a meta-analytic review to investigate social media and its relation to citizen engagement. Here, associations between social media usage and citizen engagement (social capital, civic engagement, political participation) are quantified through analysis of 22 studies that were published between 2007 and 2013. The authors find that social media use had a positive relationship with citizen engagement across the three sub-categories. A key discovery is that informational uses of social media significantly predict citizen engagement, which reinforces the idea that access to diverse political information via social media can invigorate civic participation by improving political knowledge and stimulating political discussion. The authors notably state that "social media enable users to intensify interactions with their online and offline contacts, expanding their social networks, and consequently, social capital" (Skoric et al., 2016, p. 1820). Boulianne (2020) also put forward a meta-analysis of research conducted between 1995 and 2016 on these topics, specifically on associations between digital media use and offline civic and political participation. Upward of 300 studies were investigated via multivariate modeling. A small increase in civic engagement was found and attributed to the rise of social networking sites, interactive websites, and the development of online tools that can facilitate political participation. The latter is an interesting finding, as back in 2007–2008, Bachen et al. (2008) investigated internet-based civic websites through the prism of addressing youth disengagement from civic life. A total of 73 US-based civic websites aimed at youth were investigated qualitatively and here the authors observed that many sites lacked interactive features (message boards and simulations) which conceptually would be important for engaging young users and developing civic skills. Although the authors believe that information and communication technology have the potential to enhance civic education, at the time of publication, the inquiry entailed that many websites do not employ active pedagogical techniques nor did websites adequately address topics such as freedom of speech and intellectual property rights.

Since then, internet-based content has become more functional due to the emergence of high-powered smartphones and associated Android and IOS applications. Moreover, Boulianne (2020) also observed variations in effect sizes across different countries and over different temporal periods. The average coefficient for U.S. studies is 0.130, studies outside the U.S. average 0.144, though this difference is not statistically significant ($F = 0.806$, $p = 0.370$)—this likely suggests that the U.S. is not unique in societal trends that have been considered to be induced by digital media impact(s).

Next, studying the youth as a group is important as thus far throughout the evolution of the digital realm, the youngest cohorts of society have displayed the heaviest internet usage and generally are most entrenched into the structures and systems of digital reality. Moy et al. (2005) analyzed the relationship between internet use and civic engagement via a community study with 301 respondents. The authors neatly conceptualized seven distinct dimensions of internet use: information seeking, email, household management, political participation, consumer use, social networking, and community activism. The analysis revealed that using the internet for information seeking, email, and political and community activities positively correlates with all dimensions of civic engagement. In contrast, socially based web activities and household management revealed negative relationships.

Other inquiries have come to opposite conclusions. McCarty et al. (2006) observed that decreasing civic engagement statistically correlates with increased political polarization in the U.S. as Americans participate less in community organizations they tend to become more ideologically rigid. The latter finding was also addressed in Putnam and Campbell (2010), which shows that religious and community-based civic associations have historically played a role in reducing political animosities by bringing people of different backgrounds together. Additionally, a study by Knoke (2019) highlights that the decline of local civic organizations has contributed to a rise in polarized political identities. Knoke argues that these organizations historically provided forums for deliberation and consensus-building, which are crucial for democratic stability. The erosion of such forums leaves a vacuum that is often filled by polarizing media and partisan advocacy groups, which in turn further drives political division throughout society.

Divergence in research findings across aforementioned outcomes is to be expected—as heavier entrenchment of populations into the digital realm takes place, from year to year, more and more people are using digital technology. That people's social networks are increasing is logical, but we must also not forget that these social networks are of a different nature to those found in times prior to the onset of the digital realm. By observing data on people who have experienced increases in their digital-based social networks, a given researcher studying a given population will find that people may contemplate or report greater civic activities. The key aspect here, however, is that these activities are not always analogous to classical forms of civic engagement and do not represent the same forms of community ties that were prevalent one century ago. When zooming into the actual type(s) of content that individuals consume, things become much more interesting. Individuals' entrenchment in the digital realm has been accompanied by decreases in time spent with friends, family, and neighbors. Likewise, there is a lower level trust of community that is accompanied by perceptions of greater neighborhood insecurity. Theoretically, these outcomes are not representative of random empirical occurrences. As more of society shifts into living their day-to-day lives throughout the digital realm, the structures and systems they interact with also change. In turn, this leads individual behavior to also change. Legitimation structures that feature norms and values are formed and reinforced over time online, rather than in person. Much of reality is interpreted and seen through massive increases in the total amount of content a given person comes across each day, and in consuming all of this content, an individual learns about their world, especially through signification structures in which meaning is created and communicated through symbols and discourse.

Social Interactions, Civic Association, and Trust

In this section, data drawn from the World Values Survey (Inglehart et al., 2014), as well as the US General Social Survey (GSS) (Davern et al., 2023), will be analyzed in order to obtain the broadest possible information on topics pertaining to civic engagement. This will be followed by a multifaceted analysis of digital technology. The WVS is among the more comprehensive global survey projects ever put together by social scientists. It explores people's values, beliefs, and attitudes and investigates how they change over time. The WVS features good data for studying the United States over time because of its longitudinal nature. This can enable us to track shifts in public opinion and societal values. Welzel and Inglehart (2005) notably utilized WVS data to articulate a theory of human development that associated socio-economic development with large-scale cross-national cultural changes. The World Values Survey data are widely utilized throughout social science and rely on a dependable sampling methodology. Specifically, countries that have a population that exceeds 2 million get allocated a sample size of 1200. Those with less than two million people get assigned a sample size of 1000. For nations with large and highly diverse populations (e.g., India, China or the USA, Brazil, etc.), an $N = 1500$ or more is assigned. The process that goes into sampling is done in coordination with the WVS Survey Design team and national team researchers who implement sampling frames and track each stage of sampling along with calculations on gross and net sample sizes. A very solid conceptual aspect of the WVS is that these data have been gathered, coded, and standardized with consistency across many survey waves dating back to the 1980s.

Moreover, when it comes to the US General Social Survey (GSS), this is also a long-standing sociological survey that has been used to gather data on demographic characteristics and attitudes, specifically of Americans. Initiated in 1972 and conducted nearly every year since, data have provided a plethora of insight into opinions, behaviors, and societal trends in the United States. The survey's comprehensive and consistent methodology allows researchers to analyze changes over time. Like the WVS, complex sampling strategies are utilized for the purpose of obtaining a sample of respondents that is nationally representative. Multi-stage clustering is used with the aim of taking populational distribution into consideration. Researchers also draw on rotating panels in order to track changes over time. Also similar to the WVS, the GSS features many historically standardized questions that allow for comparisons across time (Marsden et al., 2021).

We begin with the GSS and the first question under attention in which respondents have been asked (over a nearly 50-year time period) whether "generally speaking, would you say that most people can be trusted or that

Table 3.1 People can be trusted in the United States 1972–2022 (n = 12,857)

Year	*Can trust (%)*	*Can't be too careful (%)*	*Depends (%)*
1972	46.1	49.2	3.7
1980	42.5	52.6	4.4
1990	24.5	37.8	2.8
2000	23.5	39.2	4.3
2010	21.7	41.9	3.9
2022	10.2	25.6	3.6

you can't be too careful in dealing with people?" Table 3.1 lists descriptive statistics based on data from a question in the GSS that has been consistently asked to respondents from the period of 1972–2022.

A category Do not Know/Cannot Choose has been omitted from the table as less than 1% of respondents voiced this choice over time. These data reveal a major shift in American society toward decreased interpersonal trust and increased perceptions of caution as observed over the past five decades. For example, back in 1972, 46.1% of respondents believed that most people could be trusted and 49.2% felt that "you can't be too careful" in dealing with others. This indicates that a relatively balanced view of trust in relation to caution existed in the early 1970s. Yet, over time the percentage of people who believed that most people can be trusted declined in a major way as by 2022, only 10.2% of respondents expressed trust in most people. Vice versa, the percentage of respondents who felt that "you can't be too careful" increased over the same period. Figure 3.1 summarizes and visualizes these descriptive statistical tendencies and reveals that the two-fold decrease from 2010 to 2022 represents the largest decrease observable since these data were collected.

We now turn to a crucial set of variables wherein respondents were asked how much time they spend with their neighbors, relatives, and friends. In my view, these measurements provide us with what probably is the most robust proxy drawn from large-scale cross-historical survey data that can inform us of the extent to which individuals are starting to become immersed in the digital realm. These measures also can serve as a proxy for civic engagement—classical understandings of the concept entailed that an individual would be an active member of his/her community and do so on a voluntary basis. Indeed, one of the implications of the trends that will be revealed below is that people will typically feel less connected, physically, to their near community and family if they do not actually spend time with

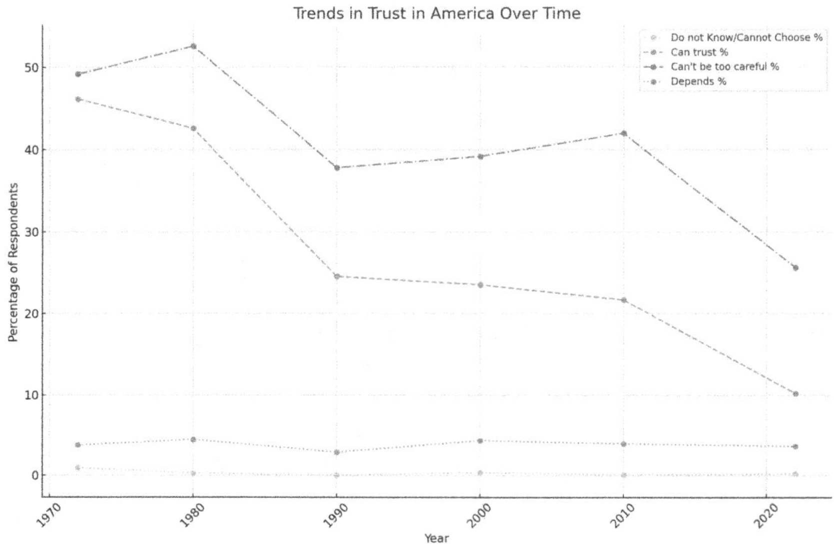

Fig. 3.1 People can be trusted in the United States 1972–2022 (n = 12,857)

them in the classical ontological material setting. Beginning with GSS data on a question that has long been asked to respondents, Fig. 3.2 visualizes descriptive statistics on how many times have respondents reported they spent an evening with friends: this question has different categories ranging from daily to yearly.

The results displayed in Fig. 3.2 suggest that there are noteworthy declines in the frequency that Americans spend time with their friends. As indicated, there is an uptick in the frequency of respondents who spent evenings with their friends very rarely—especially those who reported they only did so several times a year. Interestingly enough, the downward trend that occurred around the time of 9/11 likely indicates that the exogenous shock brought onto American society during that period brought people together, decreased polarization, and increased trust in government. Observed decreases in the frequency of Americans spending time with friends can be associated to broader trends in social interactions and the digital realm. The rise of digital technology and social media has significantly altered how people interact (Pontes et al., 2015). Pontes et al. (2015) found evidence of a de-socializing effect about digital technology

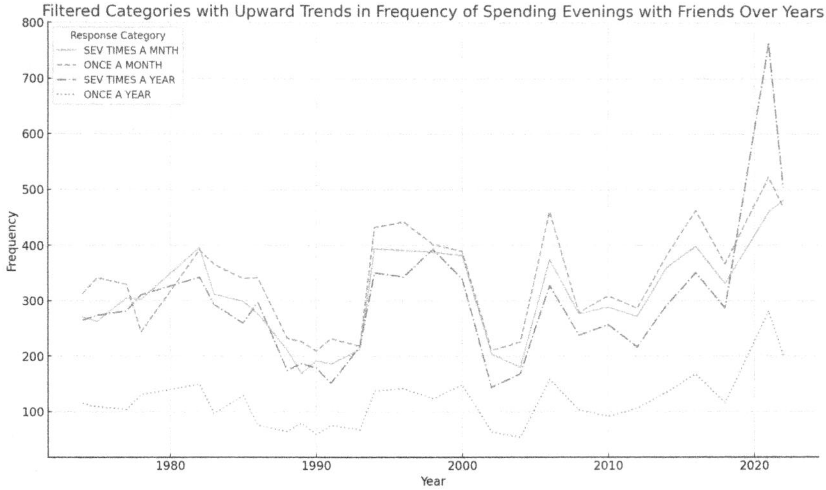

Fig. 3.2 Spending evenings with friends (1972–2022) ($N = 29{,}484$)

and civic engagement in a cross-sectional study featuring 1057 participants (aged 16–70). The authors placed focus on four outcomes: (1) participants' preferred online activities; (2) expected changes in behavior if access to these activities was restricted; (3) perceived quality of life without internet access; (4) self-diagnosed internet addiction and intensity/frequency of internet use. Their findings revealed that 51% of participants perceived themselves as being addicted to the internet, and 14.1% believed their quality of life would improve without internet access. The authors claimed that their findings imply that usage of the internet significantly influences individuals' intensity and commitment to online activities. While digital technologies provide new ways to connect masses of people, they can also displace traditional face-to-face interactions and in turn bring about declines in physical socialization, which brings us back to Putnam, who notably argued that fewer social interactions can lead to lower levels of civic engagement as individuals become less involved in community activities and organizations.

Other factors that impact individuals' behavior in the digital realm, such as the rise of remote work, might also contribute to people spending more time at home and limiting their opportunities (whether knowingly or unknowingly) for socializing in person. We now turn to the same type

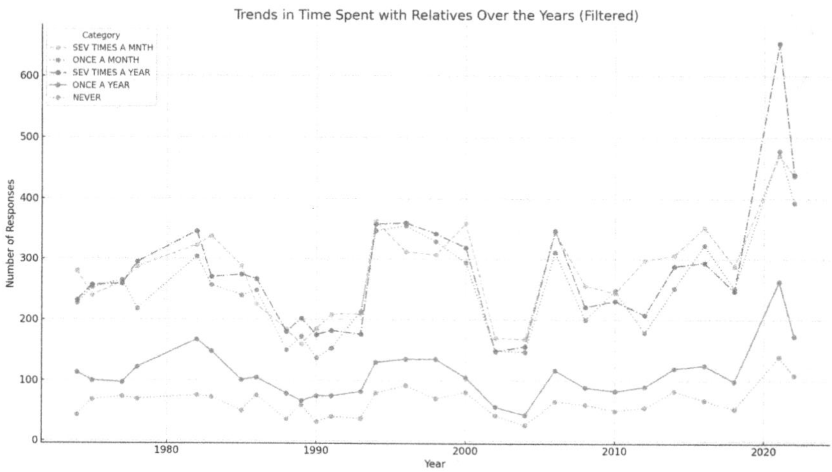

Fig. 3.3 Spend evenings with relatives (1972–2022) (N = 63,015)

of question in the GSS, but instead of asking about friends, respondents were asked about how frequently they spend time with their relatives(s).

Figure 3.3 illustrates a downtrend in how Americans' frequency of visiting relatives was observable over 1974–2022. Specifically, the categories Several Times a Month, Once a Month, Several Times a Year, Once a Year, and Never reveal a decline in more frequent visits, coupled with a rise in less frequent interactions. The categories Once a Year and Never imply that there have been increases in less frequent visits over time. Beginning with what can be considered to be relatively modest numbers in the 1970s, the responses in these categories have shown an upward trajectory, which unfortunately indicates that a growing number of Americans are either seeing their relatives only once a year or not at all. Increases started to pick up in the mid-2010s, wherein all parameters and categories in the data saw a jump in frequency.

Furthermore, we now turn to the last questions pertaining to how individuals spend time in the GSS. As to be expected, here, a similar set of trends can be observed in how much time Americans spend with their neighbors. In comparison to the previous two questions, the frequency with which Americans responded that they never spend time with their neighbors had dramatically increased. Specifically, Fig. 3.4 illustrates a

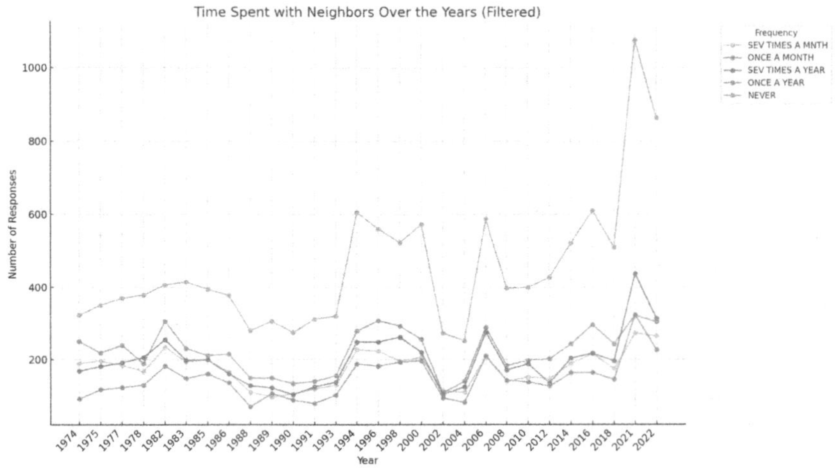

Fig. 3.4 Time spent with neighbors (1974–2022) (N = 33,457)

large pattern based on descriptive statistical tendencies of how respondents reported they spend their time in terms of being with their neighbors.

With these societal changes in mind, we must also lend consideration to the potential ways that digital communication and the expansion of digital reality have impacted how much time individuals spend with their neighbors. For example, already back in 2001, Wellman notably argued that social networks were undergoing an evolution in shifting from being primarily comprised of traditionally geographically bound communities to highly individualized connections that were mediated through technology. The rise of personalized networking constituted a shift in how people interact and form communities, argued Wellman. For example, it was noted that "we find community in networks, not groups. Although people often view the world in terms of groups, they function in networks" (Wellman, 2001, p. 9). Another transformative aspect was observed in what Wellman conceptualized as a shift from group-centric to network-centric interactions, wherein a given individual can maintain a personal community and not necessarily be categorized as fitting into a single group. Wellman notes that "most people operate in multiple, thinly-connected, partial communities as they deal with networks of kin, neighbours, friends, workmates and organizational ties" (Wellman, 2001, p. 9). Wellman's work was pioneering in the sense that he observed processes that later would blossom—computer-based communication was argued to make it possible for individuals to maintain extensive and varied social networks that are less hierarchical and have greater flexibility than those found in traditional group structures. A key point raised by Wellman pertained to social structures and the observation that traditional structures are no longer valid when observing technology-based communication.

It appears that even though individuals still place intrinsic and civic value on interactions with their family, neighborhood, and the larger community, they do not actually partake in physical interactions—or do so at less frequent rates when compared to the past. This is reflected in more survey data, this time from the WVS on individuals' viewpoints about trust and security in their neighborhoods. As interactional structures in society change, individuals spend less time with one another—this has direct implications for the evolution (or degradation) of different forms of societal trust. For example, the following data are drawn from the World Values Survey and comprise the survey's most recent three waves on the topic of trust in one's neighborhood.

As indicated in Fig. 3.5, data reflect a gradual decline in Americans' trust in their neighborhoods over three different time periods of

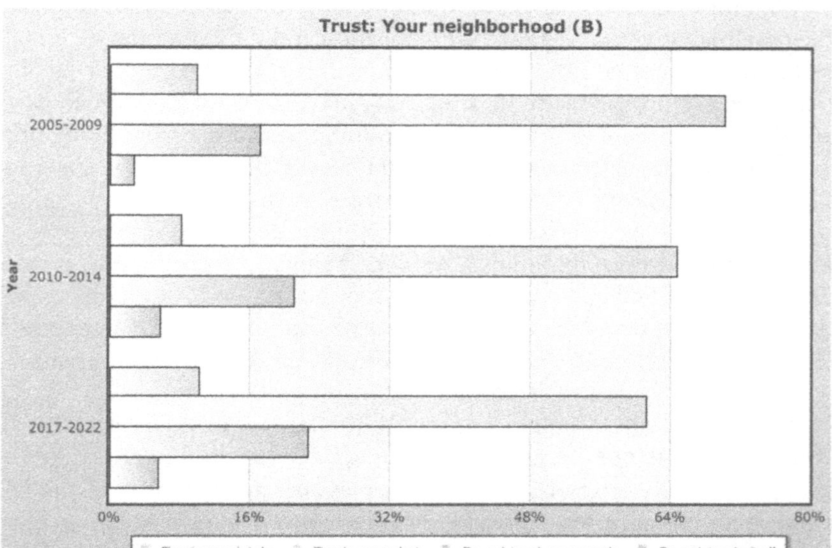

Fig. 3.5 Trust in neighborhood (WVS—2005–2022) ($N = 5998$)

surveying: 2005–2009, 2010–2014, 2017–2022. First, with the category, trust completely, there is minimal fluctuation over the three time periods. Second, with the category, trust somewhat, we can observe a clear decline as in 2005–2009, 70.2% of respondents reported somewhat trusting their neighborhood which then decreased to 64.8% (2010–2014) and even decreased further to 61.4% (2017–2022). Third, with the category, do not trust very much, the percentage of respondents who do not trust their neighborhood increased from 17.2% (2005–2009) to 21.1% (2010–2014) and then to 22.7% (2017–2022), which indicates distrust that individuals have toward their neighborhood. Fourth, with the category, do not trust at all, the percentage of individuals who do not trust their neighborhood at all increased from 2.7% (2005–2009) to 5.8% (2010–2014), then back down to 5.6% (2017–2022).

The next question was on a similar topic but was only asked in the previous two waves of the WVS (2010–2014; 2017–2022). Table 3.2 features descriptive statistics on individuals that were asked about how secure they felt in their neighborhood.

With the first category, very secure, we can observe that there is a substantial decline in the percentage of people who feel very secure in their neighborhoods, as the percentage dropped from 26.2% (2010–2014) to 11.8% (2017–2022), which is obviously a prominent decrease in perceptions of security. With the quite secure category, there also was a decrease but not as stark—in 2010–2014, 56.3% of respondents reported they felt quite secure. This then decreased to 51.5% (2017–2022). In terms of the not very secure category, here again, we can observe a substantial increase from 13.7% (2010–2014) to 32.7% (2017–2022). Next, the not-at-all-secure category also experienced an increase, but not as large. Here, the percentage of respondents who said they feel not at all secure increased from 2.7% (2010–2014) to 3.5% (2017–2022).

Table 3.2 How secure do you feel in your own neighborhood (WVS) (N = 4828)

	2010–2014	*2017–2022*
Very secure	26.2%	11.8%
Quite secure	56.3%	51.5%
Not very secure	13.7%	32.7%
Not at all secure	2.7%	3.5%
No answer	1.1%	0.4%

These results must be considered in relation to potential counter-explanations. As noted throughout this chapter, I have argued that the digital realm has changed different categories of social interaction and has fundamentally altered the structures and systems that drive and interact with agency. Over time, these recursive interactions have altered large-scale social processes and behaviors. Here we must consider Klinenberg's notable inquiry (2018) in which it is argued that individualism and privacy in modern living arrangements are marked by new values of personal space and autonomy, which take precedence over communal living. Klinenberg argued that this is primarily what has led to a decline in neighborly visits and social gatherings. The physical design of how most Americans live is not conducive to communal interaction(s), which constitutes a problem that Klinenberg believes can be addressed via the concept of social infrastructure, "the physical places and organizations that shape the way people interact" (Klinenberg, 2018, p. 5). Social infrastructure encompasses a wide range of public and semi-public spaces such as libraries, parks, schools, playgrounds, community gardens along with associations and organizations that can facilitate social interaction and community building. Such spaces are critical to the health of communities and democracy more broadly, argues Klinenberg. As such, the author contends that a decline in social infrastructure has contributed to the erosion of community ties and civic engagement. It is also argued that "investing in social infrastructure is a way to reduce inequality because these spaces provide opportunities for people to connect and support one another" (Klinenberg, 2018, p. 142).

While living arrangements are surely important, this book points attention toward a deeper set of dynamics that are embedded within structural and agency-based processes within the digital realm. Civic engagement and association were prominent in early American history and leading up until the 1950s primarily because they were enacted outside one's home, outside on the street, in town halls, community centers, and open spaces where people would gather based on shared interests. Such gatherings and interactions are very rare today, as individuals in the United States spend less physical time with their neighbors, friends, and relatives than ever before. They do nevertheless engage in civic activities, albeit in different ways and in manners that are not conducive to organic face-to-face and person-to-person real- life social interaction. This is precisely observable in any public place where individuals, especially from younger generations, gather. Smartphones are widely used most of the time when individuals are with each other. It is not uncommon to see groups of teenagers at a fast-food restaurant or Starbucks all sitting on smartphones at the same time, some even talking to one another through text or application(s) while sitting next to each other.

In Conclusion

I do not intend the analyses presented throughout this work to be polemic or overly negative. It would be a gross over-simplification to just state or argue that the internet has fundamentally changed things for the worse in American society. Like most major processes of social development and change, internet-induced change has spurred positive and negative effects—many of which require further theorization and scholarly attention. As revealed throughout this chapter, there currently are many research trajectories that are blossoming around the general pattern of investigating the impact that different facets of the digital realm have on society. Some believe digital media and the internet provide individuals with new forms and ways to engage civically and grow their social networks online. Others have found that the usage of digital media and communication decreases interpersonal trust and has other adverse impacts on society. This chapter has attempted to explain a growing trend in America—the ongoing transformation in the nature of how people interact and engage with one another. It has been argued that the rise of the internet and digital communication has fundamentally altered how people interact, which in turn has brought about "digital bowling" in which individuals are still participating in civic activities but are doing so through digital means rather than physical interactions. On the one hand, digital platforms have increased access to more information and provided heterogeneous avenues for civic participation, especially for younger generations. On the other hand, a shift away from physical interactions has led to a decline in community ties and an increase in social polarization.

As digital forms of engagement continue to evolve and the digital realm increases in the total amount of structures and systems through online-based interactions these entities have with users, it will be crucial to think about how future societies can be encouraged to engage in both online and offline interactions. For future consideration, scholars and policymakers may deliberate on how to arrive at recommendations that would enable communities and regular people to reach a potential balancing act with regard to integration of digital and physical civic engagement. For example, the creation of hybrid community spaces in which digital and physical interactions are encouraged to take place might be fruitful in helping bridge gaps between the physical world and the digital realm. Streaming events online seem to have become a new norm after the pandemic, and in times ahead, community events in this format could allow for broader participation while still maintaining some of the organic benefits that are associated with face-to-face interactions. This is already taking place in many communities as the creation of virtual town halls, online forums, and social media-based systems seems to be a route to increase local-level civic association in today's highly digitally immersed society.

References

Anisin, A. (2017). Antagonisms and the discursive sedimentation of American gun culture: A new framework. *Cultural Studies↔ Critical Methodologies, 17*(2), 133–139.

Bachen, C., Raphael, C., Lynn, K.-M., McKee, K., & Philippi, J. (2008). Civic engagement, pedagogy, and information technology on web sites for youth. *Political Communication, 25*(3), 290–310.

Boulianne, S. (2020). Twenty years of digital media effects on civic and political participation. *Communication Research, 47*(7), 947–966.

Davern, M., Bautista, R., Freese, J., Herd, P., & Morgan, S. L. (2023). *General social survey 1972–2022 [Machine-readable data file]*. NORC at the University of Chicago. Data accessed from the GSS Data Explorer website at gssdataexplorer.norc.org. This GSS Data Explorer output was created by ALEXEI ANISIN on 2024-07-11. https://gssdataexplorer.norc.org

Fairclough, A. (2001). *Better day coming: Blacks and equality, 1890–2000*. Penguin Books.

Inglehart, R., Haerpfer, C., Moreno, A., Welzel, C., Kizilova, K., Diez-Medrano, J., Lagos, M., Norris, P., Ponarin, E., & Puranen, B., et al. (Eds.). (2014). *World values survey: Round six - Country-pooled datafile version*. JD Systems Institute. https://www.worldvaluessurvey.org/WVSDocumentationWV6.jsp

Klinenberg, E. (2018). *Palaces for the people: How social infrastructure can help fight inequality, polarization, and the decline of civic life*. Crown.

Kluger, R. (1975). *Simple justice: The history of Brown v. Board of Education and Black America's struggle for equality*. Knopf.

Knoke, D. (2019). *Political networks: The structural perspective*. Cambridge University Press.

Marsden, P. V., Smith, T. W., & Hout, M. (2021). *General social survey 2018: Documentation and codebook*. NORC at the University of Chicago.

McCarty, N., Poole, K. T., & Rosenthal, H. (2006). *Polarized America: The dance of ideology and unequal riches.* Massachusetts Institute of Technology Press.

Moy, P., Manosevitch, E., Stamm, K., & Dunsmore, K. (2005). Linking dimensions of internet use and civic engagement. *Journalism & Mass Communication Quarterly, 82*(3), 571–586.

Pontes, H. M., Szabo, A., & Griffiths, M. D. (2015). The impact of internet-based specific activities on the perceptions of internet addiction, quality of life, and excessive usage: A cross-sectional study. *Addictive Behaviors Reports, 1*, 19–25.

Putnam, R. D. (2000). *Bowling alone: The collapse and revival of American community.* Simon & Schuster.

Putnam, R. D., & Campbell, D. E. (2010). *American grace: How religion divides and unites us.* Simon & Schuster.

Skocpol, T. (1997). The Tocqueville problem: Civic engagement in American democracy. *Social Science History, 21*(4), 455–479.

Skocpol, T. (2003). *Diminished democracy: From membership to Management in American Civic Life.* University of Oklahoma Press.

Skoric, M. M., Zhu, Q., Goh, D., & Pang, N. (2016). Social media and citizen engagement: A meta-analytic review. *New Media & Society, 18*(9), 1817–1839.

Smith, T. W., Marsden, P. V., Hout, M., & Kim, J. (2019). *General social survey, 1972–2018.* NORC at the University of Chicago.

Tocqueville, A. (2000). *Democracy in America* (H. Reeve, Trans.). The Pennsylvania State University. (Original work published 1835/1840).

Warren, M. R. (2001). *Dry bones rattling: Community building to revitalize American democracy.* Princeton University Press.

Wellman, B. (2001). Physical place and Cyberplace: The rise of personalized networking. *International Journal of Urban and Regional Research, 25*(2), 227–252.

Welzel, C., & Inglehart, R. (2005). Liberalism, postmaterialism, and the growth of freedom. *International Review of Sociology, 15*(1), 81–108.

CHAPTER 4

Political Polarization and Trust in Institutions

Emma used to always help her mom peel potatoes in the kitchen when preparing Thanksgiving dinner. This time of the year was guaranteed to be a pleasant period of gathering during a light Northern California fall season—kids had school off, parents took days off work, and the weather wasn't too hot or too cold. Yellow fallen leaves filled the streets as kids rode around on their bikes and skateboards around Emma's neighborhood. As with any other typical American family, Emma's Thanksgiving dinner was a pretty standard affair—everything was prepared by November 27 and the kids helped their parents tidy up the house and living and dining rooms. The usual set of interactions that would arise that evening was quite normal—conversations filled with laughter and stories from the past year were told by Emma's extended family members, including cousins, uncles, and aunts. One particular year, however, interactions unexpectedly took a turn for the worse when political topics arose. In the past, this never was a problem, things would get brushed aside and were laughed off by family members at the dinner table. Thanksgiving in 2021 turned out to be different. After having spent nearly two years in and out of lockdowns in a highly polarized political climate, the topics of vaccination, health food, diets, and January 6 collided. Emma's uncle Ron (a burly man) and his wife Jessica (a proud housewife) along with their two boys were visiting from a town that was in the agricultural farming area of California,

A. Anisin, *How the Internet Changed America*,
https://doi.org/10.1007/978-3-032-02395-7_4

inland. They wouldn't typically visit every year, but when they did, politics was never really the dominant topic of discussion.

But this time was different. Jessica and Emma's mother were seated across from each other on a long and wide mahogany table when the former made a casual remark about the 2020 election in response to a commercial that was faintly airing on the television in the living room,

"There'd have been no lockdowns if the Dems didn't steal the election," said Jessica, as she sipped on a large wine glass full of Napa Valley Cabernet Sauvignon.

"Oh c'mon, that sounds like something Tucker Carlson would say," Emma's mother lashed out in response. Both laughed off the joke, which led to an awkward moment of silence. Emma's dad then turned up their large high-definition television—a NFL football game was on. He said in a muffled voice,

"Those in D.C. are completely out of touch, regardless of what political party they represent, you all know that!"

Then one of Emma's cousins whispered to his mom,

"Mom, this stuffing taste like paper."

"It's gluten-free, not even a starving dog would eat it," Jessica replied to her son.

Voices grew louder as Emma's mother started arguing with Jessica about climate change and vaccination—the conversation escalated and people got tense. Points were made that were antagonistic to the outgroup—to the opposing political party, opposing viewpoints, and societal symbols that encompassed many different characteristics. How they were made was antecedently confrontational. Other family members tried to intervene, especially Emma's father, who unenthusiastically attempted to mediate what was a never-before-seen scenario at his family's dinner table. His efforts ended up being in vain as tensions boiled over when Jessica stood up and walked over to the kitchen counter and flung a glass of wine into the sink—crack! Small pieces of crystal were scattered all over. Chaos ensued—everyone started shouting, the kids ran to the living room, the dog started barking, and dishes clattered and chairs were knocked over. The police were not called, as Emma's aunt, uncle, and cousins left before things got even more out of hand.

Such confrontational scenarios are of course not uncommon during the holiday season in America—statistical trends long have beckoned that among the highest frequency of police visits for domestic violence tend to come during the holidays as these times of the year unite families but create conflicts at the same time. For example, according to data from the Los Angeles Police Department (LAPD) on Thanksgiving the likelihood of becoming a victim of a crime committed by a family member or acquaintance increases by over 50% (Ward, 2020). Political undertones of many societal tension points now appear to be much more salient than in times past, and it is common to come across palpable tensions in political discourse. This is a symbolic indication that American society is becoming increasingly polarized. This chapter will go through a detailed explanation of polarization and relate it to the concept of trust. It will demonstrate that the internet has impacted how individuals consume news and find out about their world, and in doing so, they interact with structures and systems in the digital realm that favor specific forms of content, much of which is antagonistic to what can be considered to be the median. Through different processes that are associated with the formation of new digital structures, polarization has increased in the last few decades in America. While political events surely have played a role in dividing society, adversities also arose in history, but they did not bring about a significant rise in polarization and distrust in government institutions such as the executive branch, Congress, and public institutions such as the press as currently observable.

When I was going over the final proof editing version of this chapter, my smartphone started receiving a plethora of incoming messages—nearly all of which were short and simply stated "Trump" "Trump!"—I opened up my web browser and the headline on every news outlet ranged from "Trump Shot" to "Trump safe but bloodied, and attacker dead, after shots fired at rally." News was live streamed across the world as an event occurred that many did not expect, but at the same time were not surprised by. An assassination attempt was carried out against former President Donald Trump at a political rally in Pennsylvania. The attacker was a 20-year-old man who managed to climb up to a rooftop with a rifle and aim from only 130 meters away from where Trump was making a speech. Shots were fired and one grazed Trump's ear and bloodied his face. Trump dropped down quickly and was bombarded by secret security agents—more shots were fired as snipers from other rooftops aimed at the attacker and killed him. Trump was quickly escorted into a vehicle and driven away. Had the bullet not hit Trump's ear and been just one centimeter to the right, a hit to the temple would have ended his life. In light of immense political polarization in American society, this event culminated what many believed to be a long cycle of increasing tension—and opened up worrisome discussions about what would follow in the 2024 election.

Indeed, political assassinations are obviously not a new phenomenon in US history—from Lincoln, to Garfield, McKinley, Roosevelt, Truman, Kennedy, Ford, and Reagan, individuals who have either attempted to shoot or have successfully shot and killed Presidents before. In recent years, there has been a wave of attempted assassination attempts aimed at incumbent politicians in America. In 2011, a mass shooting took place in a parking lot in Tucson, Arizona, in which an offender shot Representative Gabrielle Giffords in the head (who survived) during a public meeting and killed six other people. In 2013, Kaufman County District Attorney Mike McLelland (and his wife) were shot and killed in their home in Texas. In 2017, House Majority Whip Steve Scalise was shot and injured during a recreational baseball practice in Alexandria, Virginia. Also in 2017, Senator Rand Paul was attacked by his neighbor (albeit not with a gun), but the attack did injure Paul. Finally, in 2022, an attacker entered Nancy Pelosi's private residence in San Francisco and attacked her husband with a hammer—the attacker had intended to kidnap the Speaker of the House of Representatives, but she was not home.

From Donald Trump to Alex Jones, polarizing figures have entered mainstream American political culture in recent years and have fundamentally altered the political climate of the country. Much of Donald Trump's 2016 election campaign functioned through Twitter and represented among the first significant deviations from the traditional media landscape in American history. Meanwhile, fringe conspiracy theory-based news agencies such as Alex Jones' *InfoWars* gained viewership ratings that, at their height, surpassed many traditional media outlets in daily and weekly audience and reach. The internet has fostered a complete re-arrangement of how political information is disseminated, consumed, and articulated throughout American society. Podcasts are becoming the dominant medium through which hundreds of millions of people obtain information about topics they voluntarily choose to spend time engaging with. Podcasts are also increasingly contributing to the formation of political opinions and preferences. There now exist more opinions and viewpoints than ever before as a result of greater heterogeneity in the overall flow of information that is available to the populace.

This chapter demonstrates that instead of going out to town halls, community meetings, and above all, relying on newspapers and traditional television-based news media, individuals are now heavily leaning toward accessing social media and similar digital forms of communication to engage in political debate and discussion. Much of the latter transpire through digital platforms wherein individuals can post and comment anonymously and not necessarily have their name affiliated with what they write. Reading comments, anonymous posts, and following accounts that may not necessarily have a person's real name or identity affiliated with them, constitutes new types of legitimation structures that are a part of the digital realm. These structures have specific norms and social practices. With this being said, we have to keep in mind that polarization is a phenomenon that always exists in a democracy—without some degree or presence of polarization, a society would not be able to effectively deal with problems and social friction in a healthy manner. Extreme polarization, however, is not conducive to healthy democratic functionality nor is it beneficial for trust, civic engagement, socialization, and cross-cultural engagement. This chapter will demonstrate how specific functions of the digital realm, as conceptualized and observed through its structures and associated systems, have interacted with hundreds of millions of individuals in real time, which in turn has reinforced particular aspects of structure, especially in social media contexts.

Of particular prominence is the rise of digital echo chambers which are structures that have their own systems and associated interactions with human agency. Such chambers enable digital media systems to obtain more profit through sustained and increased user interactions, while, at the same time, they function through an effective reinforcing set of mechanisms that contribute adversely to political polarization.

Political Polarization in America

One need not be a political scientist to understand that in contemporary America, political polarization has become a more significant problem that is not only limited to ideological divides between mainstream political parties and their support bases. Political polarization can be defined as a set of processes that cause public opinion to be divided among key issues. Politically polarized publics have substantial ideological separation which can range from simple disagreements on topics such as abortion, economic bailouts, and social welfare funding to more severe disagreements on topics that include election fraud, corruption, and even issues such as gender identity. A polarized public is not only marked by increases in ideological distance from the median voter, but it also tends to feature palpable hostility that exists between different groups. In social science, political polarization is operationalized in specific ways for the purpose of carrying out statistical analyses. Researchers generally measure the degree of ideological divergence between groups through reliance on different sources of data which include surveys, individuals' voting records as well, and content analyses of political speeches.

Two distinct conceptual approaches are observable throughout social inquiry on polarization. The first pertains to polarization in actual politicians' behavior in Congress or a given legislature. The second is on public opinion and society more broadly. With the first, a primary reference point can be observed in Poole and Rosenthal (1997), who notably relied on ideological scores that were drawn from roll-call votes in legislative bodies and were used to place politicians on a liberal and conservative scale. Although politicians' behavior within institutional settings typically should reflect societal polarization, this is not always the case. With the second approach, populaces have been studied through survey data which heavily rely on respondents answering questions and giving their views on a variety of different topics pertaining to party membership, ideology, and social and political policies. Here, a particularly novel approach has been applied by scholars that argue gaps between in-group and out-group feelings can function as a proxy for affective polarization (Iyengar et al., 2012). Of course, we must consider that survey data are not perfect, by nature respondents in any given country may not tell the truth, and may perceive biases, stigmas, and other forces that can skew their ability to honestly respond to statements and questions. These adversities are especially likely to be prevalent with questions that are on topics of politics and issues that are already antecedently known to be polarizing. Nevertheless, the scale of contemporary surveying is so large that when gathered, major social survey projects provide us with rich data that are comparable across years and decades.

Moreover, while this chapter will not go as deep into the historical characteristics of political polarization as it did on civic association and engagement, it will attempt to provide a cohesive summary of polarization. There was a major political realignment during the middle of the twentieth century that probably had an impact on current rates of polarization. At the time of writing this book, the current political landscape in America is heavily divided between what broadly can be considered to be the left and the right. On the left, historical left-wing political factors remain prominent, but in recent decades, they have started becoming accompanied by newer phenomena. Labor, women's rights, reproductive rights, minority group rights, disabled rights, social welfare spending, universal healthcare, immigration rights, among other, classical left-wing topics still coherently are positioned within the spectrum of the left in America. Over the last several decades, greater emphasis has been placed on environmental rights (and environmental policy more broadly) on the left, specifically with regard to climatic change and global warming. Likewise, new forms of minority rights have come to the forefront, including LGBT and other iterations of sexual minority rights. Throughout historical institutional struggles, many of the aforementioned issues have been dealt with through lawsuits and court cases, with the status quo often being set by the judicial branch in the Supreme Court. When the latter's decision led to an unsatisfactory precedent, collective action would often lead to different demands being placed upon either state governments or the Federal government.

The Civil Rights Movement of the 1960s was pivotal not only because it forced the Federal government to de-segregate American society and spur concessions to groups that were long subjugated, but the movement also brought about a shift in party allegiance in the South wherein many conservative white voters transitioned from the Democratic to the Republican party (McCarty et al., 2006). Subsequently, there was an increasingly prominent alignment of political parties with specific ideological stances as Republicans wholly embraced conservatism and Democrats shifted toward liberalism. Fiorina and Abrams' (2008) inquiry neatly captures different processes in which ideological sorting occurred and solidified the homogenization of party ideologies, which was observed in partisan consistency among both elected officials and their electorate and voter base (Fiorina & Abrams, 2008). Before delving further into what became an elongated trajectory of polarization, several words about the "Right" need to be said as the divide between it and the Left seems to be at an all-time high. The right is pro-life, pro-gun, anti-regulation, anti-labor, anti-immigration, and typically the antagonistic opposite to the left across most major issues. This is not to say that the average Republican voter or individual who considers him/herself to be right-wing is necessarily racist or xenophobic, but rather, those on the right have tended to be historically in favor of states' rights over the Federal government on issues ranging from abortion to civil rights to environmental regulation and immigration. As subsequent sections will reveal, however, many of the issues that continue to polarize the American populace today are of a different character than issues of the past that tended to revolve around state versus Federal rights—there now exist large-scale digital echo chambers (Garret, 2009) and associated structures in which individuals buy into and feed into topics that would not have made into mainstream political discourse prior to the onset of the digital realm and internet-based communication.

Robertson et al. (2023b) recently cast an interesting inquiry on negative and positive words in news headlines and assessed how this impacts online news consumption. Focus was placed on click-through rates via data drawn from the Upworthy Research Archive, which include 22,743 randomized controlled trials of news headlines 2013–2015. Here, upward of 105,000 different headline variations and nearly 5.7 million clicks from 370 million impressions were analyzed through text mining and sentiment analysis. The linguistic inquiry and word count dictionary were drawn on by the authors to categorize words as either positive or negative. Statistical analysis featuring regression modeling was carried out to test the hypothesis of whether negative words in headlines would increase click rates, and vice versa, that positive words would decrease them.

In controlling for headline length, complexity as well as the age of a given story, the authors found a significant negativity bias in news consumption as each additional negative word in a given headline increased the click-through rate CTR by 2.3%. In contrast, positive words had the opposite effect (Robertson et al., 2023b, p. 816). Post-analysis robustness checks were carried out and included the usage of alternative sentiment dictionaries along with variant measures of text complexity. Such outcomes do not arise out of randomness but, rather, are a part of the repetitive character of pathways that can be traced through what Giddens refers to as "time-space" (Giddens, 1984, p. 282). There appears to have been a highly negative set of sentiments and practices that have become routinized in the digital realm within the broad sphere of digital news consumption. Such practices revolve around obtaining content on negative stories and news events—the implications of this are indeed profound as algorithms respond to negative searches by users, and then users consume more negative content, and the story goes on.

Iyengar et al. (2019) overview the origins and consequences of affective polarization in the United States and account for a growing emotional divide between Democrats and Republicans. The authors believe that party sorting is significant, in which individuals increasingly align their party affiliation with their ideological beliefs. This has intensified partisan hostility. Next, the authors also argue that social identity theory can fruitfully account for how political identities have become a primary lens through which individuals view themselves and others—this brings about the strengthening of in-group loyalty and out-group loathing. The evolutionary nature of media is also given attention—here, the authors account for the rise of partisan news outlets and the role of social media platforms wherein echo chambers function as adverse reinforcers of existing beliefs and encourage distrust of the opposing party. In its adverse totality, affective polarization has increased legislative gridlock and brought about a less willing polis of elected officials who do not want to engage in compromises with the opposing party. Affective polarization has also decreased social cohesion and stifled cross-party social interactions. Most importantly, Iyengar et al. (2019) demonstrate that this form of polarization extends beyond politics and negatively impacts personal relationships through spurring societal division.

Alternative Explanations

Throughout the last few decades' increase in polarization, there also have been issues and outcomes that are not straightforward or easy to categorize such as both Democratic and Republican parties' back-to-back bailouts of corporate sectors and failing entities during the 2007–2008 financial crisis (Bush Jr. then Obama) or both political parties' support for military conflict(s) such as the Russian-Ukraine war or Israel's ongoing military operation in Gaza in 2023–2024. There appear to be issues that are ongoing but are not adequately addressed by either party with relation to their voter base. Above all, the average American has been gravely deprived of the benefits of long-stemming economic growth over the past half-century. Real wage growth has stagnated for the past 50 years. In 1970, the average family income was $45,852, yet it only rose to $51,179 by 2012 (Schubert et al., 2015). During this period, women's workforce participation increased from 40% to 70%, which entails family incomes saw little improvement despite higher workforce participation. Additionally, the average minimum wage, when adjusted for inflation, was $7.50 per hour in 1970 and had only risen to $9.30 per hour by 2014. Estimates adjusting for inflation indicate that the real value of the minimum wage peaked at $12.12 in 1968 and has since decreased, reaching its lowest point in 66 years by 2022 (Cooper et al., 2022).

The ironic aspect of contemporary polarization is that economic factors, nevertheless, are not the typical topics that are brought up with regard to polarization, albeit they surely have played an underappreciated role in bringing about a sense of hopelessness toward the political process among the American populace. Most survey evidence points to a bold fact—that there is no focal point when it comes to any particular topic that drives polarization as there is widespread criticism of government, both political parties and political leaders (Pew Research Center, 2023b). Antagonistic rhetoric toward the out-group, however, is clearly increasing. For example, more Americans express negative opinions of both mainstream political parties than ever before. Back in 1994, only 6% of Americans had a negative view of both parties—this figure grew to 27% by 2022 (Pew Research Center, 2023a). It is estimated that almost half of young adults wish they had more parties to choose from (Pew Research Center, 2023a). The interesting dynamic here is that when it comes to the predictors of polarization, political affiliation tends to be the most robust factor as there are deep divisions between Republicans and Democrats. For example, 83% of Democrats and 69% of Republicans see the opposing party as closed-minded (Pew Research Center, 2023a). As noted by Newport (2023) political identity is strongly correlated with views on a wide range of issues. Boxell et al. (2024) even found that as of 2020, out of 12 OECD countries and a broad time period dating back the last four decades, the U.S. experienced the largest increase in polarization. This rise in partisan antipathy plays a critical role within the larger prism of polarization in America. Increasing evidence points toward a trend of both Republicans and Democrats expressing positive views of themselves, while simultaneously, there has been an intense rise in highly negative views of the opposing party. Back in 1994, 21% of Republicans held a "very unfavorable" view of the opposing party, as of 2022, this rose to 62%. Similarly, in 1994, 17% of Democrats held a "very unfavorable" view of the opposing party, which rose to 54% by 2022 (Pew Research Center, 2023a). As subsequent sections of this chapter will reveal, there are particular reasons and processes behind why such outcomes have arisen.

The most common issues (at the time of writing this book 2023–2024) that society tends to be polarized over are government size and power, climate change, environmental policy, education, abortion, foreign trade, immigration, gun laws, healthcare, and income tax fairness (Newport, 2023). Partisan gaps on these issues have widened immensely if viewed from 2003 to 2023. Democrats have become increasingly concerned about fast-moving climate change. While each of these issues surely has an associated set of causes or conditions that are sufficient for its occurrence, the overarching change that has quantitatively been present throughout two decades (and arguably more) of increasing polarization in America is a change in the medium of informational consumption.

Digital Media and Polarization

Many scholars and even members of the general public have frequently discussed the transformative role that digital media has on different social outcomes, especially political polarization. Social media platforms have amplified these effects by enabling the rapid spread of politically charged content and incentivizing the formation of ideologically homogenous online communities (Iyengar & Westwood, 2015). Among the most salient concepts in literature on digital media and polarization is the echo chamber. Echo chambers are digital environments in which individuals are exposed predominantly to opinions and information that reinforce existing beliefs. This tends to occur alongside a reduced exposure to differing viewpoints. Users interact primarily with similar-minded individuals and informational content that gets prioritized by algorithms (especially across social media platforms)—resulting in closed informational loops. Kossowska et al. (2023) investigate echo chambers in relation to what they conceptualize as micro-identities. Here it is argued that digital media usage encourages the formation of micro-identities that possess an innate propensity to erode social structures and norms. Along with echo chambers, the authors find evidence of filter bubbles that encourage fragmentation across public discourse. Micro-identities are driven by in-group self-determination and distinct epistemic characteristics that prioritize their internal ideologies. Kossowska et al. (2023) believe social disintegration (as imagined in a Durkheimian sense) is associated with micro-identities which negatively impact social structures, values, norms, and even institutions.

The concept of micro-identities captures heterogeneous outcomes that structures and systems of the digital realm currently support and facilitate. The only issue with this concept, however, is that survey data clearly indicate that party affiliation is still greatly predictive of polarization. This entails that individuals will still cling onto established grand-scale identities when it comes to political affiliation. Furthermore, Flamino et al. (2023) analyze Twitter data between two elections in the U.S. (2016 and

2020). Here the authors ask how the dissemination of politically biased content by influencers on Twitter contributes to political polarization? A longitudinal research design is implemented, which enables the authors to analyze close to one billion tweets via fact-checking tools that are proxied as measures for the volume of biased content. Data were collected continuously through Twitter's API via usage of names of presidential candidates as keywords (2020 data comprised 171 million tweets made by 11 million users; 2020 data comprised 702 million tweets put out by 20 million users). The authors discovered that between both elections, there was a decrease in fake and extremely biased content. However, echo chamber behavior and ideological polarization increased. The proportion of influencers affiliated with news media organizations decreased, while those affiliated with political organizations increased. Interestingly enough, influencers became more polarized and contributed to a higher degree of ideological separation among Twitter users. These results indicate that on the Twitter (now X) platform, there are growing divisions in political communication.

Nyhan et al. (2023) offer a different perspective in an inquiry that was carried out through collaboration between Facebook (Meta) and academic researchers to investigate the impact of reducing exposure of politically like-minded sources on Facebook. This study aimed to understand if algorithmically reducing exposure to content from like-minded sources could affect users' political attitudes, including polarization. An experimental design was deployed with participants who were randomly assigned to treatment or control groups. The treatment group experienced a downranking of content in a fashion that was predicted to share participants' political preferences and leaning, whereas the control group's news feed remained unchanged. Data included both behavioral data collected by Facebook and survey data drawn from the National Opinion Research Center (University of Chicago). Surveys included five waves (before and after the treatment period) and spanned from September 24 to December 23 (2020). A total of 23,377 American adult Facebook users then completed at least one survey post-election. Through an ordinary least squares analysis, estimates were computed based on populational average treatment effects. Here, results revealed that the intervention reduced exposure to like-minded content, but it did not significantly impact political attitudes, affective polarization, or ideological extremity. These null results were consistent across subgroups, which indicates that there were no measurable heterogeneous treatment effects. As such, the authors conclude that reducing exposure to politically like-minded content on Facebook may not necessarily lessen political polarization, which challenges dominant scholarly and public narratives that place blame on social media echo chambers.

In contrast, Katalinić et al. (2023) put forward a highly innovative inquiry on polarizing topics as observed through Twitter (now X) during the 2022 midterm elections. They ask how political polarization is reflected in the discourse of candidates from Democratic and Republican parties and specifically how this relates to outcomes of the particular election under attention. A large number of tweets (52,688) from senators, representatives, and governors that were tweeted one month before the elections are analyzed through machine learning (latent Dirichlet allocation) as well as sentiment analysis. Tweets made by political candidates between October 8 and November 8 (2022) were analyzed and results (classified on a scale ranging from −1 to 1) revealed that polarizing topics were prevalent across the board. As expected, one particularly polarizing topic was the legitimacy of the 2020 General Election. Other topics included job losses that were hypothetically related to renewable energy. Katalinić et al. (2023) conclude that political discourse during election cycles on Twitter (X) is highly polarized. Further, Robertson et al. (2023a) carried out a two-wave survey that was paired to assess exposure and engagement during the 2018 and 2020 elections. Data were drawn from observations on participants installing a custom browser extension that was able to code HTML snapshots of Google search results (exposure), which also logged their interactions with URLs (engagement). The extension was able to collect users' Google searches as well as browser history. Results revealed that identity-congruent news sources were prevalent in participant content choices. This entails that exposure and engagement with partisan (including unreliable) news via Google searches is not driven by algorithmic curation but, rather, by users' own choices.

Finally, Lorenz-Spreen et al. (2023) put out a meta-analysis that were cross-national and included observations drawn from data on China, Russia, Turkey, Egypt, Kazakhstan, Iran, Ethiopia, Hong Kong, Pakistan, Jordan, Malaysia, Kenya, Philippines, Lebanon, India, Nigeria, Mexico, Macedonia, Indonesia, Colombia, Ecuador, Hungary, Poland, Brazil, Ghana, Croatia, Taiwan, South Korea, Israel, the USA, Japan, Canada, Chile, Austria, Australia, Italy, Spain, the United Kingdom, Netherlands, France, Belgium, Germany, Finland, Switzerland, Sweden, Norway, and Denmark. The authors extracted from 496 articles (selected from a pool of 3509 articles) as identified through scientific journal article databases (e.g., Scopus/Web of Science). Primary variables that were analyzed included observations on political participation, trust, polarization, as well as the prominent topic of populism (which can be considered as a proxy for democratic backsliding). Data comprised observations drawn from self-report surveys, network analysis on social media data, URL tracking, as well as field experiments. The authors found that digital media function as a double-edged sword in terms of their impact on contemporary politics and society—while digital media have a positive influence in potentially enhancing political participation and the availability and consumption of information, they also pose detrimental effects on society. Declines in political trust were observed in established democracies by the authors who believe that citizens are starting to view democratic institutions with skepticism as a result of highly sensationalist characteristics found in online informational content. This resembles the signification structure. Overly polarizing and simplistic narratives are now easy to come by. One need not delve too deep into these dynamics to understand how they exacerbate polarization in the US context in particular.

Structures and Systems

One of the major conceptual innovations in the literature on polarization is the echo chamber—scholars from interdisciplinary fields have come to similar conclusions about the antagonistic nature of political discourse on social and digital media. Among the divergent set of findings can be observed in Robertson et al. (2023a), who tested the widely held claim that "if popular online platforms systematically expose their users to partisan and unreliable news, they could potentially contribute to societal issues such as rising political polarization"—the issue here is not in systematic exposition, but rather, the active and continuously reinforcive dynamics that exist between structures of the digital realm and human agency. There is a recursive ordering of social practices in the digital realm. It is impossible to assume beforehand whether the content hundreds of millions of internet users see is shaped by algorithms designed by tech companies or if it results from their own choices to seek information that aligns with their preferences. The digital realm is marked by immense causal complexity in its structures, systems, and their interaction with human agency. Digital platforms are designed to both influence and respond to user behavior which creates a feedback loop where technology and human agency are intertwined. As Giddens noted, "it is the specifically reflexive form of the knowledgeability of human agents that is most deeply involved in the recursive ordering of social practices" (Giddens, 1984, p. 3).

Polarization is not a one-shot process but, rather, has continuously evolved and intensified as political events have occurred and users' time spent interpreting and communicating them in the digital realm has increased. Individuals' digital footprints mirror a complex blend of algorithmically curated content and self-directed information seeking. If we are to understand the flow of information and its relationship to polarization in the digital age, we must acknowledge that there exists an intricate interplay between human agency and technological structures—both are integral to the digital experience. At the time of writing this book, there likely is a symbiotic relationship between users and the many algorithms that they interact with in online environments throughout the digital realm. As Giddens noted, "as social actors, all human beings are highly 'learned' in respect of knowledge which they possess, and apply, in the production and reproduction of day-to-day encounters: the vast bulk of such knowledge is practical rather than theoretical in character" (Giddens, 1984, p. 22). By transposing the "day-to-day encounters" aspect of Giddens' statement, we can assume the same to hold true for the digital realm. A noteworthy development that has contributed to new and significant changes in the medium through which consumers obtain information in the last decade, especially for content that is political in nature, can be observed in the rise of podcasting. Edmond (2015) described how radio consumption shifted toward digital mediums wherein listeners access content through online podcasts. In doing so, consumers break free from traditional scheduled programming and experience an expansion into physical and interactive online spaces. The evolution of cross-media production of radio-related content has fostered greater community involvement and is encouraging of a participatory culture, argued Edmond. Retrospectively, Edmond's (2015) study effectively foresaw how interactive connections between creators and audiences would gain prominence.[1]

[1] Such technological developments, importantly, are not limited to media content but also include transformations in high education and education as a whole. Back in 2009, Ragusa, Chan, and Crampton came to the conclusion that socio-cultural digital transformations based around podcasting held significant promise in the educational field and that podcasting exemplifies technological innovation and an evolution of practices in higher education.

Individuals who use digital media and social media platforms to communicate about and consume informational content on political topics are aware of legitimation structures. Community guidelines, user policies, and other similar rules are in place and vary slightly depending on the platform. However, in contrast to "real-life" or physical settings wherein individuals cannot mask their identity, the digital realm is marked by clandestinity and outward posturing in which individuals purposefully put out content, comments, and other information without the necessity of disclosing their legal name or identity. It seems that with anonymity, human beings, unfortunately, are prone to show greater hostility when it comes to topics that are polarizing and socially contention. Giddens' distinction between what he referred to as social and system integration types can enable us to delve into the nature of how the digital realm impacts human agency and vice versa. Giddens conceptualized social integration as connections between people through face-to-face interactions. System integration captures connections with those "who are physically absent in time or space" (Giddens, 1984, p. 28). The latter captures multifaceted interactions that take place in the digital realm and its structures and systems.

Structuration Across Digital and Social Media

Although it is very difficult to arrive at a definitive number on how many people use social media platforms and the most popular platforms that are used on average, by some estimates (Kemp, 2023), as of 2023, the top ten social media platforms relevant to American adults include the following platforms, applications, and sites. Below, I have grouped them together by their purpose and general characteristics[2]:

[2] As time goes on, it must be acknowledged that some of these websites and applications will decline in their frequency of usage across the population—for those that remember, America Online (AOL) and Yahoo were dominant in the late 1990s and early 2000s until the emergence of Google, Skype, and subsequently, Facebook. Likewise, Myspace was by far the hegemon for social networking in the early era of this phenomenon, it was then taken over by Facebook, which itself was surpassed by Instagram and until Facebook bought it out and acquired it. The emergence of TikTok seems to have led to younger generations favoring this platform—similar processes will continue to unfold.

Social Networking

Meta (Facebook) 75.3%
Instagram 63.9%
TikTok 50.2%
X (Twitter) 41%
Reddit 31.2% of the population
LinkedIn (unknown)
Nextdoor 13.5%

Communication

Facebook Messenger 61.3%;
WhatsApp—used by 27.3% of adults
Snapchat—used by 37.6% of the population
Discord—engages 15.7% of U.S. adults
Telegram—used by 13.5% of adults
Skype—used by 15% of users

According to surveys carried out in 2023 by the Pew Research Center (2023c), Americans primarily turn to Facebook for consumption of news content with an estimated 30% of U.S. adults saying they regularly use it for this purpose. YouTube sees an estimated 26% of people turning to it for getting news there. Comparatively, fewer people use other social media platforms for news as estimates indicate that 16% use Instagram, 14% TikTok, 12% X (formerly Twitter), and 8% use Reddit. Smaller percentages of Americans get news from Nextdoor (5%), LinkedIn (5%), Snapchat (4%), WhatsApp (3%), or Twitch (1%). Importantly, some social media platforms have a high proportion of users who regularly turn to them for news such as the estimated 53% for X (formerly Twitter) who turn to it for news. In comparison, it is estimated that only 15% of Snapchat users do the same. It is also critical to be cognizant of the changing nature of the medium of news consumption—estimates place the overwhelming percentage of news consumption moving toward being primarily driven by digital device usage versus television—as of 2023, 86% of adults reported they got news from a smartphone, computer, or tablet (Pew Research Center, 2023d).

Human beings are, as Giddens put it, knowledgeable agents (Giddens, 1984, p. 281). People willingly purchase smartphones, computers, and tablets in mass, and many pay attention to consumer developments in technology. Throughout their day-to-day life, hundreds of millions engage with technological platforms and applications in the digital realm and there now exist large-scale datasets and hundreds of millions to billions of observations of user behavior. New forms of media, such as the aforementioned prism of podcasting, also have paved the way for interesting processes where creators can target transnational audiences and blend local cultural elements with global visions. Royston (2023) neatly demonstrates how this has already arisen in diaspora networks in the U.S., which use innovative formats to attract significant audiences and reach through podcasting.

Giddens argued that individuals' knowledgeability is bounded by the unconscious, on one hand, and by unacknowledged conditions or unintended consequences of action, on the other (Giddens, 1984, p. 282). One of the primary aims of social science is to investigate these boundaries and the significance of consequences for system reproduction as well as the ideological connotations of those boundaries (Giddens, 1984, p. 282). At this point in time, we have enough evidence to tell us that throughout individuals' day-to-day lives using the internet to consume digital content and news, people generally seek out negative stories and content. Although the antecedent characteristics of why this is so are unclear, there is an overwhelming amount of evidence which tells us that individuals, in the digital realm, are drawn to negative stories and even seek them out.

More recently, the systems at play in digital and social media platforms have shifted to shorter content—especially after the rise of TikTok. With shorter content, individuals can see more, and at the same time, engineers and data architects benefit from gathering greater amounts of user behavioral data. Digital platforms including Twitter, Instagram, and of course TikTok have effectively optimized their content to be short and dynamically interactive. Algorithms are critical to this attention-based set of dynamics. As noted by Fernández-Rovira and Giraldo-Luque (2022), user personalization is based on extensive data collection and large-scale analyses, where data feed into complex systems that predict future behavior and tailor content (Fernández-Rovira & Giraldo-Luque, 2022, p. 11). Within the broad context of how individuals obtain and consume news stories and information in the digital realm, the duality of structure and agency is palpable. The aforementioned algorithms and their associated trajectories would not be empirically possible to implement without the actual interactions and behaviors of users on these platforms. Social phenomena in the digital realm, just as in the physical world, are produced and reproduced through a duality between structure and agency. Structures (rules and resources) and their associated systems shape individual agency which itself, in turn, shapes structures.

When compared to news consumption and informational sharing on socio-political topics prior to the onset of the digital realm (and even early in its evolutionary stages), there are structural and systemic differences in how Americans obtain their news, interpret their news, and communicate about news in the digital realm. The subsequent section will demonstrate how these changes have influenced polarization and trust across American society.

Empirical Analysis

Instead of discussing their world throughout their neighborhood, in community centers, town halls, and organically organized social venues, individuals have turned to online platforms to interact with heaps of information that flows throughout the digital realm on a 24/7 basis. I begin this empirical analysis with trust—a phenomenon that represents individuals' viewpoints and assumptions about another entity, person, group, or organization. Although a perceived lack of trust is not necessarily a causal factor that brings about polarization, it is nevertheless conceptually relevant to consider. Trust and polarization are interlinked. At this current point in time, we cannot definitively say that trust causes polarization or vice versa, but we do know that Americans trust one another increasingly less (as demonstrated in the previous chapter).

The following questions were drawn from the General Social Survey and captured how much confidence individuals had toward different institutions. I assume that a low level of confidence is indicative of a low level of trust—as individuals who are not confident in a given institution or service do not trust the information or output that it provides. We begin with a question on confidence in the press that was stated to respondents in the following way, "I am going to name some institutions in this country. As far as the people running these institutions are concerned, would you say you have a great deal of confidence, only some confidence, or hardly any confidence at all in them?" These data are shown by age group in Fig. 4.1.

As visualized data reveal, the amount of respondents (from all age groups) who stated they have "hardly any" confidence in the press is at a

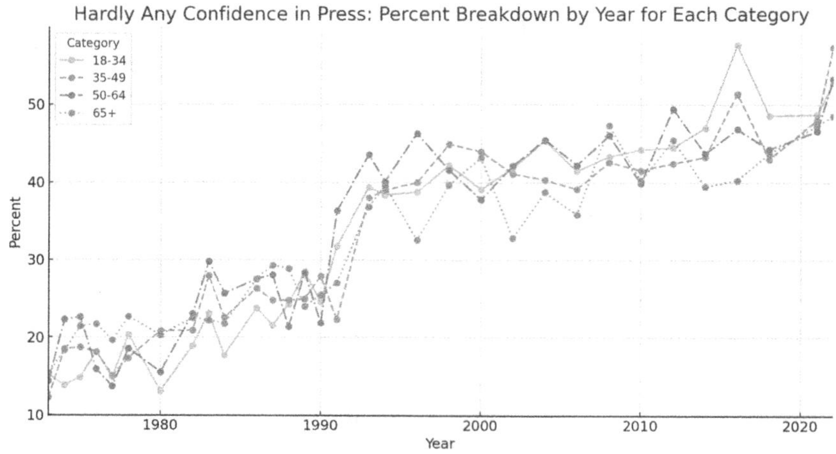

Fig. 4.1 "Hardly Any" confidence in the press (1973–2022)

record high. The most surprising aspect of this is that it is at nearly the same level for all age groups, including those aged 65+. Before 2015, this age group tended to have a bit more confidence in the press.

Jones (2004) observed that many Americans believe that the media is biased and that journalists often report with political agendas. Likewise, McChesney and Nichols (2010) argued that the changing nature of commercial imperatives of media corporations has shifted reporting from substantive to entertainment-driven content (i.e., clickbait and sensationalist content). This shift was demonstrated to privilege and prioritize profits over public service, which the authors hinted could have diminishing negative effects on the public's perception of the press as a watchdog. We must also consider these findings in relation to the changing nature of viewership—most adults now get their news and stories about the world through social media platforms. While mainstream news agencies all have social media accounts and simply analogously circulate content in an analogous manner to keep up with the 24/7 flow of information in the digital realm, the difference between today and eras of the past is that (1) news agencies are not the only bearers of news, and (2) news agencies compete with other organizations, institutions, and persons who also put out viewpoints on a given story. What this has resulted in is a plethora of user interactions on platforms that are no longer structured in the same way

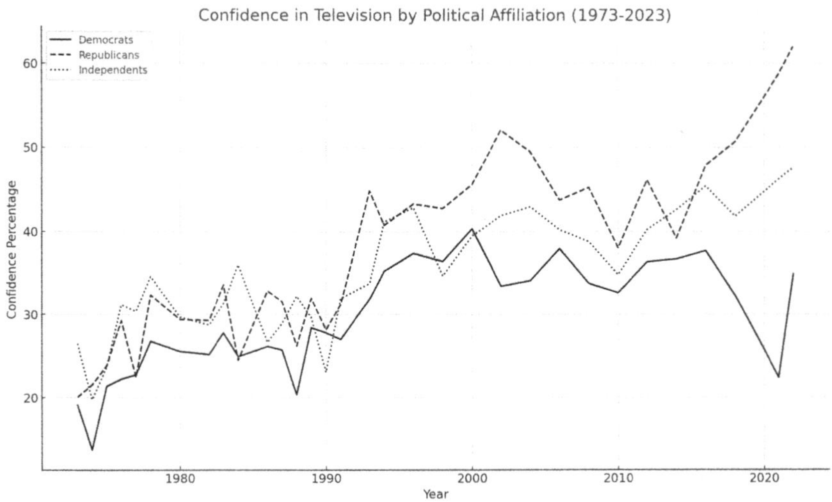

Fig. 4.2 Confident in television (hardly any) by political affiliation (1973–2022) ($N = 24{,}194$)

when compared to traditional media viewing—from radio, to newspapers, to television.

Further evidence of these outcomes can be observed in Fig. 4.2, in which respondents in the GSS were asked how confident they were in television, "I am going to name some institutions in this country. As far as the people running these institutions are concerned, would you say you have a great deal of confidence, only some confidence, or hardly any confidence at all in them?"

These data on confidence in television are presented alongside political affiliations (Democrats, Republicans, Independents) of respondents. Figure 4.2 reveals that there are significant trends that can be observed the past five decades. While all three groups have less confidence in television than in times past, the data show that there might be differences between groups. For this reason, I run an Analysis of Variance (ANOVA) to compare the means of groups for the purpose of identifying potentially significant differences between them. Table 4.1 provides statistical output on this test.

The highly significant p value indicates that there is a statistical difference in confidence levels in television among Democrats, Republicans,

Table 4.1 ANOVA results for confidence in television by political affiliation

	Sum of squares	*Degrees of freedom*	*Mean square*	*F*	*P value*
Between groups	708.72	2	7.62		0.0009
Within groups	723.96	93	7.62		
Total	716.34	95	7.62		

and Independents. This reveals that Democrats tend to not be as skeptical of television in comparison to the other groups, yet they still show a high degree of skepticism. Also, these observed variations between groups are unlikely due to random chance. The *F* value (7.62) informs us of how much confidence levels differ between the groups compared to how much they vary within each group.[3] The *p* value (0.0009) is much smaller than 0.05; hence, we can be confident that the observed differences between groups did not arise by chance. This particular result lends support to the overall claim that polarization is increasing, even in relation to a phenomenon (confidence in television) that some may perceive to be one-sided. All groups experienced decreases, and while Democrats experienced less of a decrease, they still have less confidence in television now than ever before.

Next, we turn to a question from the GSS in which individuals were asked about their confidence in the executive branch of Federal government. The statement was presented to respondents as follows, "I am going to name some institutions in this country. As far as the people running these institutions are concerned, would you say you have a great deal of confidence, only some confidence, or hardly any confidence at all in them?"—below, I again report the "Hardly Any" category.

Figure 4.3 reveals that there have been fluctuating levels of public confidence in the executive branch of the U.S. government from the mid-1970s onward. In years when confidence noticeably declined, there were often political scandals (e.g., Clinton's impeachment in the 1990s) and economic downturns (e.g., the 2007–2008 global economic crisis). In the beginning of the time period under attention, the post-Watergate era and associated economic challenges of the late 1970s (oil crisis) contributed to lower confidence levels (Citrin & Green, 1986). The global financial crisis of the late 2000s significantly impacted public trust, and political scientists have demonstrated that economic instability is strongly

[3] A higher *F* value is interpreted as constituting a bigger difference between groups.

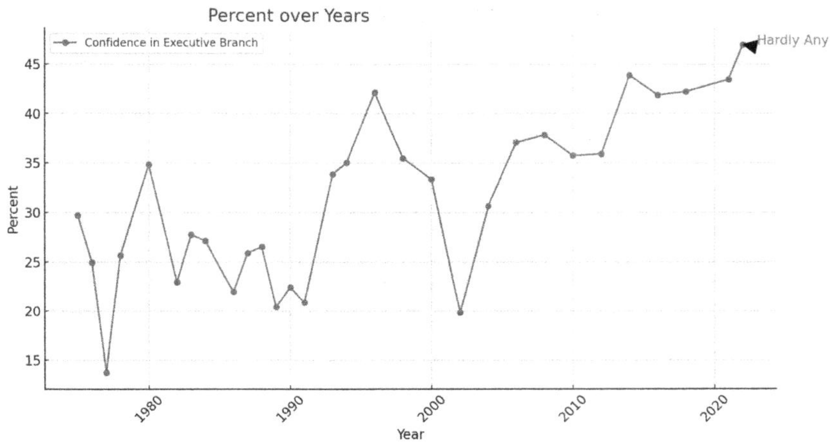

Fig. 4.3 "Hardly any" Confidence in the Executive Branch of the Federal Government (1975–2002) ($N = 23{,}064$)

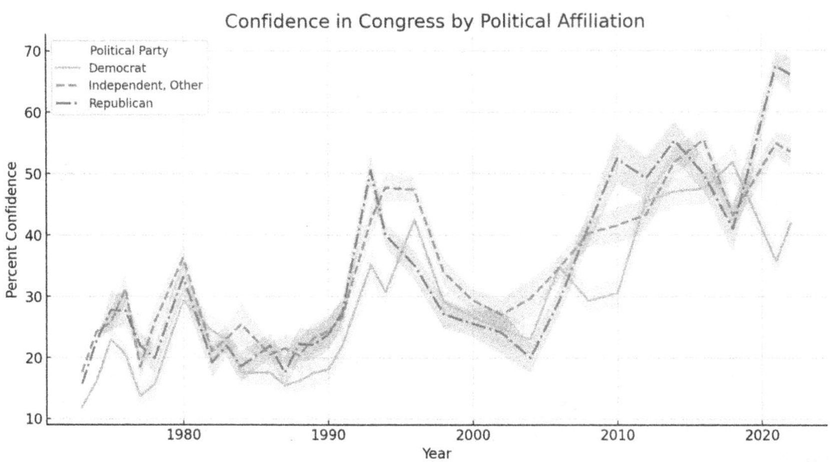

Fig. 4.4 "Hardly Any" Confidence in Congress (1975–2002)

correlated with diminished confidence in governmental institutions (Bartels, 2013). As time has gone on, individuals have grown to be less confident in the executive branch. The most recent wave of the GSS (2022), the percentage of Americans who stated they had hardly any

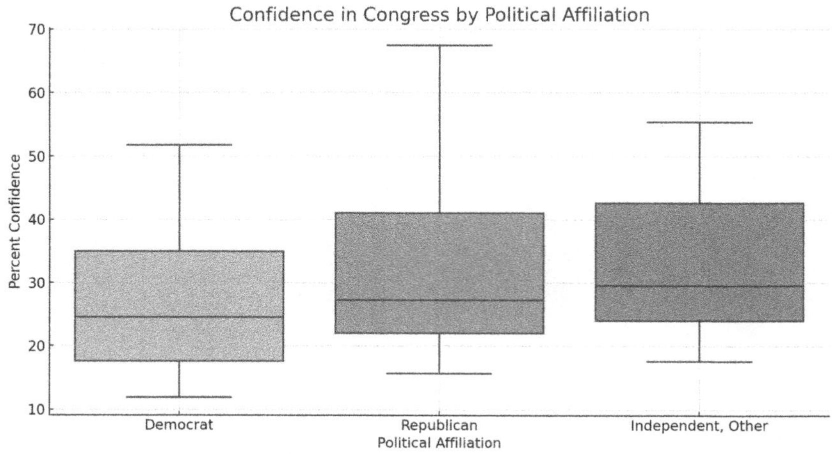

Fig. 4.5 Box plot

Table 4.2 How often respondent discusses political matters with friends 1981–2022 ($N = 9502$)

	1981–1984	*1989–1993*	*1994–1998*	*1999–2004*	*2017–2022*
Frequently	11.10%	14.70%	15.00%	16.60%	68.20%
Occasionally	56.50%	57.40%	56.50%	57.60%	20.80%
Never	31.50%	27.80%	27.00%	25.30%	9.50%
Don't know	–	–	1.50%	0.40%	0.10%
No answer	0.90%	0.10%	–	–	1.40%

confidence in the executive branch is higher than ever reported. What's more, Fig. 4.4. features descriptive statistical tendencies on the "hardly any" category on respondents' confidence in Congress from 1975 to 2022 and here, a vast uptick can be observed.

We now move on to a similar question that was posed, but this time about Congress. Here I stratified the data based on political affiliation (Democrat, Republican, and Independent). Results are provided in Fig. 4.5 and Table 4.2.

As evident, the results here are very similar to those on the question of confidence in television. However, we do not know if there are statistically significant differences between groups; thus, I will run tests. Figure 4.5 is stratified by political affiliation and also shows confidence intervals.

Here we can see that voters from all political affiliations have an increasing level of hardly any confidence in Congress. As with previous results, these trends are worrying. To see if there were any differences in group means, I also ran an identical ANOVA as before, which revealed that there were no significant differences between political affiliations. A follow-up test was run to probe these results. Here, I ran a Kruskal-Wallis test which revealed a 4.390 Kruskal-Wallis Statistic: 4.390 and a p value of 0.111—the latter is greater than 0.05 which tells us that there are no statistically significant differences in the mean confidence levels in Congress among Democrats, Republicans, and Independents. Figure 4.5 visualizes these results in a box plot, which provides us with an illustrated comparison of confidence in Congress across different political affiliations.[4]

We now shift over to the World Values Survey data and here, attention is drawn to the increasing frequency with which individuals are discussing political matters with their friends. A time series on this question (which is AO62 in the data) reveals a very strong trend.

Respondents have considerably reported that they frequently discuss political matters with their friends. Although the question does not capture if the discussions are in person or via digital platforms, these results are nevertheless telling—politics have become more frequently discussed in American society throughout the evolution and increasing prominence of the digital realm. The near seven-fold increase from the first wave of the WVS (1981–1984) to the most recent wave (2017–2022) indicates that Americans are much more deeply embedded within political discourse than ever before in the last half-century. It seems that Americans are seeking out negative content through their interactions with digital media and news stories. If this is the case, then the structural and systemic responses of digital media platforms logically will promote and reinforce such behavior for their users. Sequentially, this will result in a polarized populace and a significant amount of self-righteousness that is embedded within news cycles that are of a negative and partisan nature. These results also indicate that polarization is not only ideological. They provide evidence for the

[4] Boxes represent the interquartile range which ranges between the first quartile (the 25th percentile) and the third quartile (the 75th percentile). The line inside each box indicates the median (the 50th percentile) of the data. The whiskers extend from the smallest and largest values within 1.5 times the IQR from the lower and upper quartiles.

prevalence of affective polarization and growing emotional and social divisions between members of opposing social identities and groups throughout American society. It is clear that divisions have arisen that are not only limited to policy positions, but digital media and internet-based technologies have fostered significant in-group and out-group hostility and animosity (Iyengar et al., 2012). The role of online anonymity plays a latent, albeit crucial impact here because digital interactions are differentiated from face-to-face engagements.

A rich research trajectory in psychology dating back to Zimbardo (1969) and the notion of "deindividuation" entail that a given individual, when in an anonymous situation, will show a greater propensity to act impulsively and less decently. When individuals are in conditions that foster a diminished sense of accountability, the likelihood of social norms being abandoned increases and aggression can even follow. Postmes and Spears (1998) carried out a meta-analysis on deindividuation and discovered that anonymity increases the likelihood that individuals will engage in behaviors inconsistent with societal norms—the interesting dynamic here is that Postmes and Spears observed that such an outcome was even likelier to arise in conditions where group norms are antisocial. If a given individual perceives that she/he is less identifiable and accountable, they are likelier to act with impulse or aggressively in relation to group norms. Crucially, the psychological impact of anonymity is mediated by other factors that stem from group identity along with contextual expectations about the behaviors and expectations of groups they associate with. As noted throughout this chapter, since many interactions that individuals have with other members of their society are now online and take place in algorithmic systems and structures of social media, it is clear why such digital spaces have brought about more hostile exchanges. A lack of direct accountability in online settings has heightened antagonistic behavior that outspreads beyond political debates.

The key aspect here is that social cohesion has been undermined. The American public is no longer confident in television and media institutions, state institutions, and importantly, it appears that the public is seeking out personal discussions on divisive topics to a much greater extent than in the past. In future research, different types of social inquiries would need to be carried out in the future to understand why individuals are drawn to negativity, and if results such as those above are largely driven by individual agency and its interactions with structure, or if there are exogenous forces at play. From an ethical perspective, there remains much to be discerned about human vulnerability and the potentiality of moral growth in digital spaces. Lippitt (2020, 2023) notably argues that resentment is corrosive to the well-being of society and that community building can manifest through personal development, albeit social media constitutes among the most difficult of terrains with which these conditions can be fruitfully developed. Constructive dialogue and forgiveness can foster mutual respect and understanding and counteract significant alienation and hostility that currently dominate polarized digital spaces.

In Conclusion

This chapter has examined the intensifying issue of political polarization and an erosion of trust in government within American society. I have explored how the internet and digital media have reshaped political information—both in terms of dissemination and consumption. This has fostered digital echo chambers where individuals are exposed predominantly to viewpoints that reinforce their existing beliefs. Such echo chambers are just one systematic example of the structural characteristics that currently operate throughout the digital realm and impact digital and social media consumption. These structures and their associated systems are driven by algorithms that are designed to maximize user engagement. They have contributed to the amplification of societal political polarization because they curate content that aligns with users' preferences and interactions. Such selective exposure breeds feedback loops that reinforce existing partisan biases and exacerbate ideological cleavages and antagonisms. To gain an empirical sense on how this all unfolds, this chapter has drawn on data from the GSS and WVS. Results revealed a growing mistrust in traditional media and government institutions. Trust in the press and television has significantly declined across all age groups and is paralleled by a decline in confidence in the executive branch and Congress. The rise and current dominance of digital media has shifted political discourse from physical spaces such as classical town halls to online platforms where anonymity and a lack of face-to-face interaction are prone to breed more extreme and hostile exchanges.

Theoretically, structuration enables us to understand different dynamics of political polarization and trust in government within the context of digital media and the internet. As scholars have pointed out, American society is experiencing a surge in in-group loyalty and out-group antagonisms. Such outcomes and their associated dynamics are not exclusively the result of algorithmic design but are also shaped by users' active choices to seek out content that aligns with their beliefs. Individuals are knowledgeable agents in how they navigate their way through an array of digital platforms. Coupled with individuals seeking out negative content (more so than positive), historically high rates of polarization may be the new norm moving forward. Ultimately, we know that political polarization is a natural feature of democracy; however, the current outcomes and trends we are seeing reflect a distressing set of phenomena that have been induced by internet-based connectivity.

References

Bartels, L. M. (2013). *Unequal democracy: The political economy of the new gilded age*. Princeton University Press.

Boxell, L., Gentzkow, M., & Shapiro, J. M. (2024). Cross-country trends in affective polarization. *Review of Economics and Statistics, 106*(2), 557–565.

Citrin, J., & Green, D. P. (1986). Presidential leadership and the resurgence of trust in government. *British Journal of Political Science, 16*(4), 431–453.

Cooper, D., Hickey, S. M., & Zipperer, B. (2022, July 14). The value of the federal minimum wage is at its lowest point in 66 years. *Economic Policy Institute*. https://www.epi.org/blog/the-value-of-the-federal-minimum-wage-is-at-its-lowest-point-in-66-years/

Edmond, M. (2015). All platforms considered: Contemporary radio and transmedia engagement. *New Media & Society, 17*(9), 1566–1582.

Fernández-Rovira, C., & Giraldo-Luque, S. (2022). *Predictive Technology in Social Media*. CRC Press.

Fiorina, M. P., & Abrams, S. J. (2008). Political polarization in the American public. *Annual Review of Political Science, 11*, 563–588.

Flamino, J., Galeazzi, A., Feldman, S., Macy, M. W., Cross, B., Zhou, Z., et al. (2023). Political polarization of news media and influencers on twitter in the 2016 and 2020 US presidential elections. *Nature Human Behaviour, 7*(6), 904–916.

Garrett, R. K. (2009). Echo chambers online?: Politically motivated selective exposure among Internet news users. *Journal of Computer-mediated Communication, 14*(2), 265–285.

Giddens, A. (1984). *The constitution of society: Outline of the theory of structuration*. University of California Press.

Iyengar, S., & Westwood, S. J. (2015). Fear and loathing across party lines: New evidence on group polarization. *American Journal of Political Science, 59*(3), 690–707.

Iyengar, S., Lelkes, Y., Levendusky, M., Malhotra, N., & Westwood, S. J. (2019). The origins and consequences of affective polarization in the United States. *Annual Review of Political Science, 22*, 129–146.

Iyengar, S., Sood, G., & Lelkes, Y. (2012). Affect, not ideology: A social identity perspective on polarization. *Public Opinion Quarterly, 76*(3), 405–431.

Jones, D. A. (2004). Why Americans don't trust the media: A preliminary analysis. *Harvard International Journal of Press/Politics, 9*(2), 60–75.

Katalinić, J., Dunđer, I., & Seljan, S. (2023). Polarizing topics on twitter in the 2022 United States elections. *Information, 14*(11), 2078–2498.

Kemp, S. (2023). Digital 2023: The United States of America. *DataReportal.* https://datareportal.com/reports/digital-2023-united-states-of-america

Kossowska, M., Kłodkowski, P., Siewierska-Chmaj, A., Guinote, A., Kessels, U., Moyano, M., & Strömbäck, J. (2023). Internet-based micro-identities as a driver of societal disintegration. *Humanities and Social Sciences Communications, 10*, 955.

Lippitt, J. (2020). *Love's forgiveness: Kierkegaard, resentment, humility, and Hope.* Oxford University Press.

Lippitt, J. (2023). Kierkegaard, "the public", and the vices of virtue-signaling: The dangers of social comparison. *Religions, 14*(11), 1370.

Lorenz-Spreen, P., Oswald, L., Lewandowsky, S., & Hertwig, R. (2023). A systematic review of worldwide causal and correlational evidence on digital media and democracy. *Nature Human Behaviour, 7*(1), 74–101.

McCarty, N., Poole, K. T., & Rosenthal, H. (2006). *Polarized America: The dance of ideology and unequal riches.* Massachusetts Institute of Technology Press.

McChesney, R. W., & Nichols, J. (2010). *The death and life of American journalism: The media revolution that will begin the world again.* Nation Books.

Newport, F. (2023, August 7). Update: Partisan gaps expand most on government power, climate. *Gallup.* https://news.gallup.com/poll/509129/update-partisan-gaps-expand-government-power-climate.aspx

Nyhan, B., Settle, J., Thorson, E., Wojcieszak, M., Barberá, P., Chen, A. Y., Allcott, H., Brown, T., Crespo-Tenorio, A., Dimmery, D., Freelon, D., Gentzkow, M., González-Bailón, S., Guess, A. M., Kennedy, E., Kim, Y. M., Lazer, D., Malhotra, N., Moehler, D., & Tucker, J. A. (2023). Like-minded sources on Facebook are prevalent but not polarizing. *Nature, 620*(7950), 137–143.

Pew Research Center. (2023a). *Partisan hostility grows amid signs of frustration with two-party system.* https://www.pewresearch.org/politics/2022/08/09/as-partisan-hostility-grows-signs-of-frustration-with-the-two-party-system/

Pew Research Center. (2023b). *Highly negative views of American politics in 2023.* https://www.pewresearch.org/politics/2023/09/19/americans-dismal-views-of-the-nations-politics/#:~:text=An%20increasing%20share%20of%20Americans,parties%20in%20nearly%20three%20decades

Pew Research Center. (2023c, November 15). *Social media and news fact sheet.* https://www.pewresearch.org/journalism/fact-sheet/social-media-and-news-fact-sheet/

Pew Research Center. (2023d, November 15). *News platform fact sheet.* https://www.pewresearch.org/journalism/fact-sheet/news-platform-fact-sheet/

Poole, K. T., & Rosenthal, H. (1997). *Congress: A political-economic history of roll call voting.* Oxford University Press.

Postmes, T., & Spears, R. (1998). Deindividuation and antinormative behavior: A meta-analysis. *Psychological Bulletin, 123*(3), 238–259.

Ragusa, A. T., Chan, A., & Crampton, A. (2009). iPods aren't just for tunes: Exploring podcasting as a socio-cultural technology facilitating student experiences of higher education in rural Australia. *Information, Communication & Society, 12*(5), 678–690.

Robertson, C. E., Pröllochs, N., Schwarzenegger, K., Pärnamets, P., Van Bavel, J. J., & Feuerriegel, S. (2023b). Negativity drives online news consumption. *Nature Human Behaviour, 7,* 812–822.

Robertson, R. E., Green, J., Ruck, D. J., Ognyanova, K., Wilson, C., & Lazer, D. (2023a). Users choose to engage with more partisan news than they are exposed to on Google search. *Nature, 618*(7964), 342–348.

Royston, R. A. (2023). Podcasts and new orality in the African mediascape. *New Media & Society, 25*(9), 2455–2474.

Schubert, L., Dye, T. R., & Zeigler, H. (2015). *The irony of democracy: An uncommon introduction to American politics.* Cengage Learning.

Ward, E. (2020, November 24). *When the cops are called on thanksgiving day.* Crosstown. https://xtown.la/2020/11/24/thanksgiving-family-tension/

Zimbardo, P. G. (1969). The human choice: Individuation, reason, and order versus deindividuation, impulse, and chaos. *Nebraska Symposium on Motivation, 17,* 237–307.

CHAPTER 5

Reading

When Emma was ten years old, she visited her grandpa's summer cottage. He gave her one of the Chronicles of Narnia books. She looked at the cover of the book—it was blank and appeared dull, the only things that were written on it were, "The Lion, the Witch and the Wardrobe" by "C.S. Lewis." Emma put the book on her shelf next to her stuff and then watched TV for the rest of the day. The next morning, the power was out because some of the electrical lines in the area got thrashed by fallen trees in an overnight storm. The sun was shining bright through the window as Emma grabbed the blank-covered book, opened it up, and read,

> ONCE THERE WERE FOUR CHILDREN whose names were Peter, Susan, Edmund and Lucy. This story is about something that happened to them when they were sent away from London during the war because of the air-raids. They were sent to the house of an old Professor who lived in the heart of the country, ten miles from the nearest railway station and two miles from the nearest post office.

Emma proceeded reading. The day went by fast and before she knew it, Emma was imagining what she would do if she had stumbled into a magical wardrobe that had a portal to the land of Narnia—a land that where fog constantly rolls over giant rocks and through thick enchanted forests. She imagined befriending Aslan (the noble lion and king of Narnia) and

A. Anisin, *How the Internet Changed America*,
https://doi.org/10.1007/978-3-032-02395-7_5

thought about the story for days while finishing the book and moving onto the next in the series.

Emma never read so much ever again after her experiences with the Narnia chronicles—she got older, started using a tablet to look at fashion magazines, and once Instagram became popular, she spent her days mostly on her smartphone scrolling through photos and videos. Later on, the Narnia books were adapted into a film series of three movies. Emma watched all of them with her friends and came upon a common reflection, the books were better.

This chapter, unlike the others, is on a topic that has not received as much scholarly and public attention in discussion about the internet, digital technology, and social media—that of reading. While it is indeed the case that individuals consume more informational content than ever before, they also are reading at historically low rates when compared to the last half-century. Among the most underappreciated (but significant) impacts that the internet has had on American society can be observed in how it has changed patterns of reading behavior. The print newspaper industry has long but disappeared while the book publishing industry has taken substantial hits over the last two decades due to shifts in consumer preferences toward electronic and audiobooks. Individuals are bombarded with news, stories, updates, and advertisements from different digital and social media platforms at rates that far surpass any previous era in history. This has led to a fundamental shift in not only the extent that an individual spends interacting with text-based information but to the average attention span and the types of content that individuals come across.

According to the Environmental Protection Agency (2023), Americans now spend an estimated 90% of their time indoors—this is a record-level percentage that constitutes a very important change in social behaviors across a spectrum of different contexts. Yet time spent indoors is mostly centered around looking at screens or doing something related to consuming content that is digitally derived. The rise of TikTok, YouTube Shorts, Facebook Stories, etc., all have contributed to a shortening of the population's attention span and likewise have disabled many people from utilizing something that has always been inherently human—our creative capacity as espoused in an intrinsic desire to read physical books. These examples are just a few but are nevertheless representative of the profound effects brought on by the digital realm.

The Benefits of Reading

Reading is widely known to be beneficial for different development characteristics in children that range from psychological to neurological and behavioral. Of all the academic literatures I have ever reviewed, research on reading in youth and children and its relation to positive outcomes is probably the most solidified and robust I have come across. Reading books and stories has benefits for children's development, and there is no confounding factor that can put a damper on this relationship. First and foremost, when children are read to or read themselves, they typically encounter stories that have a very positive and hopeful message. Arslan et al. (2022) refer to this as a positive psychology storytelling which has been observed to increase adolescents' mindfulness, optimism, happiness, and other positive emotions. Such stories also can reduce depression, anxiety, and negative emotions as observed by the authors over five weeks. Sun et al. (2024) delved into the long-term effects of early initiated reading for pleasure and investigated cognitive development, mental health, and brain structure outcomes in young adolescents. Data from the Adolescent Brain Cognitive Development project were analyzed and included more than 10,000 subjects from the U.S. Statistical analyses revealed that early initiated reading for pleasure practices are significantly associated with higher cognitive performance such as better scores on verbal learning, memory, as well as performance in school. Likewise, early reading is negatively correlated with mental health problems which include reduced scores on dimensional psychopathology along with attention issues. The authors' inquiry on brain imaging data revealed how early reading for pleasure is even linked to larger cortical and subcortical volumes in regions of the brain that deal with language and cognitive processing. As noted by Sun et al. (2024), "early RfP experiences appear to foster cognitive development and mental well-being, potentially through enhanced brain structures" (Sun et al., 2024, p. 364).

Along similar lines, Mak and Fancourt (2020) also assess the relationship between reading for pleasure and children's psychological and behavioral adjustment at the onset of adolescence. Through analyzing data drawn from the Millennium Cohort Study (8936 children, aged 7 and 11), the authors utilized propensity score matching to create a treatment group (comprised children who read frequently) and a control group (comprised children who read less frequently). Their analysis also controlled for individual, social, and familial-based behavioral factors in an attempt to imitate an experimental approach. The results of this computationally complex but fruitful inquiry revealed that daily reading for pleasure (at age 7) was significantly associated with lower levels of hyperactivity and inattention and better prosocial behavior (at age 11). This result remained consistent even among children who had a history of hyperactivity and inattention at age 7. The authors also discovered that daily reading was linked with lower levels of emotional problems. Encouraging regular reading from an early age can thus have long-lasting positive effects on an individual's overall development because it enhances cognitive abilities, improves mental health, and fosters better behavioral adjustment. Furthermore, Lenhart et al. (2023) also investigated adolescent leisure reading and its association with prosocial behavior. Here, the authors asked whether leisure reading in earlier grades can predict future prosocial behavior and social adjustment. Data taken from the National Educational Panel Study were analyzed (comprised observations of 5152 students ranging from grades 5 to 9). The statistical analyses controlled for nonverbal intelligence, socio-economic status, as well as migration background. It was discovered that general leisure reading did not predict positive social outcomes, but, interestingly enough, reading modern classic literature was correlated with increased prosocial behavior and better social adjustment. This may echo Reese and Cox' (1999) classical findings that stated the quality and type of books that get read are important with regard to children's development and literacy. Here, three styles of adult book reading were conceptualized—a describer style (focused on describing pictures during the reading), a comprehender style (focused on story meaning); performance-oriented style. The authors found that the describer style of reading resulted in the greatest overall benefits for children's vocabulary and print skills. Additionally, the performance-oriented style was also beneficial when children's initial skill levels were taken into account.

Li et al. (2024) investigated the interaction of screen use and reading on brain development, cognitive skills, and behavioral outcomes in early adolescents. Data from the Adolescent Brain Cognitive Development study comprised 12,000 participants (ages 9–13) were analyzed. It was discovered that screen use has both direct and indirect negative effects on cognitive skills and brain volume, especially when it comes to language-related regions. Reading, in contrast, showed positive causal effects on language ability and brain volume. Li et al. (2024) noted that "our study further revealed that increased engagement in activities such as Video and

SNS may result in reduced reading habits, thereby diminishing the cognitive and brain volume benefits from reading in children" (Li et al., 2024, p. 9). In detail, watching television shows and movies and playing video games were associated with adverse cognitive outcomes. Specifically, TV and movie series were negatively associated with crystallized intelligence scores such as picture vocabulary and oral reading recognition. Video game use was linked to poorer performance in picture sequence memory and attention problems. Importantly, the authors found that these associations were robust at both baseline and the two-year follow-up. Both were also correlated with behavioral problems, social problems, attention problems, rule-breaking behavior, and even aggressive behavior. Above all, the authors' findings on the indirect effects of screen time on brain development were traced through observations on changes in reading habits. Screen use was found to displace time that could have been spent on reading. Empirically this leads to a reduction in cognitive and brain volume benefits that reading provides. This displacement effect was significant across various types of screen activities, suggesting that increased screen use indirectly hampers cognitive and brain development by reducing engagement in reading. The authors argue there is a significant need for monitoring and regulating screen use among adolescents to mitigate its negative impacts on cognitive and behavioral development.

Although not directly related to the mental and psychological aspects of reading and its benefits (but more so to increase in screen time), the tragic irony of mass societal-wide declines in reading is that they have been accompanied by a newly forming epidemic of myopia. Screen time contributes to myopia through several important mechanisms (Zong et al., 2024). First, prolonged periods of focusing on screens require the eyes to maintain focus on close objects (known as near work)—this has been observed to lead to eye strain and influence the eye's growth in youth. Second, increased screen time almost always means less time spent outdoors. It has long been known that exposure to bright outdoor light is crucial in preventing myopia because it stimulates the release of dopamine in the retina (which helps to regulate eye growth). Indoor environments have lower light levels compared to outdoor settings, which can spur improper eye development and elongation—both are key characteristics of myopia. Third, continuous focus on screens requires an individual's muscles in the eye to stay contracted for long periods (known as accommodation). This can lead to structural changes in the eye. Fourth, usage of screens commonly involves poor posture and close viewing distances which exacerbate eye strain.

Along these lines, the number of people (globally) with myopia is projected to increase from 1.950 billion in 2010 to 4.758 billion by 2050. In Asia, the prevalence of myopia among teenagers has been reported to be as high as 96.5%. It is now extensively believed that due to the rapid increase in myopia prevalence within a single generation is traceable to increased near-work activity (screen time) and reduced outdoor activity (Dirani et al., 2019). Dolgin (2015) notes how in the 1960s only 10–20% of the Chinese population was short-sighted, but now up to 90% of teenagers and young adults are affected. Similarly, 96.5% of 19-year-old men in Seoul, South Korea, are myopic. The trend is also evident globally, with about half of young adults in the United States and Europe now affected.

Reading and Content in the Digital Realm

As mentioned, a contradictory scenario has arisen in which hundreds of millions of Americans are encountering and consuming record levels of information and content on a daily basis through various types of internet sources and different technological devices ranging from smartphones to tablets to computers and even smartwatches. Yet by being exposed to more content, individuals are reading less and less as each year goes by. An overwhelming incursion of content and information has arguably fostered shorter attention spans and a preference for temporally constricted and easily digestible content. At the time of writing this book, social media platforms, applications, and video streaming services heavily prioritize temporally constricted and sensationalist snippets of video instead of longer-form content. These changes have arisen through structuration—through interactions of structures, systems, and human agency. Different significant and legitimation structures have evolved as time has gone by in the digital realm. For example, for those that can recall the structures of either Facebook or Twitter in their early days, content tended to be in written form with photos—there were fewer sensationalist experiences overall when compared to contemporary offerings that are highly geared toward 15- to 60-second clips. Another critical change can be observed in the overall tendency of such applications to de-personalize content to users in terms of getting access to information from their friends and people within their actual social network. In the past, a given Facebook news feed would be full of stories and posts from individuals' actual friends, family, etc., whereas now, a user will be fed (by algorithmic systems) content that is globally broad and curtailed to their past viewing history. Such content, again, is quite sensationalist and meant to grab users' attention for a limited period of time.

The aforementioned processes did not arise out of thin air—digital media companies, especially social media, have learned that users will stay on their platforms longer if they are provided with certain types of content. The rise of TikTok was a key development in spurring this process as this highly addictive application provided a wealth of data on how users could view even more content—shortly after, Facebook "stories" emerged as did Instagram stories, YouTube Shorts, etc. These developments, of course, have led to users skimming rather than reading into content on deeper and more time-consuming levels. People across American society are reading less but consuming more visual and audio information. While doing this, users tend to multitask across multiple devices, which in turn leads to an increase in cognitive load and also makes sustained reading more challenging. There is substantial evidence that individuals' attention spans have been shortened in the digital age. Back in 2009, Ophir et al. (2009) already had observed that chronic media multitasking was becoming "ubiquitous" through individuals exposing themselves to multiple incoming streams of information. The authors hypothesized that heavy media multitaskers process information differently in comparison to light media multitaskers. These claims were tested on control groups made up of 262 university students. Results revealed that the heavy media multitasking group was more prone to interference from irrelevant stimuli and representations in memory. In turn, this was observed to lead to poorer performance in tasks that require cognitive control. This group had greater difficulty in filtering out distractions and demonstrated higher false alarm rates in memory tasks. What's more, this group also had a slower response time in task-switching scenarios which the authors argue is indicative of a reduced ability to filter out irrelevant task sets, "heavy media multitaskers are distracted by the multiple streams of media they are consuming, or … those who infrequently multitask are more effective at volitionally allocating their attention in the face of distractions" (Ophir et al., 2009, p. 1585). Similarly, a seminal study by Cain and Mitroff (2011) found evidence for what many at the time were already believing was starting to happen about smartphone use.

Here, a comparable research design was utilized to investigate 85 individuals at Duke University, who were categorized based on media multitasking index scores. Subjects were given a visual search task to identify symbols within a target shape while ignoring irrelevant color singletons. Their performance was measured by response times and error rates. Low-media multitask users effectively used top-down information to filter out distractions, while high-rate users showed no significant difference in performance between the two conditions, which indicates that they had a deficit in their ability to apply top-down attentional control. As noted by Cain and Mitroff (2011), "HMMs maintain a wider attentional scope than LMMs, even when instructed otherwise" (Cain & Mitroff, 2011, p. 1183). Differences in being able to hold one's attention are significant between those who regularly engage in high rates of media multitasking and those who do not.

Increased multitasking of digital content has led to increased information consumption on a broad level. This massive shift cannot be understated. Back in 2019, it was estimated that on average, Americans check their phones 52 times a day, which has led some psychologists to refer to contemporary human beings as "informavores"—human informavores are said to engage in advanced information consumption for survival, cultural, scientific, and social advancements (Haladjian, 2019). Heim and Keil (2017) note that human beings consume around 74GB of information per day and that each year it seems to increase by 5%. This is a stark contrast to times of past human history where 74GB of information would be unlikely to get consumed by an individual in his/her lifetime, note Heim and Keil (2017). The technological organization of the internet and digital applications represent a set of structures that shape and are shaped by individual behaviors and agency. Over time, we have seen how digital and social media companies have adapted to user preferences and have capitalized upon mass amounts of data to recreate their products for the purpose of spurring greater user engagement. As agents, individuals use such technologies to access and share information, and more broadly, to simply live substantial portions of their life in the digital realm. With greater usage and time spent in the digital realm by the populace, the evolution of its structures and systems has continuously been driven by reinforcive processes, some of which have resulted in content curation that prioritizes fast multimedia content.

Over time, the desire to view fast-paced media content has taken over other forms of entertainment practices and this has become routinized and embedded in individual behavior and social practices on the internet. There now is a preference for quick and easily consumable content throughout individuals' daily lives. As noted, social media platforms and other digital content providers design their interfaces and algorithms to cater to and perpetuate these consumption patterns. The shift to short-formed content was justified by CEOs of tech companies (such as Susan Wojcicki of YouTube) as being beneficial for not only shareholders of the company but also for content creators. Each year, YouTube shorts amass trillions of views. In 2022, YouTube's CEO noted, "We're working every day to improve how we help creators get started and reach an audience faster on Shorts" (Spangler, 2022).

The structural properties of digital technology and interaction between those who create digital structures and systems (in this example, tech corporations) with individual agency (consumerist pushes for continuous engagement) influence societies to routinize their time and attention in new ways when compared to eras of the past. As people have adapted to the immediacy of internet-based multimedia content, their content consumption habits have changed, including their reading habits. It is not difficult to see how routinization and norms that prioritize efficiency and productivity can discourage extensive reading because of its time-consuming character. Reading is not possible to do if multitasking, and more importantly, reading a physical book is markedly different than reading an electronic text on a screen. Individuals now widely prefer to engage in passive forms of media consumption such as watching videos or scrolling through social media feeds. As such, the duality between structure and agency involves factors that both enable and constrain individual agency with regard to reading. The same technologies that are utilized by hundreds of millions of people offer unprecedented access to information and content and also create environments and settings that discourage deep and reflective behaviors such as sustained reading. Downtrends in reading can be observed amidst a vastly evolving highly sensationalist and informationally rich digital environment. Such outcomes have empirically arisen continuously and recursively.

Empirical Analysis

The primary data under attention in this chapter are drawn from U.S. Bureau of Labor Statistics (2024), which collects information on how Americans spend their time through the American Time Use Survey (ATUS). This survey has been administered since 2003 and is designed to provide data on the activities that people engage in and the amount of time they spend on these activities. The ATUS provides us with arguably the most comprehensive data on how Americans allocate their time. It utilizes a multi-stage stratified random sampling approach to arrive at a representative sample of U.S. civilian respondents aged 15 and up. Specifically, the survey administrators and team draw its sample from households that have completed the eighth and final interview of the Current Population Survey stemming from the U.S. Census Bureau. Survey responses are weighted in order to reflect their proportional representation in relation to the U.S. population. Here, adjustments for nonresponses are made.

Data are collected via a nationally representative sample of individuals wherein participants are asked to recall their activities over a 24-hour period—beginning at 4:00 a.m. the previous day and ending at 4:00 a.m. on the day of the interview. Households are randomly selected by researchers from those who have completed their participation in the Current Population Survey and selected participants are then contacted and asked to participate. The survey uses a time diary method, where respondents provide a sequential account of their activities throughout the day, including details such as the start and end times of each activity, where they were, and who else was present. A very helpful set of characteristics is also coded in these data pertaining to demographics, gender, and age. Observations for the year 2020 are not in the data (due to the pandemic).

This chapter's analysis will first delve into general patterns in how individuals reported they read for personal interest. Afterward, age and gender-specific characteristics will be assessed. We begin with the average hours per day individuals reported reading for personal interest. Figure 5.1 visualizes the results and the profound decrease that can be observed since 2003.

This visualization of the average time spent reading by Americans from 2003 to 2022 reveals a perceptible decline. Back in 2003 the average time spent reading was approximately 0.36 hours per day. By 2022 this average had decreased to around 0.28 hours per day, which is indicative of a decline of 22.2% over the 19-year period. The widespread utilization of smartphones, social media, and streaming services has radically transformed how people consume information which has led to a contradictory scenario wherein individuals are exposed to more information than ever, but read less. We now turn to the average hours per day that men and women spend reading. These data are provided in Table 5.1.

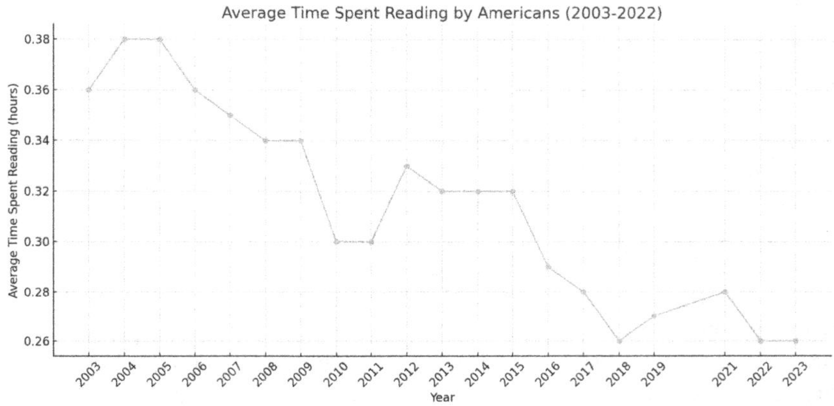

Fig. 5.1 Average time spent reading (2003–2023)

Table 5.1 Average minutes spent reading female and male (2003–2023)

Year	*Men*	*Women*
2003	32	41
2004	33	44
2005	32	43
2006	31	42
2007	28	42
2008	29	40
2009	27	42
2010	25	35
2011	24	35
2012	26	38
2013	26	38
2014	27	37
2015	27	37
2016	25	33
2017	22	33
2018	24	29
2019	23	31
2021	23	32
2022	21	32
2023	20	32

These data reveal that both women and men read less now for pleasure than they did in the early 2000s. Women also have, on average, spent more time reading for pleasure per day compared to men. In 2003, women read for an average of 41 minutes per day and men read for 32 minutes (a difference of 28%). We now turn to a visualization of all age groups provided in Fig. 5.2.

These results reveal that older age groups consistently spend more time reading per day compared to younger generations. The 65–74 has averaged around 0.66 hours per day. As one would expect, the 55–64 age group also demonstrates high daily reading times at around 0.40 hours per day. With this being said, when comparing these two groups, the 65–74 age group substantially more time reading daily than the 55–64 age group. Table 5.2 displays descriptive statistics on average daily reading time according to different age group.

These differences, nevertheless, are minor when contrasted to younger age groups (such as the 15–19 group or the 20–24). The 15–19 age group averages approximately 0.13 hours per day, while the 20–24 age group averages around 0.14 hours. Compared to the 65–74 age group, the 15–19 age group reads about 82% less per day. Among the more surprising findings here is that the age 25–34 and 35–44 groups hardly

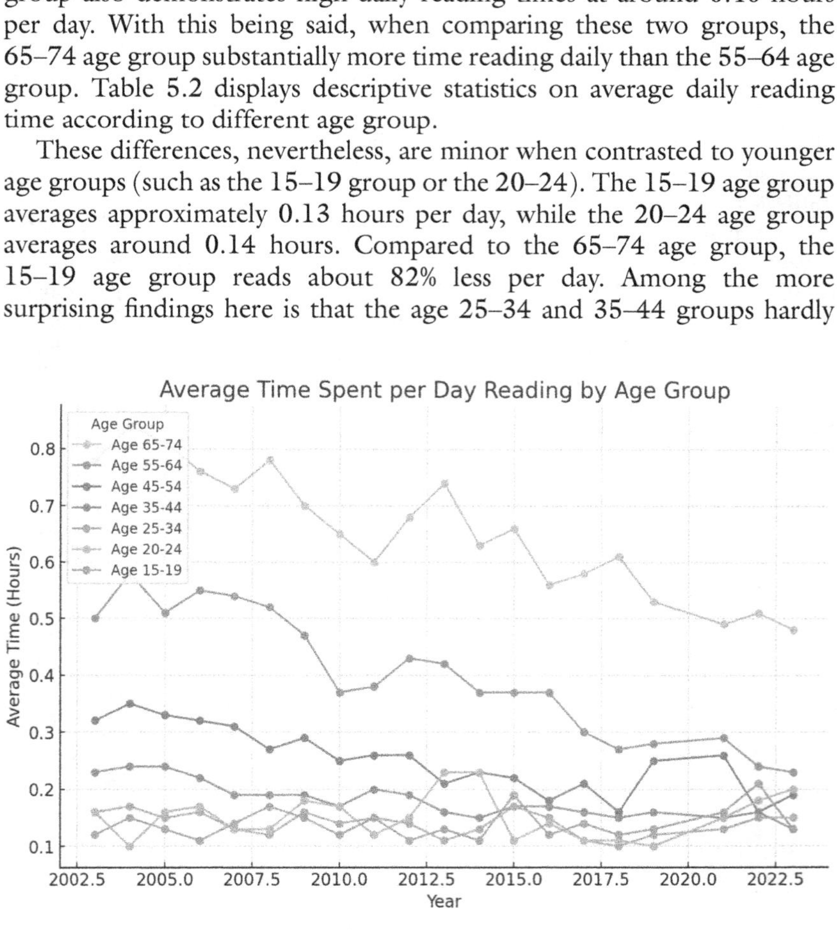

Fig. 5.2 Average time spent reading all age groups (2003–2023)

Table 5.2 Average time spent reading all age groups (2003–2023)

Age group	*Avg. daily reading time (hours)*	*Avg. daily reading time (minutes)*
Age 65–74	0.66	39.6
Age 55–64	0.40	24.0
Age 45–54	0.25	15.0
Age 35–44	0.18	10.8
Age 25–34	0.14	8.4
Age 20–24	0.14	8.4
Age 15–19	0.13	7.8

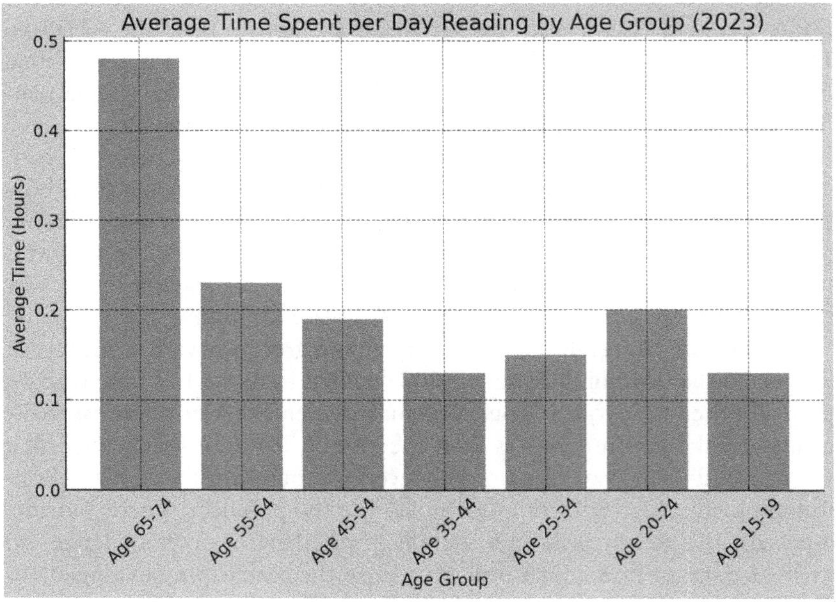

Fig. 5.3 Average time spent reading by age group bar chart (2023)

have spent more time reading than the two youngest age groups. If viewed across 2003–2023, it is not until the age 45–54 age group that we can observe individuals start reading an average of 25 minutes per day. Next, Fig. 5.3 illustrates the most recent data (for the year 2023) by age group.

Here, we can observe that the 2023 data are still dominated by the age 65–74 age group when it comes to the most robust readers. The age

20–24 group which reported it read slightly more than the 45–54 age group.

Furthermore, we now turn to perhaps the most provocative aspect of this chapter's analysis through investigating estimates on time spent on social media by age group. Here, there is no unified source of data comparable to the data used above, but different institutions can provide us with at least attempts at estimates. Beginning with the Pew Research Center, data from 2023 reveal that the percentage of U.S. teens aged 13–17 that report using the internet almost constantly throughout their day is 46% for boys and 45% for girls (Pew Research Center, 2024). Likewise, according to 2023 data from Gallup of a survey of 1500 adolescents, over half of U.S. teenagers (51%) reported that they spent at least 4 hours per day using various social media apps (YouTube, TikTok, Instagram, Facebook, and Twitter). On average the data reveal that American teens spend 4.8 hours per day across seven social media platforms. Zooming into these age groups, the average time spent ranged from 4.1 hours per day for 13-year-olds to 5.8 hours per day for 17-year-olds. Girls spent approximately an hour more on social media than boys (5.3 hours compared to 4.4 hours) (Rothwell, 2023). To put this into perspective, the average of 4.8 hours spent on social media (288 minutes) per day when compared to the 8 or so minutes spent reading per day by the youthful age group(s) represents an increase of 3500%.

Indeed, we can recall that the younger age groups have historically (at least since the beginning of data, 2003) tended to spend less time reading than all other age groups. Thus, one may contend that nothing has really changed—the youth read less than the elderly, it might be the case that such a trend will always remain. However, we must consider a major confounding factor in terms of how much time the populace spends outside, especially the youth. Although there is, to the best of my knowledge, no existent data on how much individuals use their smartphones outside of their homes or simply outdoors, there are valid estimates of the total number of time individuals spend outdoors. According to a 2019 survey (N = 1000) carried out by the APM Research Lab (2019), which is a member of the American Association for Public Opinion Research's Transparency, around two-thirds of American adults engage in outdoor activities and spend their free time in nature anywhere from once to twice per month. In contrast, approximately one in six American adults reported that they never spend their free time in nature. Those who spent most time in nature were from the age 18–34 age group had college or graduate degrees, and lived in the North Central and Western states—here, one-third of respondents said they spent time in nature several times a week. Those who stated they never spend time in nature are from the age 65+ group, low-income individuals, and African Americans.

When surveyors asked respondents, "What is the single biggest thing that keeps you from spending more free time in nature?" the most common responses (31%) were linked to individuals' jobs or work. Around 9% were linked to health issues or disability. The most startling finding here was that 22% stated that "nothing keeps me from going outside more." Beyer et al. (2018) carried out a more complex inquiry on the time Americans spend outdoors, their physical activity levels, and chronic disease risk. Data on American adults aged 20–59 (N = 7914) were drawn from the National Health and Nutrition Examination Survey (2009–2012). This inquiry sought to determine whether outdoor time on work and non-work days was associated with chronic disease indicators such as body-mass-index (BMI), allostatic load, diabetes, and cancer. The authors found that more time spent outdoors was significantly associated with less sedentary time and more physical activity. On non-work days, an additional hour outdoors was linked to a nine-minute reduction in sedentary time and a two-minute increase in physical activity. For work days, the reductions in sedentary time were even more pronounced. Importantly, non-work day outdoor time was significantly associated with lower body-mass-index, reduced allostatic load, and lower diabetes risk (but not cancer).

Specifically, Beyer et al. (2018) found that for every hour spent outdoors, sedentary time decreased by approximately 15 minutes. For each additional hour outdoors individuals spent, a 0.20 decrease in BMI was observed as well as a highly significant reduction in allostatic load. What's more, the odds ratio for diabetes decreased by 0.87 per hour spent outdoors. Beyer et al. (2018) point to the necessity of promoting outdoor activities as part of public health initiatives—increased time spent outdoors is associated with greater physical activity and reduced risk of chronic disease. The internet and structures and systems of the digital realm have brought about a significant decline in reading habits across all demographics which to date has been driven largely by the rise of digital media and associated changes in individual agency and consumption patterns. Short-form videos on platforms such as TikTok and YouTube Shorts have led to constricted attention spans among hundreds of millions of people and a growing salience in preferences for easily digestible information. This shift has resulted in individuals consuming more visual and audio content at the expense of more difficult and reflective activities such as reading or even spending time outdoors in nature.

In Conclusion

This chapter has examined the impact that the internet has had on reading patterns in American society over the last two decades. It has found that there is a marked decline in reading throughout all age groups. The evolution of digital technologies has significantly influenced individual behavioral patterns and has reshaped societal norms and practices. In empirically investigating how these outcomes have arisen throughout American society, this chapter drew upon data from the U.S. Bureau of Labor Statistics' American Time Use Survey. Results revealed that a significant decline in reading habits among Americans (as observed from 2003 to 2023) has occurred. The average time spent reading per day by Americans decreased by 22.2%. While women consistently read more than men, both groups experienced an overall decline. Older adults read more than younger generations. The 65–74 age group averaged 0.66 hours (39.6 minutes) per day, while the 15–19 age group averaged only 0.13 hours (7.8 minutes) per day—this is a major difference of 82%. The 25–34 and 35–44 age groups read only slightly more than the youngest age groups, with an average daily reading time of 14–18 minutes. Compared to how much time teenagers and youth spend on social media, the amount they read per day is astronomically less. This is a vast discrepancy that highlights a shift in content consumption from reading to digital media.

Internet-based forms of digital entertainment, communication, and lifestyle pursuits are tied to an increasing tendency of media multitasking, which is a phenomenon that is not conducive to reading physical books or concentrating on one subject for marked periods of time. It is evident that those who frequently engage with multiple streams of information perform worse in tasks requiring cognitive control and are more susceptible to distractions. The processes and mechanisms underlying the causal relationship between the internet and reading levels are easily identifiable. High amounts of screen time have universally been correlated with decreased concentration, decreased time spent not looking at screens, and ultimately, adverse mental health outcomes (such as a lack of concentration and irritability). The historically salient decline in reading rates among Americans that we are currently witnessing is, nevertheless, a complex phenomenon that has been brought about and influenced by evolving social structures in the digital realm which intersect with technological advancements and changing behavioral patterns. The rise of digital technology and social media has significantly altered how individuals pursue their daily lives and consume information. These changes reflect behavioral patterns that have arisen at the expense of traditional reading. Instead of going outside, hundreds of millions of Americans spend the majority of their time in the digital realm.

References

APM Research Lab. (2019, July 15). *APM survey: How often do Americans spend free time in nature?* https://www.apmresearchlab.org/nature

Arslan, G., Yıldırım, M., Zangeneh, M., & Ak, İ. (2022). Benefits of positive psychology-based story reading on adolescent mental health and well-being. *Child Indicators Research, 15*(3), 781–793.

Beyer, K. M., Szabo, A., Hoormann, K., & Stolley, M. (2018). Time spent outdoors, activity levels, and chronic disease among American adults. *Journal of Behavioral Medicine, 41*, 494–503.

Cain, M. S., & Mitroff, S. R. (2011). Distractor filtering in media multitaskers. *Proceedings of the National Academy of Sciences, 108*(10), 4243–4248.

Dirani, M., Crowston, J. G., & Wong, T. Y. (2019). From reading books to increased smart device screen time. *British Journal of Ophthalmology, 103*(1), 1–2.

Dolgin, E. (2015). The myopia boom. *Nature, 519*(7543), 276.

Environmental Protection Agency. (2023). *Improving your indoor environment.* https://www.epa.gov/indoor-air-quality-iaq/improving-your-indoor-environment#:~:text=Your%20Indoor%20Environment-,Did%20you%20know%20we%20spend%20about%2090%25%20of%20our%20time,disease%20can%20be%20more%20vulnerable

Giddens, A. (1984). *The constitution of society: Outline of the theory of structuration.* University of California Press.

Haladjian, H. H. (2019, March 28). Informavores: Beings that produce and consume information. *Psychology Today.* https://www.psychologytoday.com/us/blog/theory-consciousness/201903/informavores-beings-produce-and-consume-information

Heim, S., & Keil, A. (2017, June 1). Too much information, too little time: How the brain separates important from unimportant things in our fast-paced media world. *Frontiers for Young Minds.* https://kids.frontiersin.org/articles/10.3389/frym.2017.00023#:~:text=Scientists%20have%20measured%20the%20amount,billboards%2C%20and%20many%20other%20gadgets

Lenhart, J., Richter, T., Appel, M., & Mar, R. A. (2023). Adolescent leisure reading and its longitudinal association with prosocial behavior and social adjustment. *Scientific Reports, 13*(1), 9695.

Li, M., Zhao, R., Dang, X., Xu, X., Chen, R., Chen, Y., & Wu, D. (2024). Causal relationships between screen use, reading, and brain development in early adolescents. *Advanced Science, 11*(11), 2307540.

Mak, H. W., & Fancourt, D. (2020). Longitudinal associations between reading for pleasure and child maladjustment: Results from a propensity score matching analysis. *Social Science & Medicine, 253*, 112971.

Ophir, E., Nass, C., & Wagner, A. D. (2009). Cognitive control in media multitaskers. *Proceedings of the National Academy of Sciences, 106*(37), 15583–15587.

Pew Research Center. (2024, January 5). *Teens and social media fact sheet.* https://www.pewresearch.org/internet/fact-sheet/teens-and-social-media-fact-sheet/

Reese, E., & Cox, A. (1999). Quality of adult book reading affects children's emergent literacy. *Developmental Psychology, 35*(1), 20.

Rothwell, J. (2023, October 13). Teens spend average of 4.8 hours on social media per day. *Gallup.* https://news.gallup.com/poll/512576/teens-spend-average-hours-social-media-per-day.aspx

Spangler, T. (2022, January 25). YouTube shorts tops 5 trillion views to date, platform to test shopping and branded content for TikTok-Style videos. *Variety.* https://variety.com/2022/digital/news/youtube-shorts-5-trillion-views-shopping-branded-content-1235162043/

Sun, Y. J., Sahakian, B. J., Langley, C., Yang, A., Jiang, Y., Kang, J., Zhao, X., Li, C., Cheng, W., & Feng, J. (2024). Early-initiated childhood reading for pleasure: Associations with better cognitive performance, mental well-being and brain structure in young adolescence. *Psychological Medicine, 54*(2), 359–373.

U.S. Bureau of Labor Statistics. (2024). DataFinder. https://data.bls.gov/dataQuery/find?st=0&r=20&q=reading&more=0&fq=cg:[Time]

Zong, Z., Zhang, Y., Qiao, J., Tian, Y., & Xu, S. (2024). The association between screen time exposure and myopia in children and adolescents: A meta-analysis. *BMC Public Health, 24*(1), 1625.

CHAPTER 6

Idols as Influencers

Masses have turned to the digital realm to obtain guidance and advice from internet influencers. Emma's experience with this first came during college with a fitness influencer who recommended her followers should exercise 6 days a week and eat a high-protein diet. Emma wasn't overweight, but she also didn't have a defined body and would often be anxious about going to the swimming pool or beach in the summer months. Although she was highly focused on achieving good grades so she could have a chance at different scholarships and internship placements, Emma increasingly became subconscious about her body. Scrolling through her Instagram throughout the day, Emma frequently saw chiseled bodies of female fitness influencers with defined abs and tight yoga pants—pants she purposely wouldn't wear because they were too tight on the lower part of her stomach. Emma felt as if she needed to do something about her physique, especially since nearly all of the lectures she had on a weekly basis were full of girls who would wear those same yoga pants to class. Emma's favorite influencer sold her own brand of supplements, diet, and workout plans—only 29.99$ per month. Having followed this routine for a few months, Emma burned herself out and her anxiety worsened. She started having trouble sleeping, especially during periods of the college semester that were stressful—before midterms or exams. This led to an adverse spiral in which Emma would continue seeking out influencers' content on

A. Anisin, *How the Internet Changed America*,
https://doi.org/10.1007/978-3-032-02395-7_6

how to be healthy, even at the expense of her mental and physical well-being.

This chapter delves into a very underdeveloped consequence of how the internet has impacted popular culture—the rise of idols and internet influencers. Ranging from nutrition and health industry influencers to motivational speakers and a heterogeneous collection of newfound internet celebrities, a fresh frontier has been nurtured with the rise of social media. This frontier has enabled individuals to gain large-scale followings and digital stardom. The key dynamic behind internet influencers is that they would likely never have achieved such a large following without the aid of digital internet-based technology. Many of these individuals have large-scale followings and reach that surpass the domestic context of the United States. Influencers tend to advocate their "brand" and it is common for these individuals to not only collect money through "patronage" drawn from their followers but also sell supplements, merchandise, and many other affiliated products that they either create on their own or promote through sponsorship.

While a significant amount of scholarly research has been attributed to the economic and marketing-based factors associated with the rise of influencers, this chapter places attention on a different set of trends that are more sociological in their underpinning. It explains how the internet has directly facilitated the rise of idols and influencers and conceptualizes the processes that have enabled tens of millions of Americans to follow these idols and take cues from them throughout their day-to-day lives.

The Rise of Influencers

Prior to the emergence of the digital realm, there were only a few pathways that individuals could take in an attempt to gain societal fame. The most common pathways were rooted in the entertainment industry—in film, acting, singing, and to some extent theater. Athletics were also a route for some (depending on the era). Other less prominent trajectories to fame include literary authors, individuals who achieved great feats in life (astronauts, scientists, etc.), and even those who committed heinous crimes sometimes would leave a mark on society and be remembered for years. By the early 2000s, internet usage in households began to increase and as mobile-based connectivity became more and more widespread, the amount of time individuals spent on digital platforms and social media grew exponentially and continues to grow today. With an estimated

5.35 billion people in the world using the internet and spending an average of 6.5 hours a day on it (Pelchen, 2024), the evolution of the digital realm is currently taking place in rapid fashion. It is also estimated that individuals across the globe spend close to four hours a day on their smartphones, and 5.04 billion are on social media as of 2024.

Within the complex structures and systems of the digital realm are many opportunities for individuals to become what is referred to as "influencers"—or users on a given platform that have extensive reach through their social network and following. The most common digital setting that internet influencers operate in is social media. Influencers are particularly known for their ability to convey messages, content, and information to their followers. Influencers' content has been observed to have the capacity to impact attitudes, behaviors, and most significantly, purchasing and consumer decision-making of their audience. Scholarly research on internet influencers traces the genealogy of this phenomenon (expectedly) back to the late 1990s and early 2000s—a time which was marked by bloggers. Bloggers would create their own website or use a hosting service to put out content (usually in the form of written text and photographs) on specialized niche topics that ranged from fashion, to music, video games, film, technology, and countless other lifestyle themes. Blogs would (in their most successful manifestation) attract hundreds of thousands of viewers per week and get millions of hits over the course of a month.

By the time YouTube got launched in 2005, the nature of user-driven video content creation fundamentally changed. This led to the rise of vloggers who would record content (about their lives, opinions, and expertise) through videos. By 2010, Instagram paved the way for a process of revolutionizing the digital landscape of influencers as this platform was primarily smartphone-based and heavily prioritized visual content in which users could share curated images and short videos (Abidin, 2016). As such, internet influencers have been observed to be able to effectively leverage perceptions of authenticity and relatability with their audience(s) through intricate mechanisms that enable them to build trust with followers. Unlike traditional celebrities, influencers tend to interact directly with their audience in heterogeneous communication channels and ways that range from comments, direct messages, to live streams and private interactions throughout different financial donation platforms. Influencers are known to be able to foster a sense of community and personal connection for users. This tends to occur within the structure(s) and system(s) of a given digital application.

Miyake (2024) argues that virtual influencers are representative of a phenomenon that is situated at a convergence of social media, consumer culture, artificial intelligence (AI), and digital technology. Virtual influencers represent an intersection of multiple realities and have contributed to the naturalization of contemporary identities with virtuality—as mediated by digital technology. Miyake also makes a plausible claim by noting that influencers represent much more than just digital avatars but, rather, are a reflection of contemporary digital society and an increasingly complex relationship that this society has with identity. Along these lines, Miyake illustrates numerous ways in which influencers are operationalized within an AI-driven algorithmic capitalistic economy. In this regard, influencers are symbolic to society because they are representative of stylized, visible, and visual digital interfaces that reinforce normative ideologies of identity.

Senft (2013) already observed that influencers operate through the establishment of a perceived sense of accessibility that is necessary for users to feel and pursue genuine engagement. In turn, this can enable an influencer to shape individuals' behavior and preferences (Senft, 2013). As a result of this dynamic, a variety of different businesses and brands have grown to recognize the empirical value of influencers. This has fostered a burgeoning industry or phenomenon of influencer-led marketing strategies. Anything from high-profile corporations to local-based shops have cooperated with different tiers of internet and social media influencers to promote products and services—such strategies have grown to be quite sophisticated and even computational (data-driven) in recent years as companies now have data to engage in targeted demographics via influencers in what Boerman et al. (2017) reasonably describe as a more trusted manner in comparison to traditional advertising. Along these lines, influencers commonly share product reviews, tutorials, and even endorse products. This can influence their followers to make consumption and purchasing decisions. Depending on the context under attention, research has generally found that influencers do positively impact consumer decisions when applied to a specific product or industry. Such a shift exemplifies a decrease in influence of traditional advertising and the increasing importance of social proof and validity that marks social interactions in the digital realm.

As of 2024, estimates indicate that 49% of all consumers make daily, weekly, or monthly purchases as a result of influencer posts. Most notably, the generation of society that spends the greatest amount of time on the internet as a part of growing up (Gen Z) constitutes a set of consumers that trust influencers at a higher rate than other generations and thus are more likely to make daily or weekly purchases due to influencer-led marketing strategies. For example, estimates indicate that 87% of Gen Z consumers are more willing to buy from brands that partner with influencers. Researchers indicate that this has to do with trust—as followers of influencers tend to trust their viewpoints more. Another important dynamic here pertains to feedback. Gen Z and frequent influencer-based consumers have reported that they are more likely to share product feedback with influencers than with the brands they bought from. Customer engagement is now being combined with a rising level of trust. Finally, American consumers are most likely to engage with influencer content on Instagram, TikTok, and to a lesser extent, Facebook. Millennial and Gen Z consumers are more interested in fitness and gaming, while Gen X consumers prefer movies, television, and sports content at a greater rate than younger audiences (Yahoo Finance, 2024). In interviews with 63 teenagers, Lajnef (2023) found that there was a significant sense of trustworthiness between teens and their perception of the influencers they follow. It was also observed that psychological and emotional factors significantly impact and drive teens' interactions with social media influencers.

Furthermore, Engel et al. (2024) carry out a meta-analysis to investigate the relationship between social media influencers and adolescent health through 51 eligible articles (that were published between 2012 and 2022). The authors observed that social media influencers significantly impact adolescents' health behaviors and perceptions. Most studies focused on social media influencers' roles in promoting unrealistic body images, unhealthy food content, substance use, and inaccurate health information. Influencers offer personal stories, heterogeneous accounts of reality, and life histories to their followers that make them appear to be closer or more in touch with their followers. A key aspect to this pertains to an influencer's ability to make themselves relatable to their followers—this was, by and large, missing prior to the emergence of digital and social media platforms as there always were significant mediums that made communication between followers and idols commonly blocked or heavily filtered.

Structuration and Influencers

At the time of writing this book, the prominence of internet influencers in American society continues to grow and there does not appear to be any mechanism or barrier that would disable this trend from increasing in both scope and frequency. The monetary components associated with influencers and their role to the larger economy is of course a massive topic in itself, but there is more than simple economic and marketing-based profit that can be observed with regard to the rise of influencers and their positioning in the digital realm. Structuration theory tells us that human actions are both constrained and enabled by structures, which are concurrently produced and reproduced through these actions. Structures (rules and resources) are both the medium and the outcome of the practices that they recursively organize. Social media platforms represent the most common structures that shape influencer behavior and their interactions with followers. These platforms provide (1) rules such as community guidelines and algorithmic systems, as well as (2) norms that tend to be industry-specific, along with (3) resources that include audience reach, monetization tools, and content creation capabilities. Through these three factors, influencers navigate structures of the digital realm and build their presence online by putting out content.

Indeed, the rise of influencers is easily attributable to their ability to effectively utilize these structures and gain a following through their looks, personality, humor, their ability to find unfilled or underexploited niches, their intellectual, scientific, or spiritual contributions, among many other factors. Influencers navigate their way through systems and algorithms of platforms including Instagram, YouTube, TikTok, and to a lesser extent, Facebook. They prioritize the creation of content that is considered to be of high quality (video, audio, acoustics, shading, etc.). Social media structures also incentivize influencers to produce visually appealing and interactive posts that attend to the constant demands of users in an attention-driven online economy. In turn, influencers contribute to shaping these structures and their associated algorithmic systems by driving user engagement and this feeds back into the platform's structure to reinforce the prominence of influencers. Such a cyclical relationship exemplifies how structures are both the medium and the outcome of social practices. Importantly, as noted, the interactive features of social media platforms enable influencers to build direct and personal relationships with their followers. This fosters a sense of digital community. It must also be noted that the monetary gain that many of the most successful influencers experience does not trickle down and that there are ideologies that are associated with perceptions of social media activity as being an accessible path toward acquiring fame. Such perceptions, argues Fuchs (2021), fail to consider underlying economic and power dynamics akin to influencer capitalism and neoliberal ideals of individualism (Fuchs, 2021).

The relationship between influencers and their followers can be theorized as constituting an empirical manifestation of structuration. Influencers exercise their agency through the curation of content and their larger persona to both attract and retain followers. Here, we can observe strategic usage of speech, text, aesthetics, as well as other engagement tactics that they know (and hope) will resonate with their target audience along with potentially new users that may end up increasing their following. Influencers' agency is not exercised in a vacuum because it is shaped by actual feedback and highly fluid expectations of followers. Followers thus constitute a part of the structure within which influencers operate as they are not passive recipients, but rather, they actively engage with influencers and can challenge their content. Interactions of this sort play a role in creative decisions underlying influencers' future content strategies via recursive processes of structuration. Recall that Giddens' theoretical framework (1984) is marked by a division of time-space which sought to explain the ways in which different social interactions can get stretched across time and space through technological processes. With the phenomena under attention, influencers and their role on social media platforms exemplify Giddens' space-time distinction because such platforms clearly enable influencers to connect with not only audiences in the U.S. but across many parts of the globe. A global reach of this sort empirically amplifies the reach of these individuals and even allows cultural trends and norms to be disseminated across diverse regions of the planet.

Conceptually, the temporal aspect here is palpable in the constant demand of users for fresh content. This drives influencers to produce and put out content and continuously update their online presence. There also are several deeper dynamics that drive influencers to put out specific forms of content. Here, Bishop's (2023) recent conceptualization of the notion of influencer creep is useful for understanding how influencers engage in self-branding and optimization. Bishop argues that creative forms of labor have effectively permeated artistic domains digitally and have likewise reshaped the nature of creative work. Yet, there are also adverse outcomes that have arisen as a result of these processes as influencers have to live up to heightened expectations of personal visibility which are often predicated on systemic inequality pertaining to gender, class, as well as race. In the context of Instagram, Bishop observes how influencer creep breeds constant demand for self-promotion and strategic engagement with algorithmic systems that are opaque with relation to different artists' nature. Artists on this platform are compelled to divert away from their focus through engaging with putting out content based on emotional narratives. The latter often results in self-branding that aligns with societal biases, especially for women.

Furthermore, interestingly enough, Miyake's (2024) conceptualization of influencers' activities online captures the affective and intimate dimensions of online interactions which share similarities with Giddens' theorization of routines and everyday practices and their role in sustaining social structures. Influencers engage in performative acts that aim to bring about emotional and intimate connections with their followers. This can be considered to be somewhat of a parasocial relationship that seeks to replicate real-life interactions, but in the digital realm. Although these routines and practices are somewhat artificial because they take place digitally, they nevertheless contribute to the maintenance and reinforcement of social media norms and expectations. As such, influencers help to sustain the structures of digital interaction in similar ways to how everyday routines in Giddens' theory are assumed to perpetuate social norms and institutions. An important dynamic to consider here pertains to cross-platform variance. The behaviors of influencers vary according to the platform. Abidin's (2021) inquiry into influencer behaviors on TikTok reveals how the platform differs in comparison to the previous hegemon, Instagram. TikTok is much more "viral" in its nature because it requires influencers to engage in personal branding that seeks to complement its vast amount of meme-like content, especially audio memes featuring remixed sound clips. This pertains to the platform's discoverability mechanisms which, Abidin contends, have contributed to democratizing the standing of internet celebrities. Engaging short videos allows diverse content creators to gain visibility in ways that were not possible with Instagram. In turn, this has led to outcomes that challenge the highly traditionalist beauty standards that are prevalent across Instagram.

The structural prevalence of influencers in the digital realm (as observed in the U.S. context) can be observed in the sheer frequency with which young people want to become influencers as their primary occupation. According to the survey, more than a majority of young people regularly state that they want to become influencers. For example, a 2019 survey (by Morning Consult) revealed that 86% of young Americans are interested in trying social media influencing. In 2019, the social media influencing business was already valued at $6.5 billion, and the aspiration to become a "social media star" was the fourth-most popular career goal for children (Min, 2019). Another survey in 2023 of 2204 U.S. adults and Gen Z aged 13–26 who use Twitter, Facebook, Snapchat, Instagram, TikTok, Twitch, or YouTube revealed that 57% of Gen Z and 41% of adults expressed a desire to become influencers if given the opportunity. What's more, 53% of Gen Z respondents view this as a reputable career choice and a similar percentage would leave their current jobs to become influencers if it could sustain their lifestyle (Liu, 2023). These numbers reveal much more than the simple preferences of younger generations—they enable us to decipher the extent to which individuals are embedded in structures and systems in the digital realm, and more significantly, the extent to which individual agency (as a whole) is increasingly becoming exercised by Americans through digital rather than physical contexts. As of 2023, a majority of teens and youth have reported that they not only use YouTube and TikTok daily, but many use these sites on a constant basis (Vogels & Gelles-Watnick, 2023). Duffy et al. (2022) even identify a fascinating set of dynamics in hateblogs featuring interactions between users and their thoughts about certain influencers. In an inquiry into a blog called "Get Off My Internets (GOMI)" wherein women engage in gender-coded critiques of female influencers, the authors analyze upward of 400 comments and dozens of threads and observe how user critiques actually end up reproducing narrow ideals of womanhood (such as those based around cosmetic surgery, photo editing, and regressive beauty standards). In turn, user interactions on this hateblog bring about processes that retell gendered symbolic violence via public shaming and adverse discourse.

A final but key dynamic that can be associated with influencers and their explanatory relevance to structuration theory is in how the influencer phenomenon as a whole is reflective of broader trends in late modernity that Giddens deeply emphasized. Here, the reflexivity of modernity was said to be marked by individuals constantly reflecting on and altering their actions in response to new information. Perhaps there is nothing more revealing of this than the current iterative nature of influencer interactions they have with their followers in the digital realm.

Empirical Analysis

This chapter's empirical analysis is slightly different when compared to those in the previous chapters as there is no time series-based data on society's relationship to influencers in the United States. The topic of influencers in the digital realm is also incredibly new when compared to previous topics that have been covered in this book. For these reasons, this chapter will gauge the extent to which top influencers have reached over society and the typical types of content they put out. It will also touch on some non-American influencers, as current trends in followers are not limited to one single country or context. Typically, content from influencers from countries that are in the English-speaking world (ranging from the U.S. to Canada, Australia, Britain, etc.) tends to be disseminated through algorithmic processes. Afterward, case studies on two different influencers and their interactions with followers and society will be investigated—one of which stems from the early 2010s, the other from the early 2020s.

We begin with an attempt to map out the top 25 influencers in the U.S. as of 2024. For explanatory purposes, I will include individuals who were not celebrities, musicians, or actors before gaining a large following on social media platforms. Table 6.1 contains the top 25 leading influencers in the United States (valid as of 2024). The total number of followers each individual has is not listed—as there are significant fluctuations of follower amounts and current numbers will not be of explanatory relevance as time goes on.

These influencers have impacted American society across a heterogeneous collection of domains that range from modeling, lifestyle, high fashion, beauty ideals, dance trends, viral stunts, large-scale charitable initiatives, sports, do-it-yourself (DIY) content, comedy, music, magic, prank-based, and comedic videos. Collectively, they have contributed to the reshaping of cultural norms, trends, and even entire industries.

Next, I categorize the most prominent influencers from the fitness and health industries. These particular segments of the digital space are of particular relevance because they arguably represent industries that have the largest impact on people's bodies. Specifically, not only is it common for influencers in digital fitness and health spaces to sell products, clothing, supplements, but they also sell books, diet plans, workout plans, coaching programs, and put out many different material and ideational products that get consumed and implemented by their followers. This can then lead to followers trying to lose weight, get muscular, get toned, become more

Table 6.1 Top 25 influencers (2024)

Influencer	*Platform*	*Content type*
Kendall Jenner	Instagram	Modeling, lifestyle
Charli D'Amelio	TikTok	Dance, lifestyle
Gigi Hadid	Instagram	Modeling, fashion
MrBeast	YouTube	Stunts, philanthropy
Kylie Jenner	Instagram	Modeling, lifestyle
Huda Kattan	Instagram	Beauty, makeup
Hailey Bieber	Instagram	Modeling, lifestyle
Addison Rae	TikTok	Dance, lifestyle
Liza Koshy	YouTube	Comedy, lifestyle
James Charles	YouTube	Beauty, makeup
Jake Paul	YouTube	Vlogs, boxing
Logan Paul	YouTube	Vlogs, boxing
Cameron Dallas	Instagram	Comedy, lifestyle
David Dobrik	YouTube	Comedy, lifestyle
Nash Grier	Instagram	Comedy
Emma Chamberlain	YouTube	Lifestyle, comedy
Lauren Riihimaki	YouTube	DIY, craft
JoJo Siwa	YouTube	Dance, singing
Lele Pons	Instagram	Comedy, music
Emma Chamberlain	YouTube	Lifestyle, comedy
Lauren Riihimaki	YouTube	DIY, craft
JoJo Siwa	YouTube	Dance, singing
Jenna Marbles	YouTube	Comedy
Bretman Rock	Instagram	Beauty, comedy
Casey Neistat	YouTube	Vlogs

physically fit, and get a variety of other different outcomes, depending on the context and type of fitness or health space. From cycling to yoga, Zimba, pilates, fishing, jiu-jitsu, MMA, boxing, rock climbing to bodybuilding and longevity, the digital realm has influencers that have followers stemming to literally every topic, sport, hobby, and niche. The platform column emphasizes the type of digital application that a given influencer has gained the most prominence. Table 6.2 lists each of these influencers alongside their niche in the fitness and health industries.

It is worthwhile to consider a recent study by Lawrence (2022a) who conceptualizes influencers as belonging to a larger phenomenon of digital Guru Media. Here it is argued that the emergence of health and fitness influencers is reflective of broader societal shifts from a reliance on traditional expertise and the concurrent rise of post-truth narratives. The role

Table 6.2 Top influencers health and fitness (2024)

Influencer	*Platform*	*Content type*
Michelle Lewin	Instagram	Fitness, bodybuilding
Jen Selter	Instagram	Fitness, lifestyle
Kayla Itsines	Instagram	Fitness, workouts
Simeon Panda	Instagram	Fitness, bodybuilding
Chris Bumstead	Instagram	Fitness, bodybuilding
Blogilates	YouTube	Fitness, workouts
Joe Wicks	YouTube	Fitness, nutrition
Emily Skye	Instagram	Fitness, workouts
Liver King	Instagram	Fitness, lifestyle
Massy Arias	Instagram	Fitness, lifestyle
Cassey Ho	YouTube	Fitness, workouts
Rachel Brathen	Instagram	Yoga, wellness
Kelsey Wells	Instagram	Fitness, workouts
Anna Victoria	Instagram	Fitness, workouts
Sarah's Day	YouTube	Fitness, lifestyle
Shaun T	Instagram	Fitness, motivation
Sam Sulek	Instagram	Fitness, bodybuilding
James Haskell	Instagram	Fitness, sports

of metrics is also critical, as it fosters a culture that can shape public trust and enhance the appeal of alternative digital sources of content and knowledge. Wymer (2022) similarly argues that the digital shift has blurred boundaries between professional and personal domains across fitness and health contexts.

Case Studies

Now shifting onto case studies of influencers and their interactions with users, we begin with Belle Gibson. This represents quite an "old" case in the grand scheme of the evolution of the digital realm and social media influencers' interactions with users. Back in 2013, Instagram was gaining prominence and Facebook was still widely used. YouTube was also relevant, but there was no TikTok. Belle Gibson (born October 1991) is an Australian wellness influencer who manipulated her followers to rake in huge monetary gains. With strawberry blond hair and a captivating smile, Gibson constructed herself and image as representing an unlucky young woman who was dealt a bad hand in life—terminal cancer via a brain tumor. She gained eminence in the digital wellness scene in 2013—her original story was that she overcame terminal brain cancer through implementing holistic and natural remedies as well as a healthy lifestyle. Gibson said her tumor was inoperable and thus, she rejected conventional medical treatments that doctors prescribed to her, which resonated with many individuals that seek out alternative health solutions. It also appealed to those who are emerged in what scholars describe as an increasingly prominent era of post-truth. Moreover, Gibson's constructed story stated that she rejected chemotherapy after two months and pursued "alternative" forms of medicine. She then chronicled her falsified journey on social media with hundreds of posts that were very emotionally catered—she successfully gained a large following on platforms including Instagram and Facebook. While encouraging fans to drink green juices and eat organic produce, Gibson claimed her tumor went away holistically.

As one would expect with wellness and alternative medicine social media influencers, her posts were filled with vibrant and filtered images of healthy foods and holistic practices. Over time, her construction of a mindful holistic approach enabled Gibson to create a large community of loyal followers who admired her falsified resilience and embraced her message of hope and healing through the power of nature, rather than formal medicine. Gibson launched an application (that was available on Android and IOS). The app was called "The Whole Pantry" and provided users with access to recipes, lifestyle tips, and behavioral activities related to her lifestyle. At its peak, the app was at the top of the Apple App Store chart and provided Gibson with substantial profit. As expected, a book was also released with the same name and was published by Penguin Australia (Gibson, 2014)—Gibson became among the most prominent wellness gurus in the digital realm. The book deal was reported to have been valued at upward of GBP 220,000. In multiple ways, such lucrative financial outcomes echo what Fuchs (2014) referred to as a capitalist regime of time—a regime that is marked by a relentless drive for accumulation and acceleration. The time that influencers and users spend on social media platforms is not simply representative of leisure but is productive labor that gets commoditized into great amounts of profit for corporations. Moreover, things started to fall apart relatively quickly. In 2015 several investigative journalists probed Gibson's story and found that there were numerous discrepancies—it was discovered that she fabricated her cancer diagnosis as well as the strategies of treatment. One of Gibson's best friends watched her fake a seizure in which she fell to the ground, pretended to have a violent attack, then quickly got up and recovered on her own (Adamou, 2024). Gibson then publicly admitted to lying about her illness and subsequently encountered widespread condemnation from the public and the media which led to the collapse of her business ventures. The app was removed from app stores and her book was also removed off of shelves. Additionally, she was fined $410,000 by the Federal Court of Australia for deceptive conduct and false representations—by 2021, she was reported to own upward of $500,000 in fines and penalties—leading to internationally read media referring to her as the "cancer conwoman" (The Guardian, 2021).

Gibson's manipulation of her followers was insidious and it is important to keep in mind that this is not representative of the average influencer-follower experience. Nevertheless, this case was chosen as a case study because it elucidates the vast scope of the influencer phenomenon and specifically provides us with great evidence for how followings can develop in the digital realm through the current structures and systems associated with social media platforms. Along similar lines, Gibson's deceptive behavior is representative of not only a personal betrayal but also emblematic of a more dangerous set of manipulations that unfortunately are not that uncommon in the health, wellness, and fitness digital spaces. The wellness industry is, to the best of my knowledge, scarcely regulated and can thus enable con-artists to attract followers by riding societal trends and exploiting the fears and desires of masses of people that are looking for quick and easy fixes to their health via health solutions. Specifically, there are consumer protection laws (depending on the country) that are garnered toward protecting populations from purchasing bad or faulty products—yet there are no laws or regulatory parameters that would prevent a given individual from creating a fake and even malicious persona and amassing a larger following on social media to sell products based on a constructed set of pretexts. There is an obvious (faulty) allure of quick fixes and miracle cures at play here, and unfortunately, tens of millions of people have shown that they are susceptible to deceptive practices.

In recent years, structure and systems associated with social media platforms have enabled the rise of many fitness influencers who promise transformative health benefits through specific diets, workouts, and lifestyle choices. The Liver King (Brian Johnson, born April 1977) gained prominence during the pandemic through his espousal of what he referred to as a "primal" lifestyle. The Liver King would never be seen with his shirt on, and this brawny man would walk around his ranch (property in Texas) eating raw meat, eggs, animal testicles, and of course, raw liver. Many of his meals were filmed in sensationalist format and uploaded to his social media channels—as expected, they attracted millions of views and followers. The Liver King espoused (and continues to espouse) a lifestyle of consuming raw organ meats as a principal food source. Arguably, the Liver King's video content was among the most effective put out to date if gauged in the context of sensationalist content—even people that did not have any particular interest in fitness or bodybuilding often would talk about the Liver King's highly viral videos of eating a bull's testicle or raw liver. This "primal" lifestyle was also comprised of exposing one's self to cold temperatures, water (cold plunges), and barefoot walking on the ground. The Liver King would frequently visit symbolic places, such as Times Square in New York City, where he would be recorded walking around with a kettlebell weight or a similar strength training object.

Johnson conceptualized what he referred to as nine "ancestral tenets" that he then marketed as a part of his supplement and lifestyle business—these included: sleep, eat, move, shield, connect, cold, sun, fight, bond. For more than a year, millions of followers and fans believed that the Liver King's physique was achieved through adherence to his "ancestral" lifestyle practices. His line of supplements was sold throughout the United States and included more than 30 different products (different groups that targeted different proposed health benefits) such as Beef Liver which was marketed as a nutrient-dense superfood containing rich sources of vitamins A and B12, iron as well as many essential nutrients; Beef Organs which similarly was marketed and included a blend of liver, heart, kidney, pancreas, and spleen; Bone Marrow was marked at as a product that can promote joint health, immune function, and overall "primal" vitality; Beef Heart was marketed as a product containing CoQ10 which, Johnson said, supports heart health and energy levels; Beef Brain was a supplement that was claimed to support cognitive function and mental clarity.

Through purchasing these supplements, Johnson recommended his followers to break away from the shackles of modern society and return to their "primal" state of optimal health. Importantly, Johnson's ability to market his products tapped into another set of dynamics that have gained prominence in the digital realm—that of fad diets and associated marketing campaigns. Since the emergence of the ketogenic diet in the mid-2010s, there has been a growing market of consumers that are interested in dietary plans ranging from paleo (similar to an underdefined "primal" diet) to ketogenic (restriction of carbohydrates) to carnivore (only meat and organs) and other diets such as vegan or plant-based. It is indeed ironic that the most statistically obese population in the world is situated in a context that is marked by massive amounts of duplicitous dietary behaviors, groups, and individuals. Without a doubt, the Liver King knew what marketing tactics to utilize to tap into a particular dietary and wellness digital space and sought to differentiate his supplements from competitors—not only through the actual creation of supplements but through acting out what he conceptualized as "primal" behaviors in a format that would appeal to algorithmic processes and viral content.

As with Gibson, Johnson experienced his world crashing down on him at the tail end of 2022 when it became known that he not only used anabolic steroids to attain his physique (something which he repeatedly had denied to his followers) but that he had been spending $11,000 per month on steroids (Xie, 2023), growth hormone, and other advanced chemical forms of enhancement which included a high-tech form of growth hormone called Omnitrope. It turned out that eating raw organ meats on a daily basis was not the primary causal factor that was responsible for Johnson's excessive energy and chiseled abdominal section. Johnson was sued in $25 million class action lawsuit that claimed he maliciously made upward of $100 million from his supplement brand. Johnson later said he "regretted" lying about steroid use in light of the lawsuit (Landsverk, 2023), as tens of thousands of consumers who bought his products felt cheated.

The interesting aspect here is that in comparison to Gibson, the Liver King's story led to condemnation from some, while others accepted his apology. That his $11,000 per month anabolic steroid and growth hormone regimen did not actually fit into the "primal" lifestyle he was promoting did not result in any termination of his social media accounts, even though the impact of these lies is surely on the same plane as those put forward by Gibson. Both cases also elucidate how behavior in the digital realm and interactions between influencers and their followers translate over into the physical realm—in how people consume food, exercise, and decide to carry out behaviors when not online.

The Intersection of Physical and Digital Reality

There is more to the influencer phenomenon than meets the eye. Influencers not only sway masses of peoples' decision-making with regard to fitness, health, diet, well-being, etc. In the most extreme or staunch of cases, the influencer phenomenon represents a larger process of idolization in the digital realm that extends beyond the confines of traditional society-media relations which once were marked by a barrier of mediums between content consumers and producers. The latter were typically corporate entities (film, music, entertainment industries). In today's highly digitalized communicational space, idolization takes on new forms that exacerbate our classical understanding of this concept. In the Judeo-Christian tradition, idolization is a concept that captures a process in which individuals or groups express excessive admiration or reverence of someone or an entity to the extent that it takes the place of a more appropriate or balanced focus of their attention. In this regard, idolization can be considered as a long-stemming historical social practice that is not limited to any particular context, culture, or setting. It can manifest as an intense and often unrealistic admiration of celebrities and public figures, which leads to individuals exhibiting dependability to the object of their admiration. Rojek (2012) makes a plausible argument by noting that idolization of celebrities reflects broader cultural and social dynamics that are driven by media which shape whom and what people idolize—values are typically promoted that center around fame, wealth, and physical appearance (Rojek, 2012).

In the digital realm, the linkage between idols and their fans and worshipers is not as loose as it was before the advent of internet-based entertainment and social media. The extent to which users and fans in the digital realm can impact real-world behavior(s) of idols represents an interesting development. Structuration here is clearly operational between social media platforms, users, and exogenous institutions. Influencers have, in recent years, been able to sway actual court cases and legal proceedings. Take, for example, the Johnny Depp and Amber Heard trial (Depp v. Heard), which was arguably the most high-profile legal trial since the OJ Simpson case of the 1990s. Depp v. Heard was a defamation case that saw both parties suing one another over claims that they were either physically abusive or verbally tarnishing toward one another's public reputations. The trial was live-streamed and saw extensive media coverage in Fairfax County, Virginia. Across YouTube, Facebook, Twitter, and especially TikTok, hundreds of millions (if not billions) of people around the globe followed each day of the trial and each piece of evidence and then subsequently articulated their own content based on legal developments. On the ground, hundreds (and by some estimates, thousands of idol worshipers) of both Depp and Heard camped outside of the courtroom in an attempt to gain access to the trial—some spectators even came from oversees and spent thousands on their travel expenses (Ballasy, 2022). Furthermore, what ended up arising as a result of widespread social media attention was the manipulation of information from the trial. This happened through selective editing and biased commentary as well as the subsequent dissemination of false information. Influencers leveraged the trial's popularity to generate content that aligned with attempts to go "viral" through distortion of facts, which led them to hoard significant monetary gain through new followers and advertisement revenue.

Selective editing involved cutting footage to create disingenuous narratives and memes. False narratives from the trial gained traction throughout the digital realm and in turn influenced public opinion. Fans of Depp and Heard struck to their respective idols and it was not uncommon to see antagonistic online interactions across different social media platforms between the two camps engaging in online spats. What's more, commentators on YouTube (such as "LegalEagle" or "Emily D. Baker") saw their channels experience significant growth during the trial. These individuals provided legal analysis and breakdowns of the daily proceedings. TikTok creators (such as "ThatUmbrellaGuy" or "Spill Sesh") also gained mass traction by posting about the trial through short sensationalist videos. These accounts themselves turned into influencers in the context of this trial and similar celebrity legal cases. At the time of writing this book, the topic "Justice for Johnny" on TikTok had amassed 96.4 million posts. The end outcome of the trial favored Depp although many considered the mass social media reaction to have skewed the jury's opinions as they were, in one way or another, exposed to public opinion and the viral nature of the trial in their life outside of the courtroom.

This case reveals how influencers navigate structures in the digital realm to build their presence online by creating sensationalist and engaging content that meets user demands. The cyclical relationship between influencers and social media platforms exemplifies how structures and practices are mutually reinforcing empirically. Such processes are starting to influence real-world contexts and institutions as emulated in the Depp v. Heard trial. These developments also pertain to an evolving set of dynamics on the nature of idolization in contemporary society. Idolization is indeed an extreme form of influencer-fan relationship, but is important and relevant to consider for scholars in future social inquiry because there now is a clear and pervasive influence that social media and digital technology have in being able to shape public opinion.

In Conclusion

This chapter has revealed how the duality between structure and agency operates in social media platforms in the specific territory of influencers' interactions with users. The former shape and are shaped by the latter. Interactions between influencers and their followers exemplify the recursive nature of social practices. There also are commodification processes at play that monetize social relationships in the digital realm. The influencer phenomenon can be seen as both a product and a producer of contemporary social and technological structures and is reflective of the profound impact influencers have on contemporary American society. Influencers promote their brands and many earn significant incomes through follower patronage and marketing sponsorships as well as merchandise sales. With billions of people spending significant amounts of their day and time online, the scope for becoming an influencer has expanded dramatically. Through several case studies of influencers (Belle Gibson and the Liver King), this chapter has illustrated the adverse societal aspects of the influencer phenomenon. Gibson fabricated a story about curing her terminal cancer with holistic remedies, while the Liver King gained fame for his "primal" lifestyle and diet of raw organ meats and was later revealed to have used anabolic steroids to achieve his physique. While not all influencers manipulate their audiences in as grotesque of ways, it is nevertheless safe to assume that most influencers produce a number of real-world consequences through altering the social behavior of their followers.

References

Abidin, C. (2016). "Aren't these just young, rich women doing vain things online?": Influencer selfies as subversive frivolity. *Social Media + Society, 2*(2), 1–17.

Abidin, C. (2021). Mapping internet celebrity on TikTok: Exploring attention economies and visibility labours. *Cultural Science Journal, 12*(1), 77–103.

Adamou, C. (2024, April 25). Chilling moment woman realises best friend is twisted con artist who faked cancer in 'web of lies'. *The Mirror*. https://www.mirror.co.uk/news/world-news/chilling-moment-woman-realises-best-32668404

Ballasy, N. (2022, May 11). Meet the fans who line up to watch Johnny Depp trial in person, including one who spent $30K. *People*. https://people.com/movies/fans-witnessing-johnny-depp-amber-heard-trial-in-person-exclusive/

Bishop, S. (2023). Influencer creep: How artists strategically navigate the platformisation of art worlds. *New Media & Society*. Onlinefirst. https://doi.org/10.1177/14614448231206090.

Boerman, S. C., Willemsen, L. M., Van Der, A., & E. P. (2017). "This post is sponsored": Effects of sponsorship disclosure on persuasion knowledge and electronic word of mouth in the context of Facebook. *Journal of Interactive Marketing, 38*, 82–92.

Duffy, B. E., Miltner, K. M., & Wahlstedt, A. (2022). Policing "fake" femininity: Authenticity, accountability, and influencer antifandom. *New Media & Society, 24*(7), 1657–1676.

Engel, E., Gell, S., Heiss, R., & Karsay, K. (2024). Social media influencers and adolescents' health: A scoping review of the research field. *Social Science & Medicine, 340*, 116387.

Fuchs, C. (2014). Digital prosumption labour on social media in the context of the capitalist regime of time. *Time & Society, 23*(1), 97–123.

Fuchs, C. (2021). *Social media: A critical introduction* (3rd ed.). SAGE Publications.

Gibson, B. (2014). *The whole pantry*. Penguin.

Giddens, A. (1984). *The constitution of society: Outline of the theory of structuration*. University of California Press.

Lajnef, K. (2023). The effect of social media influencers' on teenagers behavior: An empirical study using cognitive map technique. *Current Psychology, 42*(22), 19364–19377.

Landsverk, G. (2023, May 12). The Liver King claimed he got ripped by eating raw organs when he was really taking $11,000 worth of steroids a month. Now he says he regrets lying to his followers. *Business Insider*. https://www.businessinsider.com/liver-king-regrets-using-steroids-after-being-sued-25-million-2023-5#:~:text=%22Liver%20King%22%20Brian%20Johnson%20built,biggest%20regrets%22%20of%20his%20life

Lawrence, S. (2022a). I am not your guru: Situating digital guru media amidst the neoliberal imperative of self-health management and the 'post-truth' society. In S. Lawrence (Ed.), *Digital wellness, health, and fitness influencers: Critical perspectives on digital guru media* (pp. 1–15). Routledge.

Lawrence, S. (2022b). *Digital wellness, health, and fitness influencers: Critical perspectives on digital guru media*. Routledge.

Liu, J. (2023). CNBC. September 20, 2023. https://www.cnbc.com/2023/09/20/more-than-half-of-gen-zers-think-they-can-easily-make-a-career-in-influencing.html#:~:text=Some%2057%25%20of%20Gen%20Zers,for%20the%20emerging%20career%20path

Min, S. (2019, November 8). 86% of young Americans want to become a social media influencer. *CBS News*. https://www.cbsnews.com/news/social-media-influencers-86-of-young-americans-want-to-become-one/

Miyake, E. (2024). *Virtual influencers: Identity and Digitality in the age of multiple realities.* Routledge.

Pelchen, L. (2024, March 1). *Internet usage statistics in 2024.* Forbes. https://www.forbes.com/home-improvement/internet/internet-statistics/#:~:text=There%20are%205.35%20billion%20internet%20users%20worldwide.&text=Out%20of%20the%20nearly%208,the%20internet%2C%20according%20to%20Statista

Rojek, C. (2012). *Fame attack: The inflation of celebrity and its consequences.* Bloomsbury Academic.

Senft, T. M. (2013). Microcelebrity and the branded self. In J. Hartley, J. Burgess, & A. Bruns (Eds.), *A companion to new media dynamics* (pp. 346–354). Wiley-Blackwell.

The Guardian. (2021, May 21). *Cancer conwoman Belle Gibson's home raided to try to recoup unpaid fines.* https://www.theguardian.com/australia-news/2021/may/21/cancer-con-woman-belle-gibsons-home-raided-to-try-to-recoup-unpaid-fines

Vogels, E. A., & Gelles-Watnick, R. (2023, April 24). Teens and social media: Key findings from Pew Research Center surveys. *Pew Research Center.* https://www.pewresearch.org/short-reads/2023/04/24/teens-and-social-media-key-findings-from-pew-research-center-surveys/

Wymer, S. (2022). Fitness trainers' perceptions of social media: I'm a fitness professional, not an influencer. In S. Lawrence (Ed.), *Digital wellness, health, and fitness influencers: Critical perspectives on digital guru media* (pp. 128–143). Routledge.

Xie, T. (2023, September 22). Raw meat-eating liver king and other health influencers face mounting lawsuits. *Bloomberg.* https://www.bloomberg.com/news/articles/2023-09-22/liver-king-steroids-video-inspires-wave-of-lawsuits

Yahoo Finance. (2024, April 25). *New research reveals influencers significantly drive purchasing decisions.* https://finance.yahoo.com/news/research-reveals-influencers-significantly-drive-130300999.html?guccounter=1&guce_referrer=aHR0cHM6Ly93d3cuZ29vZ2xlLmNvbS8&guce_referrer_sig=AQAAAIpD_3tAg6IhZmEhEIhXq7YZcgRVeirAz7OhmgdP6uY1nbLfmDc1arCY625R-KBEnjmUBbm7LDyifkosBYO843g2Xa_3aFEUm-_NKiCu6UNazS058KlIWf8VlyFiyXRZqVIGa8Dtx5A3lKeazXbpxFLBNFDbDLcf2c938cayqPL0

CHAPTER 7

Digital Surveillance Structures

"Your personal data may have been compromised" was the title of an email Emma received from a cloud storage service she was using during her time as a university student. Clicking on the email, Emma realized that a bunch of documents, including those with her passport number, home address, and date of birth were in cloud storage for ease of access. The email further read, "our administrators are doing everything possible to ensure that your personal data have been retained"—Emma then thought about what this means and clicked on the website of her cloud storage service. There, a front page link to the company's press release was provided. Emma clicked on it and came across legal jargon as well as another link to the company's "privacy" policy, wherein very small shifted text read on for pages in a PDF document. Emma then closed the window on her web browser and continued to go about her day. Whether or not Emma's personal data ever made it into malicious hands is unclear, but her data, like millions of other regular people, were out there, leaked into the vastness of the digital realm. The cloud storage company paid no penalty for having its users' data breached, nor did it incur any significant costs from its shareholders—"these things happen all of the time," said one of the VPs in a follow-up interview for a press release.

It is indeed factual that data breaches are a part of contemporary digital reality—billions of people's personal information, ranging from birth dates to credit card and social security details have been hacked and leaked

A. Anisin, *How the Internet Changed America*,
https://doi.org/10.1007/978-3-032-02395-7_7

into the digital realm. Although it is unclear how many times these details get used for illicit purposes by hackers and cyber criminals, the nature of online behavior and life in the digital realm entails that things are epistemically unsecure. As such, it is plausible to assume that the status of individual privacy has been fundamentally transformed throughout the evolution of the digital realm. In part, this has been made possible by surveillance capitalism and the increasing power that technological corporations have over our personal lives, data, and wherewithal. Yet there is also much more to privacy and surveillance than the surveillance capitalistic element. A great amount of scholarly attention has rightly been attributed to surveillance capitalism, but to date, the conceptual basis of this phenomenon remains vague in relation to actors and forces that are not within the context of corporate-user relations. Structuration theory, to the best of my knowledge, has not been applied to analyze contemporary surveillance in the digital realm. This framework can advance knowledge of different dynamics that are inherent to contemporary internet surveillance.

Power is inherently tied to human agency and is not purely about direct coercive forces. It is also constitutive of a transformative capacity that is embedded within social structures and practices, specifically in domination structures that determine and influence how authority and resources are distributed. These structures are often linked to political institutions and can be observed in the digital realm through influences from lobbyists, interest groups, and state agencies. Understanding power through Giddens' theoretical framework can enable us to identify flows of causation in relation to how surveillance capitalism operates through the digital architectures of the internet. This chapter will demonstrate that even with a functioning liberal democratic system of governance, massive changes to how information is shared, stored, and utilized for profit have arisen with minimal input from voters and consumers of technological products. Examples from social media and its role in spurring socio-political outcomes will be provided based on analyses of tech corporations' handling of data and individual privacy. Tech conglomerates such as Google, Facebook, or Amazon have, throughout their histories, been deeply entrenched in ongoing relationships with military and intelligence agencies and institutions. These connections are multifaceted and symbolize an important but under-theorized dynamic between technological advancement and surveillance.

Throughout this chapter, Giddens' concept of the dialectic of control will be drawn upon to demonstrate that surveillance is not a one-way street—in light of the increasing academic and public policy relevance attributed to the phenomenon of surveillance capitalism, this chapter will, theoretically, account for processes and mechanisms that are not captured by this phenomenon but are empirically salient with regard to the duality between surveillance structures and individual agency.

Surveillance Capitalism

Digital forms of technology are widely utilized by individuals for the most basic of services such as paying one's bills, shopping for food, dating, funeral planning, vacation planning, schooling, and entertainment. In shifting from largely in-person to digital-based communication and social practices, we have succumbed to providing our data and personal information to companies and governments, often with little reflection about the implications that this may pose for our own personal interests, well-being, and collective involvement. All of these new tendencies associated with surveillance capitalism are not random but were made possible by the emergence of internet-based technologies that were developed and made available to consumers. Similar to how identities rapidly changed as a result of millions of peasants being forced from their land during economic dislocations that led to a reshaping of economies and practices during the seventeenth, eighteenth, and nineteenth centuries, the shift from a service economy to a surveillance capitalistic economy has had profound impacts on all facets of our lives (Anisin, 2022). The digitalization of social reality and the presence of what Zuboff (2019) accurately describes as an empirically salient imbalance between the accumulation and possession of information and surveillance capitalists' access to our "private" or personal data. Surveillance capitalism captures how most of the contemporary economic system is based on storage and access to personal data through commodification. These data are commodified and used to predict and modify human behavior for profit.

Zuboff defines surveillance capitalism as a new economic order that exploits human experience as free raw material for hidden commercial practices. Personal information is the new currency. This economic system subordinates traditional production to behavioral modification, which in turn results in unprecedented concentrations of knowledge and power that are in the hands of technological corporations. Surveillance capitalism is argued by Zuboff to pose a significant threat to human nature and also to democracy—as the system and its actors seek to establish a new collective order based on expropriating personal data. This phenomenon represents arguably the most significant shift we have seen in terms of socio-economic conditions thus far in the twenty-first century. This "anti-democratic and anti-egalitarian juggernaut" has emerged through various trajectories of corporate dominance, which makes it similar to a "market-driven coup from above" (Zuboff, 2019, p. 513). Historically, the last time such profound changes occurred was during the transition from agricultural and agrarian societies to urban industrial societies (Anisin, 2023). Similar to the transformative economic dislocations of the seventeenth, eighteenth, and nineteenth centuries, which forced millions of peasants off their land and reshaped economies and practices, the shift from a service economy to a surveillance capitalist economy has had profound impacts on all facets of life. Zuboff (2019) conceptualizes surveillance capitalism as a new ownership pattern of a new means of production—information.

Surveillance capitalism is multi-dimensional and intersectional. It encompasses technological components such as artificial intelligence, deep learning, machine learning, individual usage behaviors with technological tools (e.g., mobile phones, computers, smartwatches), and engagement with online ecosystems and networks. Surveillance capitalism is also marked by hidden commercial practices of extraction, prediction, and sales; a parasitic economic logic where the production of goods and services is subordinated to a new global architecture of behavioral modification; a rogue mutation of capitalism and unprecedented concentrations of wealth, knowledge, and power (Zuboff, 2019). Given its multi-dimensional nature, scholars from various disciplines have examined surveillance capitalism's impact on different outcomes. Fourcade and Healy (2017) demonstrate how digital information dragnets can yield large quantities of individual-level data used to deepen market reach and create new profit-making strategies. Profit is derived from individuals' data which they provide to tech corporations whenever they use or sign up for a given app or service. The authors argue that modern organizations follow institutional data imperatives to collect as much data as possible and then drive capital flows through digital scoring and ranking methodologies.

For our theoretical purposes, it is clear that these strategies are endogenous to the creation of technological structures and their associated systems—many of which have thus far been described in earlier chapters of this book. Along these lines, there are important implications that these processes have for socio-political outcomes in the United States. Zuboff's

(2022) content analysis identifies complex interactions between technological corporations, state authorities, and the populace. She finds that corporate entities such as Facebook and Google have, over the years, developed extensive surveillance apparatuses. These systems are used to collect, analyze, and exploit personal data with the aim of predicting user behavior and influencing it where possible—this is conceptualized by Zuboff as a form of "behavioral surplus" extraction. Personal data are widely repurposed for commercial gain without users' informed consent. What this equates to is an immense imbalance in terms of asymmetrical power dynamics that exist between surveillance capitalists and individual users. Facebook-integrated surveillance-based economic policies within its massive corporate structure under the leadership of Sheryl Sandberg who helped facilitate the extraction of behavioral surplus from users. This was done through data generated from users' activities that were collected and analyzed without their explicit consent. These data were then used to build detailed user profiles that included inferred personal information such as political orientation, interests, vulnerabilities, and other factors. In turn, these profiles enabled highly targeted advertising and made ads more effective and profitable for both the corporation and its advertisers (Zuboff, 2022, p. 19).

As one would expect, Google's exploitation of user data is similarly extensive—this monopolistic corporation, over time, has transformed its search engine into a powerful surveillance tool that can analyze the "data exhaust" from user activities to predict behavior. Behavioral surplus is used to enhance Google's targeted advertising capabilities. Zuboff demonstrates how Google's algorithms infer user preferences and habits even when explicit information is not provided and inferred data are then used to deliver highly personalized ads that increase the likelihood of user engagement and advertising revenue (Zuboff, 2022, p. 17). On a technical basis, Google's data practices were enhanced by its ability to patent early developments in data gathering that enabled it to carry out detailed methodological techniques and the construction of user profiles from behavioral data. These data and methods allowed Google to accumulate vast amounts of personal information, which underpins Google's entire business model, a model that is reliant on commodification of user data for profit (Zuboff, 2022, p. 19). Zuboff argues that such data extraction practices infringe on privacy and simultaneously erode democratic processes—specifically that "the entire economic edifice of surveillance capitalism is built on this illegitimate but not illegal foundation" (Zuboff, 2022, p. 16).

Zuboff also makes a plausible claim in noting that current regulatory frameworks are insufficient to deal with the adverse empirical outcomes brought about by surveillance capitalism.

Power and Structuration

In a 1982 monograph, Giddens developed the concept of dialectic of control, which was premised on a reciprocal nature of power relations. Social media corporations, as subsequent sections of this chapter will reveal, have been widely cooperative with government agencies and it is within digital structures (specifically, domination structures) and systems that political power has been exerted through wide-scale surveillance over behavior in the digital realm. Social media corporations not only lobby the Federal government on a continuous scale, but they also help political actors and groups engage in clandestine operations. As such, we can assume that both legal and institutional structures which facilitate surveillance capitalism are both the medium and the outcome of the practices they organize. Through billions of interactions with digital platforms, users' actions are shaped by their systems and structures, which in turn are continuously reproduced and transformed through these interactions. If we are to understand how power dynamics are exerted, we have to be able to account for processes that involve exogenous actors and their political interests. In the structures and systems of contemporary digital communication platforms, especially those of social media (Facebook, Twitter, Instagram), evidence is starting to pile up, which tells us that large-scale involvement of government agencies and actors has been occurring across high-profile political events.

Indeed, the linkage between state security institutions and tech companies is as old as the internet itself. Spy agencies have coalesced with technological companies to modify hardware and software in order to facilitate the monitoring of foreign targets (Menn, 2013). It is known that the U.S. government (and not only the U.S.) uses third parties to shield major tech companies from repercussions if such operations are uncovered. Historically, defense contracts were important through the 1950s and 1960s. In the 1960s government space and defense programs such as the Minuteman missile effort were customers for Silicon Valley's integrated circuit computer chips—Oracle Corp's first customer was the CIA. Along these lines, it has been reported that government agencies commonly demand to review software code from vendors in order to spot vulnerabilities for later exploitation. Companies provide early warnings of software vulnerabilities to intelligence agencies before informing customers (Menn, 2013). Google, Facebook, as well as Amazon are companies that have roots in military-funded research. Levine (2018) argues that Facebook's ability to create detailed behavioral profiles of its users made it an early tool for political campaigns as demonstrated during Barack Obama's 2008 presidential run. Facebook co-founder Chris Hughes drew from the platform's data for micro-targeting voters (Levine, 2018, p. 86). Along similar lines, Amazon Web Services is Amazon's cloud computing division and has long been to known to be a provider of services to the Central Intelligence Agency (CIA) and the National Security Agency (NSA). Such a partnership is argued by Levine (2018) to not just be about providing storage but comprises significant contractual and financial incentives for the corporation. Even the classical commerce platform eBay had developed specialized software for fraud detection in collaboration with law enforcement agencies. Here, Palantir Technologies (founded by PayPal's Peter Thiel) provided data-mining services to the NSA and CIA (Levine, 2018, p. 103). There are countless other examples of similar types on the influence of military and intelligence funding on the development of computer science and networking technologies.

We know that users of these platforms engage in common practices such as searching for information, sharing personal updates, making purchases, consuming content, sharing content, and many other forms of behavior. Users widely share their geolocation data (whether voluntarily or not). This brings us to an important point. While user actions are indeed shaped by structures and systems of a given digital platform and the platform is continuously reshaped by user actions, there are instances in which high-profile social, political, economic, and cultural topics that happen in the empirical world get framed and systematized within digital platforms and applications in particular ways according to political interests of power holding groups. This occurs through reflexive monitoring which involves processes of continuous review and adjustment of actions based on feedback and swaths of user data. Digital platforms in social media companies constantly analyze user data to refine their algorithms and improve their predictive accuracy. Such reflexivity enhances these platforms' ability to influence user behavior and optimize their revenue stream. Although the exploitative and coercive nature of surveillance capitalism is significant, it is crucial to recognize the multifaceted interactions that occur within the digital realm, specifically when it comes to technological conglomerates. Individuals are not merely passive victims of digital exploitation; they actively engage with social structures.

This brings us back to Giddens' concept of legitimation structures which encompass norms, values, and moral positions that justify and sustain social practices. Giddens (1984) posited that these structures encompass rules and standards that effectively demarcate acceptable and unacceptable behaviors within a society. Legitimation structures form the basis for establishing norms and expectations that direct both individual and group behaviors. These sources of legitimation encompass legal systems, religious doctrines, and cultural traditions. They play a crucial role in maintaining social cohesion and regulating conduct (Giddens, 1984, p. 31). In the digital realm, legitimation structures from the physical world continue to exert significant influence. Despite the online world's anonymity and the potential for creating content under false identities, major platforms like Amazon, Facebook, and YouTube still adhere to standards reflecting the regulatory and legal frameworks of American society. Content deemed "illegal" is promptly removed through algorithmic detection. This, to a variant (but significant) extent, ensures that digital spaces remain aligned with broader societal norms. The controversial aspect here is in latent and often clandestine activities that occur within decision-making at the top managerial levels of technological conglomerates and the influence of exogenous actors on these decisions. These outcomes form domination structures which themselves intersect with legitimation structures to impact social behavior.

If we consider a brief, but now classical example of censorship, a Senate hearing on October 28, 2020, reveals a lot about how political content is regulated and censored in contemporary America. In a statement before a Senate Commerce Committee hearing on October 28, Sundar Pichai (CEO of Google's parent company Alphabet) acknowledged that the search company has repeatedly censored the World Socialist Web Site (WSWS). Republican Senator Mike Lee (Utah) asked Pichai to name one left-wing "high profile person or entity" that had been censored by Google. Pichai cited the WSWS as an example. Importantly, this particular hearing featured testimonies from three tech CEOs: Pichai (Google), Mark Zuckerberg (Facebook), and Jack Dorsey (Twitter). Interestingly enough, Senator Lee claimed,

> I think the trend is clear that you almost always censor – meaning block content, fact-check or label content or demonetize websites – of conservative,

> Republican or pro-life individuals or groups or companies ... Can you name for me one high profile person or entity from a liberal ideology who you have censored and what particular action you took?

Dorsey and Zuckerberg did not provide names, but Pichai responded that Google has moderation policies applied equally. He mentioned that they had "compliance issues with the World Socialist Review [sic], which is a left-leaning publication." Although Pichai incorrectly referred to the WSWS as the "World Socialist Review," it was clear he meant the World Socialist Web Site as a Google search for "World Socialist Review" yields results for the WSWS (Reed, 2020). It is more than likely that Google applies similar restrictions to sites across the political spectrum that are both right and left-leaning.

Furthermore, Giddens' structural domination sought to capture dynamics of power and control that get exercised through resource-based authority. Domination structures determine how power is distributed and influence who has the ability to make decisions, allocate resources, and enforce rules (Giddens, 1984, p. 33). These structures are empirically linked to political institutions that govern the distribution of resources and power relations within a state. In intersecting with legitimation structures, domination structures capture how power is exercised. This may include political influences from lobbyists, interest groups, and other actors of the state (or connected to the state) that seek to sway behavior. Domination structures also include censorship and manipulative practices and often involve behind-the-scenes interactions between state agencies and private technological corporations. These latent processes significantly impact the regulation and control of online activities—there currently is a pervasive influence of domination structures in the digital realm. Zuboff notably argues that surveillance capitalism thrives on the asymmetry of power between users and platform owners. Users, in their daily interactions, provide data that these companies utilize to predict and modify behavior and this happens, empirically, over and over again without their explicit consent or awareness. Importantly however, within Zuboff's surveillance capitalism, the power to transform social practices and individual behaviors lies chiefly with the companies that control the data and the algorithms and a lack of emphasis is placed on exogenous actors or users themselves.

The Dialectic of Control

When it comes to political topics, news, and events, empirically more complex processes have arisen than simple corporate executives exercising power over users through the design and implementation of algorithms that operate throughout social media platforms. While it is indeed true that algorithms determine what content users see, how content gets visually presented and how it spreads through digital networks, in key instances, and during important political periods, algorithms are not only produced and implemented by those in a given social media company. Exogenous political forces come into play and such forces are not adequately theorized in the aforementioned surveillance capitalism framework. Recall that Giddens' notion of allocative resources assumes that material phenomena involved in the production and reproduction of social systems are allocative and are controlled by a given group. With social media, data and algorithms can be assumed to be allocative resources that tech executives control, but importantly, they are also, at times, dictated by exogenous actors and political interests. This brings us to Giddens' concept of the dialectic of control.

The dialectic of control helps to conceptually link power dynamics with agency and structure. At its time of articulation, Giddens challenged many traditional sociological views by arguing that even the most subordinate individuals in a social system possess the ability to influence and alter the conditions of their existence, and hence, with the dialectic of control, he sought to capture a reciprocal nature of power relations. This reciprocal nature can be observed in the ways that dominant and subordinate actors possess variant degrees of autonomy and dependence. A key dynamic in the dialectic of control is in Giddens' assumption that the "capability of the weak, in the regularized relationships of autonomy and dependence that constitute social systems, to turn their weakness back against the powerful" (Giddens, 1982, p. 39). Importantly, there is an asymmetry in power relations and,

> power relations in social systems can be regarded as relations of autonomy and dependence; but no matter how imbalanced they may be in terms of power, actors in subordinate positions are never wholly dependent, and are often very adept at converting whatever resources they possess into some degree of control over the conditions of reproduction of the system. (Giddens, 1982, p. 199)

The surveillance capitalistic framework, however, cannot account for how resources get continually shifted and impact the overall distribution of power. Social structures and systems are never empirically unidirectional, but rather, they involve constant negotiation and balancing acts of control between actors. In certain cases, this can occur regardless of the position of a given actor(s) within a given hierarchy. Giddens noted that "in all social systems, there is a dialectic of control, such that there are normally continually shifting balances of resources, altering the overall distribution of power" (Giddens, 1982, p. 199). An example provided by Giddens on imbalances in power is the relationship between prisoners in solitary confinement and their jailors. Despite an extreme imbalance of power, prisoners can exert some control through acts of resistance such as carrying out hunger strikes or dirty protests. Such actions, although seemingly minor, reveal that even the most constrained individuals retain the capacity to affect the actions of those in power, and in turn, they participate in the dialectic of control (Giddens, 1982, p. 198).

In the era that Giddens wrote his major works and articulated his theoretical framework(s), analyses of class structure were widely prominent in social science when compared to the present day. As expected, Giddens situated a lot of his conceptualizations around the prism of Marxism and frameworks that at the time were prominent (e.g., Braverman). Nevertheless, Giddens' conceptualization can easily be extended to the theme of surveillance capitalism and the current assumptions that are relevant to the study of surveillance and digital reality. Zuboff assumes that there are parallels between surveillance capitalism and Marxism which is observable in commodification processes in both economic systems. Surveillance capitalism, similar to Marxism, functions through the extraction and exploitation of resources. The difference is that contemporary digital reality is marked by personal data getting exploited rather than individuals' physical labor. Specifically, Zuboff (2022) argues that "human experience is claimed as free raw material for market action, beginning with its secret extraction and translation into behavioral data" (Zuboff, 2022, p. 12). Giddens' conceptualization of the dialectic of control demonstrated that workers can navigate and resist managerial strategies—by exercising agency and engaging in different forms of resistance (Giddens, 1982, p. 209).

This logic can be applied to contemporary surveillance capitalistic settings—as individuals in the digital realm on social media platforms do indeed possess agency and can redefine as well as assert control over their conditions. This is a dialectic of control in action and agency. Even in subordinate positions, individuals can challenge models of algorithmic control and power structures. Some of the most significant high-profile events in recent American history reveal how these dynamics unfolded during periods of political contingency.

Tech-Based State Surveillance

There is an ongoing collaboration between Silicon Valley tech companies and the U.S. defense and intelligence communities and this collaboration has deep historical roots. As digital technology and internet-based communication evolve before our eyes, the power of the state grows. The alliance between state agencies and technological companies is becoming increasingly powerful in scope and global in nature. To understand the characteristics of contemporary surveillance and privacy in the digital realm, exogenous political forces and interests have to be conceptualized within structuration and the dynamic relationship between structures, systems, and agency. While the state has been involved in internet since its creation, it has become increasingly involved in dictating how information (especially on political events) is interpreted across society. The Patriot Act (and its subsequent revision) paved the way for this. Back in 2011, President Obama authorized drone strikes that targeted and killed Anwar al-Awlaki (a U.S.-born Muslim cleric) using geolocation data. González (2023) notes that the widespread use of smartphones and digital devices has turned billions of individuals into data generators and fed information into algorithms that can be militarized. The U.S. Defense Intelligence Agency has widely utilized commercially available geolocation data from cell phones for surveillance and targeting purposes—this is often accomplished in the absence of warrants. González traces the historical relationship between the U.S. military and Silicon Valley back over 50 years. The Department of Defense (DoD) and intelligence agencies have established numerous outposts and advisory boards to capture technological innovations from tech companies. Efforts can be observed in the Defense Innovation Unit Experimental in Mountain View, California, established in 2015 by then Defense Secretary Ash Carter. The aim of institutional cooperation here was to provide the state the ability to quickly identify and invest in companies developing cutting-edge technologies that are useful to the military.

González also draws attention to an increasingly prominent phenomenon of virtual warfare, which is said to encompass robotic and autonomous weapon systems, psychological operations (psyops), predictive modeling, along with sophisticated cyberwarfare. All of these technologies rely on vast amounts of data collected from drones, satellites, and social media. Furthermore, the creation of the Defense Innovation Unit (DIU) signaled a shift toward integrating tech innovations directly into military operations. This effort parallels the establishment of In-Q-Tel, which is the CIA's venture capital firm (González, 2023). In-Q-Tel funds startups to develop surveillance and intelligence technologies. For example, Keyhole was such a startup and later was acquired by Google and was rebranded as the well-known and widely used Google Earth. Another case can be observed in Project Maven, which is an AI initiative to process and analyze vast amounts of data from military drones. While Google's involvement in Project Maven has led to internal protests and resignations from employees who opposed the company's participation in military projects, the corporation continues to proceed in developing among the most sophisticated technologies used to support warfare in human history.

There are, of course, deeper roots observable here, many of which were revealed to publics by E. Snowden's actions and subsequent writings. Snowden was the first high-profile individual to expose the degree of the U.S. government's surveillance on its populace. He leaked classified documents to journalists that revealed the NSA was conducting extensive and indiscriminate surveillance programs through collecting data in not only the United States but globally. The NSA cooperated with intelligence agencies and private companies in its systematic collection of telephone metadata and internet communication. These processes unfolded in the absence of adequate oversight or explicit consent of those being monitored (Greenwald, 2014). PRISM allowed the NSA to access the servers of tech companies including Google, Facebook, Microsoft, and Apple to collect data on users. Data encompassed emails, video chats, photos, and file transfers (Greenwald & MacAskill, 2013). AT&T had a "highly collaborative" relationship with the NSA that allowed it to access billions of emails. What's more, in 2011, AT&T handed over a billion of its domestic cellphone calling records daily to the NSA.

The thought-provoking and highly coercive dynamic pertaining to these programs is that they operated under Section 702 of the Foreign Intelligence Surveillance Act, which was, in its fundamental purpose, aimed at foreign intelligence targets. Yet it resulted in the widespread collection of American citizens' data. What's more, the XKeyscore program allowed analysts to search databases of emails, online chats, and browsing histories without prior authorization (Greenwald, 2013). Snowden revealed that the NSA's capabilities were not limited to metadata but extended to content surveillance and led to a wide-reaching debate about the balance between national security and individual privacy. Along with Snowden, Julian Assange's actions through WikiLeaks revealed systemic issues with U.S. foreign policy and also touched on domestic privacy topics. Assange argued that a lack of transparency was adverse for democracy and the public had a right to know what its government was doing overseas. WikiLeaks documents revealed that there was a gap between public statements and private actions. Extensive secrecy undermines democratic accountability and enables policies to get carried out that otherwise likely would not have withstood public scrutiny (Benkler, 2011). Secrecy was largely made possible through technology which was used to both carry out and conceal surveillance and intelligence operations. The U.S. had developed sophisticated digital tools for surveillance and data collection and used them both domestically and overseas in military conflicts such as Afghanistan and Iraq. Here, war logs with advanced tracking and reporting systems helped monitor battlefield fatalities and record incidents. Yet these logs also revealed that civilian casualties and incidents of abuse were either underreported or kept hidden from public view. Technological tools were employed by the state to create a specific narrative that suited strategic objectives. Along similar lines, domestically, extensive monitoring capabilities that were exposed by WikiLeaks pointed toward the NSA's vast surveillance programs. The NSA's bulk data collection functioned through frameworks of PRISM and XKeyscore. Via PRISM, the NSA's accessed servers of major companies including Google, Facebook, Microsoft, and Apple. The NSA proficiently collected emails, video chats, photos along with other forms of communication directly from these companies' databases (Greenwald, 2013).

The technical capabilities possessed by state agencies were made possible through internet connectivity and collaboration with tech companies that stem back decades. These applicational frameworks enable state security agencies to garner heaps of information about our private lives—much more so than in times of the past. XKeyscore has been described as the NSA's widest-reaching system that gets used to gather intelligence and information from computer networks as it can capture what a typical internet user does on the internet such as a person's content of email, websites visited, searches, and metadata as a whole. These technologies were already active and utilized as early as 2008. The training received by NSA analysts included pull-down menus that were designed for the purpose of providing communicational content reviews in real-time—empirically, this would encompass users' chats, browsing histories, and many other forms of content (Greenwald, 2013).

There are, of course, more practical examples that have had real-world impacts on American society, especially on politics. The widely discussed Cambridge Analytica scandal is a significant example of how a tech conglomerate coalesced with political actors to change social behavior and outcomes. Here, Facebook influenced the 2016 U.S. presidential election as the Trump campaign drew from data-mining processes to identify and target specific voter groups via Cambridge Analytica (a British firm). Part of the campaign's strategy was premised on suppressing voter turnout among unfavorable demographic groups through targeted ads and messages designed that aimed to dissuade them from voting (Zuboff, 2022, p. 15). It is now widely considered that this scandal constitutes significant breaches of data privacy. Estimates put the total number of people involved and impacted at 87 million individuals (BBC News, 2018). Data that were deemed "private" were used to build comprehensive psychological profiles of users to influence their voting behavior across what now are historically monumental political events including the 2016 U.S. presidential election and the Brexit referendum. Facebook's chief technology officer (Mike Schroepfer) revealed that 305,000 people had installed the "This Is Your Digital Life" quiz, which was subsequently utilized to harvest data on users' political preferences.

Readers may wonder, why is this case significant? First, Facebook executives notably claimed that they had relied on Cambridge Analytica to "self-certify" the data it had collected from users would be deleted. Empirically, however, this did not happen. Along with all of the behavioral (e.g., cookies and browsing based data), perhaps the most significant data reference point was the quiz that civilians completed called, "This Is Your Digital Life." Here, users who downloaded an app consented to provide their data for academic research purposes. Yet the app also collected data from the users' Facebook friends and increased the amount of data that was harvested exponentially. Second, as argued by Dowling (2022) digitization has empowered non-state information operations actors to interfere with democratic processes at unprecedented levels—Cambridge Analytica challenged three fundamental axioms of liberal democracy that are relevant to citizens' actions including participation, notions of pluralism, and understanding political information.

When Mark Zuckerberg was called to testify before both the U.S. Congress and the European Parliament, he attempted to justify his corporation's actions as being driven by an ethical sentiment, but to no avail. Facebook ended up paying $725 to plaintiffs of a class action lawsuit against mass data misuse by Cambridge Analytica that alleged Facebook violated consumer privacy laws by sharing personal data with firms (Cambridge Analytica) (Townsend, 2022). This particular case is exemplary and it will go down in history as being among the most pivotal and foundational in a precedential sense—Cambridge Analytica will be a reference point for future legal proceedings having to do with political actors' involvement in citizens' privacy.

Exogenous Political Actors and Algorithmic System Censorship

Most recently, during the COVID-19 pandemic, critically oriented journalists revealed the Twitter Files, which came to fruition as part of Elon Musk's efforts to de-censor Twitter and examine the company's long-standing content blocking and review policies. After Musk had acquired Twitter, journalists were invited to company headquarters and the Twitter Files were released. These files represent arguably the most significant leak of documents related to government-led surveillance since Edward Snowden's whistleblowing in 2013. Importantly, the major difference here is that not only surveillance was carried out, but exogenous political forces entered into the realm of content creation by directly influencing and dictating algorithmic systems. In this sense, comparatively, the Cambridge Analytica scandal featured a political entity (in the form of a political campaign) expending users' personal data illegally for electoral gain through collaboration with a subsidy of a tech conglomerate, whereas the Twitter Files revealed that state agencies were directly involved in regulating the type of content that was viral and able to spread on one of the most widely used social networking sites and applications in America.

These actions transpired during the most noteworthy lockdown in economic history and a year of a presidential election. Highly targeted efforts by state agencies were initiated in order to censor, de-platform, and de-monetize specific types of political speech and opinions. Complaints about these events and their associated processes eventually were submitted in a brief to the Supreme Court of the United States via Vivek H. Murthy, Surgeon General, et al., Petitioners, v. State of Missouri, et al., Respondents (No. 23-411). The brief was specifically submitted by independent journalists: Matt Taibbi, Michael Shellenberger, Lee Fang, David Zweig, Leighton Woodhouse, and Alex Gutentag. Without a doubt, this case constitutes the most significant legal battle over the extent of government influence on social media platforms in modern history. It also has immense implications for free speech.

Journalist Michael Shellenberger, through observation of state attorney general lawsuits combined with investigative reporting, revealed that censorship practices were carried out on topics that ranged from stories of the origins of COVID-19 to vaccinations to other pandemic-related issues. These examples are of theoretical relevance, as they illustrate the intricate dynamics that empirically operate between social structures and individual agency. They are particularly salient in relation to the dialectic of control—as private citizens and journalists have boldly been able to challenge power structures that are present in the digital realm. Algorithmic censorship is reflective of Giddens' concept of the reflexive monitoring of action in which social actors continuously adjust their behavior based on feedback. The Twitter Files revealed how social media platforms constantly refined their algorithms based on user data and governmental requests, which in turn skillfully shaped the informational landscape of the platform and in turn public discourse. These processes exemplify how structures and agency interact reflexively.

The aforementioned brief and its associated extensive report (Candeub, 2024) reveals the many mechanisms through which state agencies have manipulated and controlled public discourse via covert means. They have done this through circumventing constitutional protections that are supposed to safeguard free speech. There was a systematic effort by Federal agencies to engage in censorship by proxy using social media platforms' terms of service as a cover for what would otherwise be unconstitutional restrictions on speech. Here, a key issue is in how the Cybersecurity and Infrastructure Security Agency (CISA) (which was originally tasked with protecting American computer infrastructure from foreign hacking) was utilized to analyze "cognitive infrastructure" or what the aforementioned journalists describe as the thoughts and opinions of American citizens. Such a shift allowed this institution to justify its involvement in monitoring and influencing domestic social media content under the semblance of protecting national security. Emails and internal communications in the report revealed that this institution (along with others) engaged in extensive flagging of social media posts, including political speech, jokes along with hyperbolic statements that were deemed harmful or classified as misinformation. What's more, organizations such as the Stanford Internet Observatory (SIO) and the University of Washington's Center for an Informed Public (CIP) played critical roles in censorship efforts as they received funding to develop methodologies for identifying and reporting what they labeled as misinformation. Subsequently, these tools were used to pressure social media platforms into specific types of politically oriented content. The aforementioned brief claims that the collaboration between government, academia, as well as private companies helped forge a network of influence that effectively bypassed traditional checks and balances on governmental power.

These organizations and institutions were working together to monitor and report social media content. The report also reveals that CISA officials were not only aware of these efforts but actively participating in them through engaging in direct communication with social media platforms in an effort to flag content and recommend actions against users. Importantly, report documents show that these efforts were not limited to combatting foreign disinformation but widely extended to domestic political speech and often targeted conservative viewpoints (Candeub, 2024). What's more, the Twitter Files revealed that the role of the Biden Administration was significant in censorship efforts—high-ranking officials from the White House directly pressured social media companies to adjust their content moderation policies, especially regarding COVID-19 information. In the report's analysis of internal emails from Facebook, information is revealed about how actors from the White House were not only aware of what was going on but actively influenced the platform's decision to remove or label posts about vaccine hesitancy. This constitutes direct government influence on private companies and logically raises constitutional questions about the limits of state power and the protections afforded by the First Amendment.

These developments are indeed adverse. They demonstrate the multifaceted ways through which social media algorithmic systems and structures were encroached upon by exogenous political actors in order to censor and silence journalists and independent critically oriented voices. Specifically, journalists who questioned the government's COVID-19 policies or other contentious issues were flagged, shadow-banned, and even de-platformed. This represents a troubling development that has come to fruition in the digital realm—it undermines the role of the press in holding the government accountable. Perhaps the most important implication of these adverse processes can be observed in their downstream effects—the report highlights that there is now an increasing prevalence of self-censorship—as journalists and critically oriented voices are censoring themselves to avoid retribution or loss of their voice on a given digital platform.

The digital realm's structures and systems are marked by an intricate set of dynamic interactions that take place between the creators of these systems, engineers, data scientists, as well as executive decision-makers who then coalesce with government actors to oversee and attempt to the flow of informational content that the platform facilitates to the public. The public itself is not homogeneous, as there have been a range of different critical actors and investigative civilians that have sought to engage in alternative political practices by questioning and challenging political status quos. On a conceptual level, these events and processes are captured by Giddens' dialectic of control. Power is not a one-way street where dominant actors impose their will unilaterally on subordinates. The dialectic of control extends to the broader public—users of social media platforms, while assumed by many (and even the surveillance capitalist framework) to be at the mercy of both corporate and governmental surveillance, also have the power to influence structures and algorithmic systems. Civilian activist and journalist-led scrutiny of these structures scrutiny can (and has) put pressure on social media conglomerates and even government agencies. The Twitter Files led to congressional hearings, public debates, and calls for greater transparency and accountability in how social media platforms manage content and collaborate with government entities.

The duality between the digital realm and individual agency is thus much richer than a simple narrative of power, domination, and coercion. While surveillance capitalism does exert significant influence, individuals still retain the capacity to navigate and resist these structures through their actions and interactions. This dynamic interplay suggests that the digital realm is a site of both constraint and possibility and most importantly, there is an intrinsic potential for positive formations of collective action to challenge mechanisms of control and exploitation. Technological conglomerates in the digital realm are characterized by a complex interplay between coercive and cooperative processes.

In Conclusion

The digital realm is a complex ecosystem in which hundreds of millions of individuals interact with one another continuously. It comprises much more than surveillance capitalistic elements. While this chapter may be perceived to be overly critical of surveillance capitalism, I do not intend this to be the case. Surveillance capitalism is not absent of explanatory power—it is clear that practices of surveillance have become embedded in digital platforms, which clearly reflects what Giddens describes as the institutional dimensions of social life. Institutions, in Giddens' framework, are deeply embedded patterns of social practices that endure over time and space. Surveillance capitalism has institutionalized the practice of data extraction and commodification and has made these practices routine aspects of the digital economy. However, surveillance capitalism falls short in being able to account for the more complex dynamics that have arisen in recent years, specifically with relation to exogenous political actors and their role in promoting (or demoting) informational flows in the digital realm through social media structures and systems.

This chapter has drawn from Giddens' structuration theory. It has applied this framework to examine how aspects of surveillance capitalism operate within digital architectures. The concept of the dialectic of control demonstrates that surveillance processes are not a one-way street. Power is distributed across various actors and crucially, users can resist and reshape the conditions of structures. This theoretical perspective boldly contrasts with the more deterministic aspect of surveillance capitalism as it demonstrates that there is a potential for agency and resistance within increasingly exploitative and oppressive structures in the digital realm. Indeed, many digital platforms, especially those of social media, function through legitimation structures in which norms and values sustain social practices that guide corporate behaviors and continuously result in the systematic commodification of vast swaths of personal data. Commodification has led to an asymmetry of power in which technological corporations (and at times exogenous political actors) wield significant influence over individual behaviors. Conceptually, this chapter contributes contemporary knowledge on surveillance capitalism and demonstrates that this framework can be complemented by structuration theory.

References

Anisin, A. (2022). Pandemic surveillance capitalism: Authoritarian liberalism or democratic backsliding? *Journal of Political Power, 15*(2), 262–278.

Anisin, A. (2023). *Authoritarian Liberal surveillance and the COVID-19 pandemic.* Walter de Gruyter GmbH & Co KG.

BBC News. (2018, April 5). Facebook scandal 'hit 87 million users'. https://www.bbc.com/news/technology-43649018

Benkler, Y. (2011). A free irresponsible press: Wikileaks and the Battle over the soul of the networked fourth estate. *Harvard Civil Rights-Civil Liberties Law Review, 46*(2), 311–397.

Candeub, D. A. (2024). *Amicus curiae brief of the "Twitter Files" journalists: Matt Taibbi, Michael Shellenberger, Lee Fang, David Zweig, Leighton Woodhouse, Alex Gutentag in support of respondents (No. 23–411).* Supreme Court of the United States. https://www.supremecourt.gov/DocketPDF/23/23-411/300197/20240208220913623_44722%20pdf%20Candeub.pdf

Dowling, M. E. (2022). Cyber information operations: Cambridge Analytica's challenge to democratic legitimacy. *Journal of Cyber Policy, 7*(2), 230–248.

Fourcade, M., & Healy, K. (2017). Seeing like a market. *Socio-Economic Review, 15*(1), 9–29.

Giddens, A. (1982). *Profiles and critiques in social theory.* Macmillan Education UK.

Giddens, A. (1984). *The Constitution of Society: Outline of the Theory of Structuration.* University of California Press.

González, R. J. (2023). *Militarising Big Tech: The rise of Silicon Valley's digital defence industry.* State of Power 2023. https://www.ucpress.edu/book/9780520384767/

Greenwald, G. (2013, July 31). XKeyscore: NSA tool collects 'nearly everything a user does on the internet'. *The Guardian.* https://www.theguardian.com/world/2013/jul/31/nsa-top-secret-program-online-data

Greenwald, G. (2014). *No place to Hide: Edward Snowden, the NSA, and the U.S. surveillance state.* Metropolitan Books.

Greenwald, G., & MacAskill, E. (2013, June 7). NSA Prism program taps in to user data of Apple, Google and others. *The Guardian.* https://www.theguardian.com/world/2013/jun/06/us-tech-giants-nsa-data

Levine, Y. (2018). *Surveillance Valley: The secret military history of the internet.* Hachette.

Menn, J. (2013, July 3). Strong ties bind spy agencies and Silicon Valley. *Reuters.* https://www.reuters.com/article/technology/strong-ties-bind-spy-agencies-and-silicon-valley-idUSBRE96214J/

Reed, K. (2020, November 4). *Google admits to censoring the World Socialist Web Site.* https://www.wsws.org/en/articles/2020/11/04/goog-n04.html

Townsend, M. (2022, August 27). Facebook-Cambridge Analytica data breach lawsuit ends in 11th hour settlement. *The Guardian*. https://www.theguardian.com/technology/2022/aug/27/facebook-cambridge-analytica-data-breach-lawsuit-ends-in-11th-hour-settlement

Zuboff, S. (2019). *The age of surveillance capitalism: The fight for a human future at the new frontier of power*. Hachette.

Zuboff, S. (2022). Surveillance capitalism or democracy? The death match of institutional orders and the politics of knowledge in our information civilization. *Organization Theory, 3*(3), 1–79.

CHAPTER 8

Conclusion: Going Inside

It's summer and the sun is scorching down through bay trees in a local park. Emma is sitting on a bench in the shade as a group of kids race by and startle her—electric-powered scooters and skateboards. In a flash, they're gone, with the wind, into the hot summer evening. People walking around the park all have their smartphones in their hands; a group of teenagers is sitting on a lawn nearby having a picnic, taking selfies of one another. Emma's phone sounds off a notification; it's a Zoom call from one of the meetings connected to her work, although it's a voluntary meeting so she doesn't have to attend. Looking at her phone, Emma mutes the notification by decreasing the sound volume. A warm wind blows through Emma's hair and she has a flashback, decades ago, she was at that same park with her dad and her cousins, they were running through the grass and playing Frisbee—life was simple, no work, no responsibilities, no stress. We all experience nostalgia, but some of us, like Emma, may at times perceive that the nostalgia experienced in today's world about memories of the past is constituted by something extraordinary in comparison to times before. Society and the world more broadly is fundamentally different in comparison to all other periods of modern history. This is most evident when going out in public areas in contemporary developed economies and countries—smartphones, tablets, smartwatches, and other technological devices are widely present in the hands of people going about their daily routines and businesses. Most new cars also have a

A. Anisin, *How the Internet Changed America*,
https://doi.org/10.1007/978-3-032-02395-7_8

tablet-sized screen in them and it is not uncommon to come across individuals using virtual reality (VR) glasses in public settings.

The internet was not invented yesterday—it has been around since the 1960s, but its commercialization in the 1980s enabled the United States to gain technological and economic supremacy for decades to come. In today's world, apart from China, American technological companies still hold their hegemonic status over most the world's markets and in turn, most people in the world rely on and use American technology whether it is Apple, Google, or Facebook. The internet has fundamentally altered the way that Americans go about their day-to-day lives. This book has conceptualized internet-induced change through structuration theory. Many behaviors and trends that have arisen across society were not due to random changes in individual agency, but rather, new structures have arisen and old structures have dramatically changed alongside technological progress and widespread commercialization of the internet across the realms of television, entertainment, work, communication, and nearly every single personal activity. Americans no longer spend their days coalescing with neighbors or community members nor do they watch as much television as they used to. Reading books has also become a rare activity. Most young people spend close to five hours of their day on social media and screen time as a whole is increasing throughout the population.

Just three decades ago, when a problem or issue would need to be addressed, there were two routes that people would go about in attempting to deal with it. The first would be to pick up the telephone and dial a number that would provide more information about the said problem. The second, which in my personal experience appears to have been most common, would involve going outside to ask neighbors and members of one's community about what was going on. Although this example might seem intuitive or even benign in a world that is marked by Google searches and rapid informational dissemination, it elucidates the transformative power of the internet. Going outside used to encompass an attractive way to interact with and find out about the world. Surely, there were telephones, newspapers, and even email three decades ago, but the process of going outside did not yet get dislocated. Processes of this sort have been investigated throughout this book. As readers may acknowledge, these processes have thus far been interpreted differently by different groups and actors.

One could glance at these profound societal changes and automatically assume that there is a clear structural causal factor that necessarily had to be in place for such significant social change to have arisen. Yet the structural aspects of the internet and its associated systems, rules, resources, institutions, and algorithms are only but one piece of a complex puzzle—structure interacts with agency through structuration. Algorithms and their development trajectories depend on user interactions and behaviors on these platforms. Just as in the physical world, digital social phenomena are produced and reproduced through a duality between structure (rules and resources) and agency. Structures and systems shape individual actions, which in turn reshape structures. The duality between structure and agency is necessary to consider in any given attempt to explain how the internet has changed society. The internet is managed by individuals, groups, companies, and organizations. In some cases, the state and exogenous political actors get involved and use the internet in an attempt to change social behavior—these dynamics constitute a symbiotic dualism between the internet and human society. By applying structuration theory to examine internet-induced societal change, this book provides insights into the reciprocal relationship between digital structures and individual agency. This theoretical framework has allowed me to develop a multifaceted exploration of how digital technologies shape and are shaped by social practices—I have placed emphasis on complex dynamics that empirically operate between internet technologies and society.

Each chapter has engaged with specific literatures and themes that are rooted in traditions of scholarship such as research on media studies and mental health, research on polarization, or research on civic association among other topics such as surveillance capitalism and privacy. In this regard, the chapters of this book and their associated findings are meant to be interpreted alongside the literature(s) that they contribute to. With this being said, readers will likely acknowledge that many of the topics covered in this book are related to one another. Whether or not their relationships are causal can be left up to others to decide, theorize, and possibly empirically research. Along these lines, in accounting for some of the major changes that the internet has had on American society, this book has taken a diverse path through touching on topics that are broadly classifiable as belonging to social science—some to sociology, others to political science, psychology, history, philosophy, and media studies. An interdisciplinary approach was necessary to take because of the sheer causal scale within which the internet has impacted society over the last several decades. The second chapter explained the sociological ideas of structure and agency. Focus was placed on the conceptual and even ontological characteristics of how the internet affects society and individual behavior. In doing so, I explained why structuration theory was chosen instead of different social network theories and other potential explanatory frameworks including Bourdieu's theory of practice and Castells' network society. The chapter then further developed the idea of a digital realm via structuration theory. It demonstrated how the internet (structure) and individual behavior (agency) are interconnected. Reference was given to technical parameters of algorithms and artificially intelligent properties. This theoretical groundwork served as the foundation for empirical analyses that were presented in subsequent chapters.

The third chapter put forward the first empirical analysis of the book. It shifted attention to what is probably the most significant societal phenomenon in American history—that of civic association. Helping each other, working with neighbors, and contributing to the formation of community were key aspects of early American history. The establishment of civic associations early on helped form new communities, towns, and cities across the country's vast and diverse geographic landscape. These processes transpired in the absence of a large Federal government and in many cases, civic associations filled key gaps in terms of the provision of public goods that the state was simply not able to address. This chapter reviewed a range of foundational texts (from Tocqueville to Robert Putnam) and associated the impact that the internet and digital realm have had on behavioral patterns in contemporary society. Decades ago, Putnam noted that Americans were "Bowling Alone" and becoming more isolated from activities that used to be common in communities and associations across America. This chapter demonstrated how the internet fundamentally transformed civic association through digital forms of community comprising virtual realms. The chapter drew on data from the General Social Survey and the World Values Survey and found that American society has experienced significant declines in interpersonal trust and the frequency of face-to-face interactions. The percentage of Americans who believe most people can be trusted plummeted from 46.1% in 1972 to 10.2% in 2022. Similarly, the frequency of social interactions has decreased, with fewer people spending evenings with friends or feeling secure in their neighborhoods. This decline in traditional forms of social interaction has been accompanied by a rise in digital interactions that are facilitated by social media platforms and other online communication tools.

The fourth chapter delved into polarization and public distrust in institutions. Both were argued to form a nexus that is heavily dependent on individuals' entrenchment into social media algorithms and usage of the digital realm. The chapter demonstrated how the internet has completely reshaped the ways political information is consumed. Instead of relying on the morning newspaper or the evening news, individuals often check the news dozens of times a day and do so on their own, in absence of attending town halls and community meetings. Along with echo-chamber-related factors, the ability to post and comment anonymously on these platforms has contributed to increases in antagonistic rhetoric and affective polarization. In accounting for these changes, this chapter drew upon data from the General Social Survey and the World Values Survey. Findings revealed that there were significant declines in trust in the press, television, the executive branch, and Congress. Additionally, there has been a substantial increase in the frequency of political discussions among friends—rising nearly seven-fold from the early 1980s to 2022. This chapter's analyses highlighted a recursive interplay between digital media structures and user agency, which was argued to continuously perpetuate polarization and foster ideological cleavages.

The fifth chapter shifted attention onto what I believe is a highly undertheorized phenomenon and one that has simply not been talked about enough (given its importance)—that of reading. One of the most significant impacts the internet has had on American society can be seen in shifts and changes in individuals' reading habits. The print newspaper industry has nearly vanished. Meanwhile, book publishing industries have suffered substantial losses over the past two decades as consumer preferences have shifted toward electronic and audiobooks. People are constantly bombarded with news stories, updates, and advertisements from various digital and social media platforms, but the quantitative impact of this is that individuals actually read less today than ever before. Technological changes to how information is presented and consumed have fundamentally altered how most people read. The chapter analyzed data from the U.S. Bureau of Labor Statistics' American Time Use Survey and found a 22.2% decrease in average daily reading time across all age groups. Older adults were observed to read significantly more than younger generations, with the 65–74 age group averaging 0.66 hours (39.6 minutes) per day, compared to the 15–19 age group, which averaged only 0.13 hours (7.8 minutes) per day. The 25–34 and 35–44 age groups read only slightly more than the youngest age groups. In stark contrast, teenagers and youth spend 7.8 minutes of their day reading in comparison to 5 hours looking at screens.

These observations reveal a profound shift in interpersonal and social behavior across American society toward consuming fast-paced and easily digestible video content. Importantly, with less reading, individuals are transforming their ability to shape their own lifestyles and make decisions that reflect their own personality. These effects are especially noticeable across the digital realm wherein new online influencers have gained massive followings and significantly impacted how tens of millions of people go about their day-to-day lives. Next, Chap. Six presented what was among the first applications of structuration theory to the influencer phenomenon. The chapter demonstrated how influencers constitute a new phenomenon that functions by way of the digital realm, primarily through structures and systems of social media. Individuals have garnered large-scale followings and digital fame often through the promotion of their personal brand and putting out variant types of content. The chapter argued that the internet has directly enabled the rise of these influencers. Most young people now follow influencers and even make consumer decisions based on content they come across. In the most significant of cases, followers take advice on how to live their lives, contribute money and time to influencer causes, and spread their messages with enthusiasm. Along with identifying the most salient influencers in the U.S., the chapter presented several case studies of influencers who deceitfully exploited their followers for material gain and profit.

The seventh chapter focused on surveillance capitalism and privacy. This chapter explained how the digitalization of our social reality is premised upon a grave imbalance between information held by companies and our access to our own data. While technological advancements have been used for surveillance and control, power dynamics in the digital realm are more complex than commonly assumed. External political actors, such as government agencies and institutions, have played significant roles in shaping digital content and behavior. This chapter examined several high-profile cases such as the release of Wikileaks, the Twitter Files, and the Cambridge Analytica scandal to illustrate how data commodification and the political manipulation of democratic processes have been carried out by external actors in collaboration with executives of technology firms. Power is thus not just about financial resources but also about setting technical agendas and norms within a given community—through forging domination and legitimation structures.

Ultimately, it must be admitted that no single inquiry can fully capture the vast amount of ways that the internet has changed a given society—we can, through different concepts, theories, and empirical analyses, touch on observable trends and outcomes, but the totality of such a phenomenon is out of reach of any single work. This is not to say that capturing social change induced by the internet is impossible or representative of an unfeasible task. Rather, we must acknowledge the vastness of the topic being studied, while at the same time, be open to the possibility that the findings we come to in one time period may differ from those which may be observed in the future. There is contingency inherent to the relationship between structure and agency as manifested in different spheres of social reality. For this reason, the different analyses that have been put forward in this book were not meant to be representative of definitive empirical laws. In studying how the internet has altered massive societal trends such as social trust, behavioral patterns such as spending time with relatives and neighbors, on how it has impacted political polarization, and the other different outcomes that have been assessed in this book, the findings presented are intended to serve as important reference points of the particular periods of time being studied—moving forward, any single one of the trends or correlations identified can mutate due to the contingency of social reality. The findings put forward in this book are not to be interpreted as overly deterministic generalizations. Giddens notably stated that causal mechanisms in social scientific generalizations rely on actors' reasons within a "mesh" of intended and unintended consequences. The content of agents' knowledge, the context in which it is situated, and the validity of the propositional content of that knowledge—all must be considered alongside the circumstances under which generalizations apply (Giddens, 1984, p. 345). These are crucial dynamics to consider in light of the many different discussions that are currently ongoing about humanity's potential shift to a post-human existence.

Given the validity underlying many of the datasets and survey projects drawn upon in this book, it will be relatively straightforward to revisit some of the patterns and trends that have been analyzed in this book years down the line. The internet and digital connectivity are only growing in scope and power. There is nothing that appears to be impeding that can slow this process down. Short of an eschatological event such as a total nuclear war, the digital realm will endure. Indeed, the functionality of this digital realm is heavily contingent upon the availability of electricity and access to reliable power grids. Such physical infrastructure is the backbone that supports vast networks of servers, data centers that are essential for the operation of the internet. Natural disasters such as hurricanes, earthquakes, or floods can disrupt power supplies and internet connectivity in a given country or set of countries as can waves of political instability, particularly in authoritarian regimes, which thus far have revealed how incumbent leaders can cause intentional shutdowns of power grids or internet services as a means of control or censorship during. Nevertheless, thus far, history has shown that the World Wide Web cannot be disrupted on a global scale. Emergent satellite technology such as Starlink further demonstrates how autonomous internet connectivity (autonomous from planet Earth itself) may be a defining characteristic of future digital communication.

Furthermore, leading economists and many social scientists have long believed that the impact of technological change on the economy and on society would be an overwhelmingly net positive as it would let more people benefit from economic growth. As time has gone on, many are starting to believe that current technological changes we are witnessing are producing impacts that pose numerous unexpected existential questions about the nature of our relation to the economy, to inequality, and to democracy. With the onset of publicly available AI tools like ChatGPT, we can observe how AI is already starting to impact workforces as a concentrated percentage of workers with advanced degrees are probably on track to replace hordes of lesser qualified workers. As a result of AI-based tools' ability to replace worker tasks (and decrease their total frequency), the future is bound to be marked by new problems that we may not have the capacity to tackle without thorough understanding of what brought such problems about. Johnson and Acemoglu's (2023) inquiries in their recent book reveal that in other periods of history which were also marked by technological developments, masses of people did not actually experience immediate improvements in their socio-economic conditions. For example, while the invention of new mechanical equipment during the Middle Ages led to significant increases in agricultural productivity, the people who were using these devices (peasants) ended up getting overworked to death. Life expectancy dropped due to malnourishment. Similar adversities can be observed in the age of industrialization where masses were forced off of rural farms and into newfound cities where factory-based exploitation and disease were rampant. An overarching tendency, argue Johnson and Acemoglu, is that technological change leads to either human workers getting replaced or getting exploited.

In some aspects, one can plausibly lend explanatory power to various post-human notions about how the internet is involuntarily forcing us into using corporate platforms, digital banking, and an overall pattern of hegemonic reliance on app-based modes of societal interaction. In the near future, further entrenchment into digital-based technologies will be propelled through the launching of more and more 5G networks. As more generations grow up through heavy usage of internet-based technologies, Americans will continue to go inside. The increasing prominence of artificial intelligence offers us a temporally constricted but salient projection into what the future of internet usage across different cultural and social practices may entail. As artificial intelligence continues to evolve and integrate more deeply into our lives, the duality of structure and agency between the digital world and our day-to-day behaviors will become even more pronounced and significant, but it will also mutate and transform depending on the type of digital technological evolutionary processes that arise and the will of people and creativity of human agency.

References

Giddens, A. (1984). *The constitution of society: Outline of the theory of structuration.* University of California Press.

Johnson, S., & Acemoglu, D. (2023). *Power and Progress: Our thousand-year struggle over Technology and prosperity.* Hachette.

INDEX[1]

NUMBERS AND SYMBOLS

2G, 32
3G, 32
4G, 11, 32
5G, 2, 175

A

Acoustics, 128
Addiction/addicted, 2n1, 6, 7, 65
Adults, 3, 8, 84, 90, 91, 94, 110, 118–120, 131, 171
Advanced Research Projects Agency (ARPA), 5
African Americans, 119
Algocracy, 33
Algorithms/algorithmic, 7, 9, 11, 13, 17, 24, 30, 33, 34, 36–39, 41, 82, 85, 87–89, 92, 101, 111, 113, 126, 128, 132, 138, 149, 151–154, 156, 160–163, 169–171
Allocative resources, 154
Amazon, 3, 5, 37, 41, 146, 151, 152
American Psychological Association, 31
Anxiety, 41, 107, 123
Apache Spark, 41
Apple, 32, 135, 157, 158, 168
Archer, M. S., 25, 27
Arizona, 78
Asymmetrical, 149
AT&T, 157
Audiobooks, 106, 171
Australia, 87, 132, 135

B

Biden, Joseph, 162
Biology, 8
Black-Scholes, 24
BLM, 50
Bloggers, 125
Blogs, 125

[1] Note: Page numbers followed by 'n' refer to notes.

A. Anisin, *How the Internet Changed America*,
https://doi.org/10.1007/978-3-032-02395-7

Books, 7, 105–108, 120, 132, 168
Bourdieu, P., xiv, 26, 27, 45, 170
Bowling Alone, xv, 4, 55, 58, 170
Brain, 7, 107, 108, 134
Britain, 132
Bush, George Jr., 83

C
California, 1, 75, 156
Cambridge Analytica, 3, 13, 159, 160, 172
Canada, 87, 132
Capitalism, 3, 13, 146–151, 153–155, 163, 164, 169, 172
Carlson, Tucker, 76
Castells, M., 28, 29
Causation, 42, 146
Celebrities, 124, 125, 132, 139
CEOs, 113, 152
ChatGPT, 4, 174
Children, 1, 2, 49, 107, 109, 131
China, 6, 87, 168
Christianity, 56
Chromosomes, 9
Chronicles of Narnia, 105
CIA, 150, 157
Civic association, 12, 50–52, 54, 55, 57, 59, 72, 80, 169, 170
Civic engagement, 2, 12, 52, 57–63, 65, 70, 71, 79
Clickbait, 94
Climate change, 76, 84
College, 118, 123
Computer-Aided Software Engineering, 23
Conglomerates, 146, 152, 163
Congress, 3, 52, 53, 77, 97–99, 101, 160, 171
Consume, 3, 61, 77, 82, 89, 92, 106, 112, 114, 121, 138
Consumers, 126, 137–139, 146, 147
Corporations, 13, 30, 34, 38, 94, 113, 126, 146–150, 153, 164
COVID-19, 50, 160–162
Cultural norms, 57, 132
Cybersecurity and Infrastructure Security Agency (CISA), 161

D
Deliveroo, 34
Democrats, 81, 82, 84, 95, 99
Demographics, 114, 119, 126
Department of Defense (DoD), 5, 156
Depp, Johnny, 139
Depp v. Heard, 139, 140
Depression, 107
Diabetes, 119
Dialectic of control, 30, 146, 150, 154–156, 161, 163, 164
Digital age, 4, 89, 111
Digital realm, 4, 11, 12, 17, 18, 20, 25, 28–37, 39, 41, 42, 45, 51, 58–61, 63–65, 70, 71, 77, 79, 82, 85, 88–94, 99, 101, 106, 110, 112, 119, 121, 123–126, 128, 130–141, 145, 146, 150–153, 155, 156, 161, 163, 164, 168, 170–173
Discourse, 35, 36, 55, 61, 77, 82, 85, 87, 88, 99, 101, 161
DNA, 9
Domination, 29, 30, 35, 37, 146, 150, 152, 153, 163, 172
Dorsey, Jack, 152, 153
Dualism, 10, 169

Duality, 9, 10, 12, 18–21, 23–25, 27, 30, 34, 35, 39, 42, 43, 45, 92, 113, 141, 147, 163, 169, 175

E

eBay, 5, 151
Echo chambers, 79, 81, 83, 85, 87, 101
Egalitarian, 56, 148
Election, 57, 76–79, 86, 87, 159, 160
Environmental Protection Agency, 106
Ethernet, 31
Europe, 56, 57, 110
Executive branch, 77
Exogenous, 64, 139, 153, 162, 164, 169
Exploitation, 149, 151, 152, 155, 163, 174
Eye strain, 109

F

Facebook, 5, 37, 39, 59, 86, 90, 90n2, 91, 106, 110, 111, 118, 127, 128, 131, 134, 139, 146, 149–152, 157–160, 162, 168
Feedback loop, 39, 41, 88
Filter bubbles, 85
Financial crisis, 49, 83, 96
Fitness, 123, 127, 132–134, 136, 138
Followers, 3, 123–132, 134–138, 140, 141, 172
Ford, Gerald, 78
Fragmentation, 85

G

Garfield, James A., 78
General Social Survey (GSS), 52, 61, 62, 64, 66, 93, 95–97, 101, 170, 171
Generation Z (Gen Z), 31, 127, 131
Geolocation, 151, 156
Gibson, Belle, 134–136, 138, 141
Giffords, Gabrielle, 78
Google, 5, 30, 33, 87, 90n2, 146, 149, 151–153, 157, 158, 168
Gridlock, 83
GSM, 30

H

Health, 20, 21, 34, 54, 57, 70, 75, 107, 119, 124, 127, 132–138
Heard, Amber, 139
House of Representatives, 78
HTML, 87

I

Idolization, 13, 139, 140
Individualism, 2, 9, 18, 70
Influencers, 3, 13, 85, 123–136, 138, 140, 141, 172
Instagram, 5, 8, 30, 31, 59, 90–92, 90n2, 106, 111, 118, 123, 125, 127, 128, 131, 133, 134, 150
Intelligence agencies, 146, 151, 156, 157

J

Johnson, Brian, 136–138
Johnson, S., 174
Jones, Alex, 78
Judeo-Christian, 139
Jurassic Park, 9

K

Kennedy, John F., 78
King Jr., Martin Luther, 55
Kruskal-Wallis Statistic, 99

L
LAPD, 77
Lee, Mike, 152
Legitimation, 35, 37, 39, 79, 90, 110, 152, 153, 164, 172
Lewis, C.S., 105
Lincoln, Abraham, 78
Literacy, 108
Liver King, 134, 136–138, 141
LTE, 30

M
Machines, 17, 40
Manifest Destiny, 51
Manipulation, 3, 7, 136, 140, 172
Marxism, 155
McKinley, William, 78
McLelland, Mike, 78
Mechanisms, 25, 30, 37, 39, 41, 42, 79, 109, 120, 125, 147, 161, 163, 173
Mental health, 107, 108, 120, 169
Mental illness, 2n1
Merchandise, 124, 141
Microsoft, 33, 157, 158
Microsoft Word, 33
Millennial, 127
Millennium Cohort Study, 107
MLlib, 40, 41
Musicians, 132
Musk, Elon, 160
Mutation, 148

N
Napa Valley, 76
National Association for the Advancement of Colored People (NAACP), 54
Netflix, 5, 38
Network society, 28, 45, 170
NFL, 76
Nostalgia, 167
NSA, 151, 157, 158
Nuclear war, 173

O
Obama, Barack, 83, 151, 156
OECD, 84
Outdoor, 1, 109, 110, 118, 119

P
Pandemic, 50, 72, 114, 136, 160, 161
Partisan, 57, 61, 81, 82, 84, 87, 88, 99, 101
Party affiliation, 82, 85
Paul, Rand, 78
PDF, 145
Pelosi, Nancy, 78
Photos, 30, 106, 110, 157, 158
Polarization, 3, 13, 50, 60, 64, 71, 77, 79–81, 83, 85–89, 93, 96, 101, 169, 170, 173
Police, 50, 76
Political polarization, 79, 85, 86, 88, 101, 102
Power grids, 173
Predict, 59, 92, 108, 147, 149, 153
Profiles, 149, 151, 159
Putnam, R. D., xv, 4, 51, 55–60, 65, 170
P value, 95, 99

R
Read/reading, 3, 12, 13, 36, 105–111, 113–120, 136, 145, 171, 172
Reagan, Ronald, 78

Reflexive monitoring, 27, 151, 161
Republicans, 81, 82, 84, 95, 99
Roosevelt, Franklin D., 78
Routinization, 113

S

San Francisco, 78
Scalise, Steve, 78
Science fiction, 9
Screen time, 2, 3, 31, 109, 110, 120, 168
Sensationalist, 88, 94, 110, 113, 137, 140
Sentiment analysis, 40, 82, 87
Shading, 128
Shellenberger, Michael, 161
Signification, 35
Skocpol, T., 52, 54, 55, 58
Sleep, 137
Snapchat, 91, 131
Social media, 3, 5, 6, 11, 13, 31, 36, 39–41, 59, 64, 72, 78, 83, 85, 87–92, 94, 101, 106, 110–114, 118, 120, 121, 124–132, 134–136, 138–141, 146, 150, 151, 154, 155, 157, 161–164, 168, 170–172
Starbucks, 71
Supplements, 123, 124, 132, 137
Surveillance, 3, 13, 30, 146–151, 153–158, 160, 163, 164, 169, 172
  capitalism, 146–148, 150, 153, 155, 164

T

Taibbi, Matt, 161
Television (TV), 3, 76, 78, 91, 94, 95, 98, 101, 105, 109, 127, 168, 171
Thanksgiving, 75, 77
TikTok, 8, 31, 59, 90n2, 91, 92, 106, 111, 118, 119, 127, 128, 131, 133, 134, 139, 140
Tocqueville, A., 51, 55–58, 170
Transmission Control Protocol (TCP), 31
Trends, 7, 55, 60, 62–64, 66, 76, 95, 99, 102, 124, 129, 131, 132, 136, 168, 173
Truman, Harry S., 78
Trump, Donald, 77, 78, 159
Trust, 3, 12, 13, 50, 55, 61, 63, 64, 68, 71, 77, 79, 88, 93, 96, 101, 125, 127, 134, 170, 171, 173
Tucson, 78
Twitter, 3, 5, 13, 36, 40, 59, 78, 85, 87, 91, 92, 110, 118, 131, 139, 150, 152, 160–163, 172
Twitter Files, 3, 160–163, 172

U

Uber, 34
University of California, xiv, 40

V

Video games, 6, 109, 125
Visualization, 114, 116
Vloggers, 125

W

Wikileaks, 3, 13, 172
World Values Survey (WVS), 61, 62, 68, 69, 99, 101, 170, 171
World Wide Web, 17, 174

X
X, 36, 86, 87, 91, 127
XKeyscore, 158

Y
YouTube, 8, 30, 31, 37–39, 59, 91, 106, 111, 113, 118, 119, 125, 128, 131, 133, 134, 139, 140, 152

Z
Zuboff, S., 7, 13, 147–149, 153, 155, 159
Zuckerberg, Mark, 152, 153, 160

GPSR Compliance
The European Union's (EU) General Product Safety Regulation (GPSR) is a set of rules that requires consumer products to be safe and our obligations to ensure this.

If you have any concerns about our products, you can contact us on

ProductSafety@springernature.com

In case Publisher is established outside the EU, the EU authorized representative is:

Springer Nature Customer Service Center GmbH
Europaplatz 3
69115 Heidelberg, Germany

www.ingramcontent.com/pod-product-compliance
Lightning Source LLC
Chambersburg PA
CBHW071341101225
36581CB00004B/113
* 9 7 8 3 0 3 2 0 2 3 9 4 0 *